LOST IN GREY SPACE

Mark Bolton is an IT professional that has spent over twenty years working with and for many large organisations during times of large-scale transformation. His background in business intelligence, analytics, quality management and systems thinking concepts provides him with a unique perspective on how organisations operate, and where they are losing performance. He is a practitioner at heart and sees value as something gained and refuses to accept contemporary concepts based on clever marketing. This book is a thought-provoking and practical insight into how organisations can gain from their most valuable asset – their people.

Lost In Grey Space

Transforming Transformation

MARK BOLTON

4TH Gen Group

Published By 4th Gen Group

Foreword by Mike Dicks

Artwork by Charlotte Bolton
charlotteemilybolton@hotmail.com

ISDN: 9781072673545

To Jimmy Bolton (1936 – 2018)

father, life mentor and best friend

Contents

Prologue

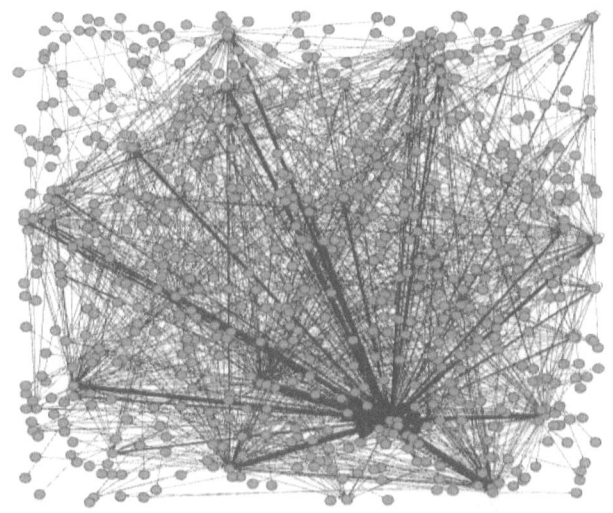

The motivation behind this book was a deep-seated feeling that there is a better way of implementing change within organisations; transformational change that gets to its very core.

In 2010 I was driving home from work. It was late on a November evening, and my mood was very dark. At that time, I was running the analytics practice for a consulting firm, implementing a large software solution. The project was in the middle of its testing phase, and things weren't exactly going to plan. The team had been working long hours, morale was low, and emotions were running high. To compound a problematic few weeks I'd been to see a few existing clients that were complaining bitterly about the value they were getting from their IT investments. One particular CIO had spent over five million on a Business Intelligence solution with the expectation of having a few hundred users all providing glowing testimonies of how their new information system was transforming their work. The reality was somewhat different. Two years had passed since the original investment and the number of people regularly using the system could be counted on one hand. All the change management and sponsorship from the executive team had all failed to get the solution embedded into their business. It might have been fine if this was an isolated case, but it wasn't, it was extremely typical. For many years I'd convinced myself that my definition of success was correct and that if things went wrong, then it was the organisation's fault for not managing the change correctly. I'd later learn that I was experiencing a very human condition called cognitive dissonance; in other words, I was telling myself what I wanted to hear. The reality was somewhat different from my biased perspective. The environment contained things that were adversely affecting the work. The problem was these *things* were hidden from view, and not just from myself but everyone, including the executive team. I'd later go on to call this phenomenon 'grey space'.

About 30 minutes from home, I turned on the radio. I was too depressed to listen to music, so I flicked over to BBC Radio 4 expecting a little light comedy, but there was a business programme airing. Listening to this was the last thing I wanted. However, the host Peter Day opened up with "*The professor this programme is all about, Russell Ackoff, would have hated the way we're going to introduce him*". It sounded interesting, so I thought I'd listen for a few moments, waiting to hear some pearls of academic wisdom that would irritate me some more. What I heard over the next thirty minutes changed me forever and would eventually lead me to write this book.

That evening Professor Russell Ackoff introduced me to a subject called Systems Thinking, and for that, I will be eternally grateful. Although he wasn't a household name, as business gurus go, he was profoundly wise about how organisations work and where most are going wrong, whether in the education system or in large global corporations (I say *are* going wrong, because they're stilling doing it).

His views were often subversive, and he didn't hold many punches when it came to mainstream thinking, such as how business schools teach, even though he was a business school professor himself. On the Peter Day programme, he explained how the interoperability of the parts within a system is more important than the individual parts themselves. A revelation to me, as I'd centred my career on implementing solutions to solve specific problems.

As I got closer to home, it felt like the proverbial scales were falling from my eyes, an expression a friend would also use many years later. I started to realise the real reasons for my sense of frustration and years of failure. How could I have not seen it? It seemed so obvious. The manner, in which I had been implementing IT systems seemed to align with what Russell Ackoff was saying, in that, introducing change in isolation would compromise, if not break a system, and ultimately lead to feelings of discontent and distrust from the people involved with that system.

Another influencer that fundamentally shaped my thinking a few years later was Nassim Taleb. His books, The Black Swan and

Antifragile, opened a door into a universally different way of thinking about analytics and prediction, that extended the concept of growth and development, to include *survival*. Growth, Development & Survival; these in combination provide a mental framework that still helps me to quickly navigate through the myriad of ambiguous and confusing messages concerning technology, especially the real-world application of machine learning and neural network analysis. Nassim Taleb's teachings reinforce the systems nature of things and tackles grey space head-on.

The principles behind Systems Thinking are timeless – universal even. Moreover, at a time when virtually every organisation is aware that they must develop a digital strategy and that without these new capabilities they're told that they're not likely to survive, it's no wonder managers are more confused than ever. IT interventions for over two decades have had a terrible track record, not merely for over-running on cost and late delivery but also for their ineffectiveness and their inability to make a transformational change, one that revolutionises the performance of an organisation. If not paradoxical, it's certainly a dilemma. Most are probably thinking, "*it must be us, and what we need is outside help to bring in the best practices that other companies have implemented.*" There's a problem with this thinking though; it's not true. There are no commonly implemented so-called 'best practices' out there – it's a myth, and most companies are struggling just like everyone else. Of course, some will prescribe to have implemented them, but when faced with the request to, "*show me your data*" they fail to produce anything that even remotely substantiates their claim - with no transformational impact to be found. Most people that promote best practices are people trying to sell them; I know I used to be one of them. However, to quote Professor Edward Deming "*Without data, you're just another person with an opinion.*" Best practices, when challenged with the data question, simply get diluted to better techniques for performing a task within a specific environment. But what works in one place isn't guaranteed to work in another.   To ensure change is transformational, it must adjust the properties of the whole system so that it operates inherently different from before. This is called systemic change.

In this book, we'll examine an alternative approach to implementing change, one that is based on the principles of Systems Thinking and one that creates change that lasts inside organisations.   We'll look at how to observe the organisation as a whole system and how to introduce systemic interventions. We'll also look at the most critical part of any change, the people within the organisation, and how their relationships shift over time in response to the unadaptable nature of the formal structures and processes.

A very human reaction, when introduced to these concepts for the first time, is to reference and even invalidate them against our core assumptions and fundamental beliefs, especially those that we hold most precious.   Moreover, it is extraordinarily hard to reflect objectively on our experiences without these biases impeding our clarity of thought. Un-learning those practices that harm our ability to improve is a much harder thing to achieve than learning them in the first place, however, doing so is far more rewarding than continuing in ways that make us frustrated and cause us to lie to ourselves.

These concepts aren't magic, they're relatively straightforward, but they do require a different train a thought, one that begins by looking from the outside in, rather than from the traditional orientation of inside out.   The truth is right there in front of us. We just need to learn how to look.

Foreword

During my career I have worked in a variety of roles leading IT functional teams, organisational change and more recently business leadership. This experience has spanned both public and private organisations with UK, European and Global reach and has allowed me the luxury of fantastic insight into how organisations are structured, how organisational change is carried out and most importantly significant practical experience of what works well and the war stories of what doesn't. Over the past 20 years I have helped organisations improve and it remains my key passion.

Back in 2014, myself and mark met while working together on a global analytics programme at a world leading manufacturer. In stereotypical IT transformation fashion, we were working to implement a significant improvement in company-wide strategic planning and operational analytics from within an IT function, using a largely outsourced team of experts partnered with an internal team. As many will have experienced this setup is common on large technology transformations due to their unique scale and complexity, however it creates such a huge conflict in people (internal and external) bringing so many different cultures together that transformational change has a very limited chance of true success. During the late nights working and many a long passionate discussion during car journeys to and from work, Mark has changed how I think about organisational structures and transformational change forever. Utilising his unique perspective, we have to worked together to overcome some of the most challenging change management issues I have seen in my career to date and this was the start of Mark's personal passion to release this book and ensure everyone who reads it can benefit.

As a reader of this book whether you are an organisational leader, a functional leader/team member, a change expert, consultant or just an everyday reader, I urge you to read this book with the intention to understand Mark's thoughts and challenge yourself. Mark has combined biology, psychology, internationally recognised methods and his own very practical experiences together with some humour to create a really unique book that will have something for everyone. During this very interesting read, challenge your thought process to understand why you should firstly think and secondly act on encouraging organisations/colleagues to focus more on joining the dots between your organisational functions/teams, consider how the interconnecting parts work together and ultimately now you have this view, understand if you could change anything to improve your organisation, especially in areas of grey space. From my experience of applying Mark's thoughts to my everyday job, I can honestly say I believe you will be able to see opportunities you didn't think existed and you will have the opportunity to influence change in your organisation to improve its success. Thinking about the world as a system of interconnected parts and applying that to everyday challenges was genuinely a light bulb moment I experienced and just like many who read this book I still to this day question why I couldn't see this before.

For many years my learning and experiences had conditioned my thinking into standard ways organisations are structured and standard ways to drive change including where I fit into this. Throughout the years, I often wondered why technology led change is considered so different to business change, why many organisations and their teams focus on following frameworks and processes rather than the simple practices to combine outcomes of IT and business change and why almost all organisations I have seen tell you they operate in one way and when you get into the detail of change you see that the reality is different. In recent times, we have seen a greater ratio of success in organisational change using more agile delivery methods and in digital transformations that focus on the customer/consumer experience, designing improvements on real organisational step changes that are tangible outcomes. Mark's amazing thought leadership has helped me see organisations and therefore change in a completely different perspective since our first connection in 2014, which in turn has allowed me to understand how to get the best value from varying organisational structures and why some approaches to change have more success than others.

Furthermore, as we look towards the next generation of organisations, the world is about to go on to a new chapter in how we work every day. Change itself has always been considered as a 'high risk' part of a business operation, challenging this paradigm digital transformation has encouraged people to understand that not changing is the biggest risk to an organisation. However, to truly deliver an organisation that successfully changes at the pace of markets, change must become a regular part of everyone's day to day operation.

Mark's insights, approaches and methods included in this book were the missing part to my thoughts on how we can make this happen.

Finally, I agreed to write this foreword for the book as my experience of understanding Mark's insights and applying them to my everyday job has had a profound impact on organisations and people I work with. I can honestly say your own work and ultimately your organisation will gain hugely if you take time to understand the unique views and then apply them to your organisation/situation.

To achieve this, it is vitally important to recognise people are the diamonds who make it all happen or in the worst-case examples make it all fail. To enable the next generation of organisations to include delivery of change as a core operational responsibility in everyone's day to day job requires organisations full of change agents. This will lead to a new relentless focus in organisational culture, processes and methods that can be readily used by all, and for organisations they will adjust their business performance focus to assess the results of change in a systematic way rather than via annual planning cycles.

Please enjoy the book, do let Mark and me have any suggestions for improving it. Our intention is to evolve this over the coming months and years and any experiences you have will enable us to make it even greater value for future readers.

Mike Dicks

When I was a young man, I wanted to change the world.

I found it was difficult to change the world, so I tried to change my nation.

When I found I couldn't change the nation, I began to focus on my town. I couldn't change the town, and as an older man, I tried to change my family.

Now, as an old man, I realise the only thing I can change is myself, and suddenly I realise that if long ago I had changed myself, I could have made an impact on my family. My family and I could have made an impact on our town. Their impact could have changed the nation, and I could indeed have changed the world

1200 AD, author unknown

Introduction

Many years ago before I began thinking about my work and the world around me, if someone would have asked what I thought about the future and my career I would have probably answered, *"it's about planning and being clear about my goals and aspirations"*. After all, isn't this what all the contemporary business guru's and psychologists tell us that we improve our future by training our mind to focus on affirmations of a better life. It is a kind of Ptolemaic model of life that is shaped by positioning ourselves in the centre and framing events around us to engineer more favourable outcomes. With an overly simplified lens that categorises situations into intended and unintended consequences, where seemingly random exceptions to our predefined expectations are simply put down to misfortune. An existence where our emotions are like waves that suddenly appear and then disappear, without a trace of where they came from and where they went. Like the pea that Hans Christian Anderson placed under the Princess's mattress, this way of living plagues us with an uncomfortable dissonance, where life itself doesn't seem to understand the rules of the game. We want to believe in a simplified and linear existence, but happenstance keeps on twisting and turning in ways that we cannot explain – it's all so unclear. As a result, we give this nonlinear reality a wide berth, keeping up the pretence that we can predict future events, and that we can avoid complexity without implication. We can see it out of the corner of our mind's eye, but we choose to ignore it, even deny its existence. Stop! was my only answer, turn and look at it was my response. Face the truth. Face the uncertainty and the randomness of life.

Directly looking at it has brought me through what I can only describe as a sort of Copernican revolution — realising that I am not the centre of my universe and that life is truly a complex web of interconnectedness, theory, and unsubstantiated dogma, where cause and effect creates an infinite whole. One that encapsulates everything from the fabled flap of a butterfly wing in the east, causing a tornado in the west, to the impact of climate change on the habitat of polar bears, and the demise of the humble bumblebee in my back garden. Everything is connected. At times I've felt like an observer looking on in, while most continue with their rituals that carry them from day to day. I'm by no means saying that somehow, I've been enlightened, but I have come to understand that questioning everything and accepting nothing unless proven is quite liberating.

At the beginning of my journey thinking about interconnectedness, I stumbled on a problem with what I thought was the most basic and unquestionable universal concept, the concept of analysis, the process of inquiry.

In a paradigm where problem-solving is the analytical process of disassembling the whole down into its constituent components, studying these components to understand their function and then reassembling them to see how their aggregation affects the whole, there only seemed to be an answer to the questions about *what*, and finding the answers to *why* was beyond my reach. Everything I questioned had this problem, the *what* was attainable through degrees of deduction but the *why* was generally unattainable with a classical analytical approach.

Here was my problem. When I was a child, my dad taught me how to wire an electrical plug (British). He showed me the fuse, the blue neutral wire, the brown live wire and the green and yellow earth wire. A few years later, I had my first holiday to Europe and was surprised to see a much smaller plug with no fuse. My first reaction was, *"Is this safe?"*. My dad had taught me that the fuse was there to protect the appliance from an electrical surge. He taught me the *what* of the British plug design but not the *why*. The reason *why* a British plug has a fuse has nothing to do with the plug. Its design came from the desire to wire as many homes as possible after the second world war during a copper shortage. To save copper, the British adopted the ring main system using a ring topology. A ring topology has sequentially connected sockets that are centrally connected to the fuse box, like Christmas tree lights, whereas in a star system every socket is individually connected to the fuse box. This means that in a ring system each connection needs a fuse and to make maintenance easier it was decided in the 1940s to place it in the plug rather than the wall socket. This also had the effect of making British plugs much larger than those in Europe and the US.

The problem with using an analytical approach to understand the British plug system or anything else for that matter is twofold.

Firstly, it's not possible to explain the reason for a design by analysing the parts of a system, for example, an electrician from a different part of the world would have to guess that a fuse in the plug or the wall socket is required because of a sequential ring main system, and they wouldn't be entirely sure unless they took a look at the topology of the circuit directly. They also wouldn't be able to explain why the ring topology had been chosen in the first place. They'd probably say that this was a poor decision and advise against it in favour of a star topology. But more importantly, the foreign electrician would not be able to describe what problem the British were trying to solve by their design, namely, to provide electrical supply into so many homes at a time when there was a national copper shortage.

The second problem of analysis resides in cause and effect. Cause and effect is the process of trying to find the ultimate or root cause of a phenomenon by treating each effect as a cause. We start with an effect, and once we find its cause, we then treat that as another effect to determine its cause, and so on until we're satisfied, we've reached a plausible end. The result is a conclusion that nothing occurs by chance, and everything must have a cause. This is the doctrine of determinism, the theory that a previous event always determines a recent event. By using cause and effect in combination, we falsely assert that through analysis, we can find the cause of a problem within a greater whole, assuming that the further down we go the more we will understand how the whole is affected.

The problem with this is that it places the boundary of analysis around the system under examination, with the premise that the cause to the effect experienced, must be found within the system. My plug example shows that to understand how to replace an expired fuse, I first needed to pull it apart to know how to fix it. The consequence of this is that it separates the analysis (understanding the plug) from the wider environment (the circuit topology). In other words, to replace the fuse in a plug I don't need to understand the topology of the circuit, I need only to know how to replace a fuse. In science, we would perform such an analysis under laboratory conditions. Under laboratory conditions, we deliberately exclude the environment to understand function and not purpose. Function is a description of *what* happens. Purpose is the reason for something existing in the first place, the *why*. So, in summary, the second problem I found with analysis is that it doesn't determine purpose and it can't answer the questions, *"why does the design of the system look the way it does?"* and *"what problem were the designers trying to solve?"*.

The inability to explain the reasons for both the purpose and the design of a system was a logical dead-end for my thinking. There had to be another way, and fortunately, I found the answer in the teachings of Russell Ackoff. He taught that it is not possible to understand the nature of a system by analysis and that another method of thinking is required. This method he called synthesis, and it is the *"exact opposite of analysis"*.

To understand the nature of a system requires us to understand the properties it can only possess when it is a whole, and therefore, that it can't possess when it is not. For example, placing all the parts of a bicycle on a table does not provide us with a bicycle. Only assembling those parts into a whole bicycle makes them a bicycle. The fundamental property of a bicycle is to carry its passenger from point A to point B, a property only the whole possesses and not any of its parts taken in isolation. When we disassemble a whole system, it loses its essential properties, and so does its parts. The bicycle in pieces can no longer carry a passenger, and the wheel sitting on the table can no longer perform its designed function. Taken apart the whole and its parts lose all their essential properties.

Questioning the properties of the whole takes us down a completely different line of inquiry, not one of function predicated on what effects what, but one of, *why* do the properties of a system exist.

If we examine the differences between a synergistic and an analytical approach, we can break it down into three simple points:

1. The first step of analysis begins by breaking the system down into smaller parts to be examined. The first step of synthesis starts by defining the containing system. For example, *why* does the electrical system require that a fuse be placed inside the plug? Alternatively, if the focus were on the improvement of a department, the starting point would be *why* had the structures, processes and policies been implemented, and what problem were they trying to solve?

2. The second step of analysis is to analyse the construct and functionality of each part taken individually. The second step of synthesis is to understand the containing system. For example, where does our department sit within the larger organisation, and what are the interactions (communications) between it and those other areas; typically left, right, above and below.

3. The third step of analysis is to aggregate the parts to determine the impact on the whole. The third step of synthesis is to disaggregate the understanding of the whole into an understanding of the parts. For example,

in a ring main system, every connection requires a fuse. Alternatively, in an organisation with no central control mechanism for a given situation, each area would need its own.

Comparing the two approaches in this way exposes a fundamental difference between them. Analysis reveals the structure of a system and explains *how* it works, while synthesis reveals *why* a system is designed the way it is. Put another way; analysis is required to gain knowledge of a system and its parts to determine how the individual parts work to enable the whole to function. Whereas synthesis provides an understanding of why the system exists and what purpose it was designed to fulfil.

In the case of the British plug system, the problem it was intended to solve no longer exists (there is no longer a copper shortage). Nevertheless, the system still exists. Designing an electrical circuit topology in Britain today would most certainly produce a very different result.

The difference between analysis and synthesis can also separate the meaning of knowledge and understanding. *Knowledge* is gained by working down a system and *understanding* is gained by working up and out beyond the boundary of the system.

A consequence that surfaces, when we include the environment in an assessment of a system, is that it becomes clear that while the system itself is necessary for its purpose, it isn't sufficient. This situation was first described by Edgar A. Singer, of which Russell Ackoff was a former student. He used the example of an acorn and an oak tree. He deduced that although the acorn is necessary to produce an oak tree, it isn't sufficient. To make an oak tree, other elements are also required such as soil, water and sunshine. All these additional elements he categorised as the environment, and he called this way of thinking producer-product. He stated that there's no such thing as a universal law and that all systems are environmentally relative; meaning that there is never an environment-free explanation, only an environment-fault explanation. This became one of the foundations of quality management in the decades to come and brought its founders like Taiichi Ohno, Edward Deming, Eli Goldratt and others to conclude that it is system conditions, the environment, that determines how people perform not the people themselves. To paraphrase Stringer, people are necessary but not sufficient to increase performance.

It also throws a spanner in the works of contemporary thinking that describes how standardisation predicated on universal laws is what creates organisational transformation possible. This book describes a way of considering transformation from a systemic perspective and challenges the unquestioned paradigms that have been cemented into contemporary organisations, mainly sold by management consultants and software companies. To transform transformation, analytical thinking is necessary but not sufficient; it also requires the environment to be recognised and understood.

The reward of improvement is addictive, and although we enjoy the journey, success is the real thrill, regardless of what people say. Running a marathon is always much more pleasurable after the event than during it (especially, when your wife gives your mid-race drink away to the kids because it's a warm day – I'm not affected by that at all). These kinds of successes last a lifetime.

SECTION 1

PERSPECTIVES

CHAPTER 1

Systems Thinking

"We shape our buildings, and afterwards, our buildings shape us."

Sir Winston Churchill

THINKING IN SYSTEMS

"Systems that are designed by their parts will always perform at significantly suboptimal levels than systems designed as a whole."

Professor Russell Ackoff

Before we can begin to understand how things work it's important to view things not just in isolation, but also how they're connected to other things and how each influences the other. This opening chapter provides a perspective that considers the collective over the individual and how ultimately this translates into the way we think about organisations.

What a mess!

Systems Thinking is a way of approaching the world full of things that are interconnected. Russell Ackoff said *"managers don't solve problems, they manage messes"*, meaning the workplace is full of interconnection, and everything is connected to something else in some way, and the sum of all these things is a mess.

Basic common sense would confirm that our environment impacts us, but this way of thinking has had little traction in modern organisations, and the overwhelming paradigm in most remains a reductionist approach by breaking everything down into smaller parts. The reasons for this are many, but there are three that stand out as significant contributors; science, education and practicality. We'll discuss these themes throughout this book but to start with its important to start with what a system is and the difference between the different types of system.

The nature of a system is described as a whole when it consists of two or more parts and meets the following criteria:

- The whole has at least one defining function
- Every part can affect the behaviour of the whole
- Every part is necessary for the whole to carry out its function but insufficient to do so alone
- The behaviour of each part depends on at least one other part

When we ponder the meaning behind these points taken collectively, two things happen. Firstly, we agree with them. They seem intuitive and straightforward enough to comprehend. Secondly, though, the deeper we reflect, the more a kind of unsettling feeling sets in, something a little lower down than logical thought. A sense that the bigger the system, the more difficult these points are to comprehend, and that in larger systems like an organisation, with an immense amount of complexity these words seem to morph from their intuitive nature into a statement of impractical platitudes. Further contemplation to explore the reason for our apprehension is a dull foreboding of uncertainty and ambiguity that arises in our mind, so we back away quickly and rationalise it as interesting but irrelevant.

One of these things is not like the other ♫

People inside organisations have been fed a diet of People, Systems and Processes to help them solidify and simplify the conceptual task of problem-solving. The word *systems* in this phrase mean machines or IT. It's a way of breaking down our world into understandable and manageable components.

In this process, we regard all of them equally with a view that each coexists with parity. It's why most pictures used to describe their relationship are usually drawn as an equilateral triangle with each of the words at each angle, (People, Systems, Processes) — presented in this way they're regarded equally, in a similar mechanistic nature. The issue, in the abiding words of Sesame

Street, is that "*one of these things is not like the other*". And, one is missing (Sesame Street had four things). The phrase should be (Environment, People, Mechanisms, and Processes).

System types can be classified in four ways:

Type	Parts	Whole	Example
Deterministic	No Choice	No Choice	Computer
Ecological	Choice	No Choice	Nature
Animate	No Choice	Choice	Person
Social	Choice	Choice	Organisation

Social systems are unique in this classification of systems, not only because their parts can exert choice (a person), but also because so can the whole (the people). This ability makes for a dynamic and complex situation, one that can be incredibly unpredictable. Therefore, without an understanding that people are not deterministic machines like computers, we will seriously misjudge the considerations needed to create systemic and sustainable change.

All systems can be classified as a *system* because they share the same set of properties described above. It is the relationships between the parts or their interconnectedness, that determines their function that influences the performance of the whole. Interconnectedness is the interface between two parts that trigger an action or response of some kind. Information in a deterministic system, in the form of instruction, from one part to another typically influences a physical flow, like material flowing through a plant or a sales order flowing through a software system. Information in a social system comes in the form of communication and influences choice.

Talk to me Goose

For systems to be autonomous, the system must possess the ability to *feedback* information from one part to another. Let's take a simple example: imagine for a moment a thermostat in your home. Let's say you've set the thermostat to twenty degrees. The room cools down, so the thermostat turns the heating on. The room temperature rises to twenty degrees, and the thermostat turns the heating off. The room cools again, and the thermostat turns the heating on. This cycle continues. The problem is that one of the children has left the window wide open, so you shut it, and the room temperature stabilises at twenty degrees.

This is an example of a single flow of information. Depending on the temperature of the room determines what the thermostat does. It has no idea that the window has been left open or that a window even exists, it's just a simple thermostat. Now, imagine if you had an intelligent window that could inform the thermostat it was open, and imagine if the thermostat could request the window to close itself as a stabilising measure. This is information-feedback. A loop of communication between two or more parts to fulfil an objective.

Like our simple thermostat, not all systems have information-feedback capabilities. However, the kind of systems we're interested in discussing here, do. The feedback capabilities inside an organisation are the single most contributor to performance over anything else. It is worth pausing for a moment to think this over. How many times do we experience organisational performance spoken about in terms of people, departments, functions, IT, processes, and so on? This perspective is ubiquitous. We hardly ever hear performance spoken about in terms of feedback or communication. We see these as necessary interfaces, not the primary driver of performance. But a systems approach would say the exact opposite, that the performance of the whole is an outcome of the synergies or interconnectedness of the parts that make up the whole. To emphasise the importance of this, systems thinking prioritises an understanding of the synergies between the parts of a system over the analysis of each part taken individually. In more practical words, the quality of the communication between two departments is more critical than the performance of each of the departments taken separately. Think about the shift in thinking that needs to take place to allow that to happen. It requires looking at organisational improvement in the reverse order in which most do today. Instead of looking into each department as an individual unit, we'd first take them collectively and assess the gaps between them. This way of thinking places the flow of information at the centre of an assessment.

For those that are firmly grounded in a reductionist way of thinking, the implication can seem somewhat counterintuitive, that a system will perform sub-optimally when the focus of attention is on the parts rather than on the relationships between the parts. Let's take a straightforward factory example. Imagine we have a production line made up of three machines. The first two machines are state-of-the-art and can process hundreds of pieces an hour. The third machine (C), however, is older, and it can only process half the amount of the other two newer machines. After a while, a pile of pieces builds up at machine C as machines A and B produce more than machine C can process in the same period. Eventually, the pile is so large the whole production line comes to a halt.

The feedback from machine C to machines A and B to hold off on production until it is finished is far more important to the performance of the production line than the maximum capacity of machines A and B taken in isolation.

The feedback from machine C to pause production on machines A and B is called a stabilising or balancing feedback because it regulates the flow and is, therefore, a control mechanism.

Now picture this as service departments processing demand. The same situation occurs. The first two departments have become very efficient and produce a great deal of throughput, while the third department isn't so capable and melts down under pressure. Now also image, given this scenario, that the first two departments were asked to slow down, and help the third department become capable of handling their throughput rather than continuing at the same pace.

In contrast to duplex systems, systems with one-way information flow have no self-correcting capability. Think of a time when you've described a situation as out-of-control or spiralling out of control. We call this kind of feedback, reinforcement-feedback or a reinforcing-loop because over some time this situation continues in the same increasing trend.

So, the two forms of communication we see between the parts of a system are:

- The reinforcing loop, that over time creates an increasing situation
- The balancing-loop that puts in place an intervention or control to regulate the effects of a reinforcement-loop. Making balancing-loops a regulatory measure.

We see these kinds of feedback loops all around us. Recall the trend over the last ten years of the increase in pedestrian zones within town centres to lower traffic pollution, and controls such as GDPR that have been put in place inside organisations to regulate the flow of personal data.

A complex and dynamic system is made possible because of the presence of finely tuned reinforcement and balancing loops.

Nature has a peculiar way of applying balancing loops to reinforcing situations that are detrimental to the health of the planet. We think of an ecosystem as being in a stabilised state. The definition of homeostasis is the regulation of conditions maintained by living things and is often referred to as the 'cycle-of-life'. The Gala theory proposes that life on our planet is self-regulated by the synergistic interactions between living organisms and their organic and inorganic surroundings. Populations, for example, are regulated by a balance between eat or be eaten. When a species like ours disturbs that balance, then the ecosystem can become unstable.

Between 1980 and 2000 a community of around a hundred thousand otters on the Aleutian Islands thrived. The ecosystem provided them with a healthy diet of small fish, crab, shrimp and sea urchins, all supported by a healthy kelp forest. But suddenly, in ecological terms, the otter population dramatically decreased, and the kelp forests seriously depleted with much higher numbers of sea urchins appearing. After years of research, it was determined that fishing quotas had significantly depleted the population of fish, the staple diet of seals and sea lions, and as their numbers fell orcas turned their attention to the otters. In just five years, forty thousand otters had disappeared. As the otter numbers fell so sea urchins increased, and the sea urchins consumed so much kelp, it destroyed the ecosystem. To reverse this, they imposed much smaller fishing quotas.

Presenting feedback in a picture or diagram is a compelling way of visualising balancing and reinforcing effects. If we take a very simple diagram of births and deaths, deaths act as a reinforcement loop to births keeping the population under control.

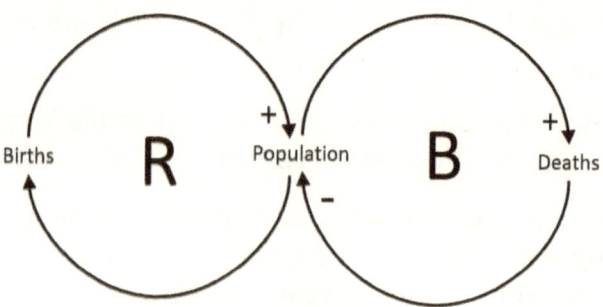

In our ecosystem example we have a slightly more complicated diagram, but again we have a balancing effect brought in by the fisheries commission to stabilise the fish population by controlling the fishing quotas, this, in turn, has a positive effect on the seal population, that ultimately results in more otters, (less being eaten by orcas), that eat more urchins, and eventually, helps the kelp forest recover.

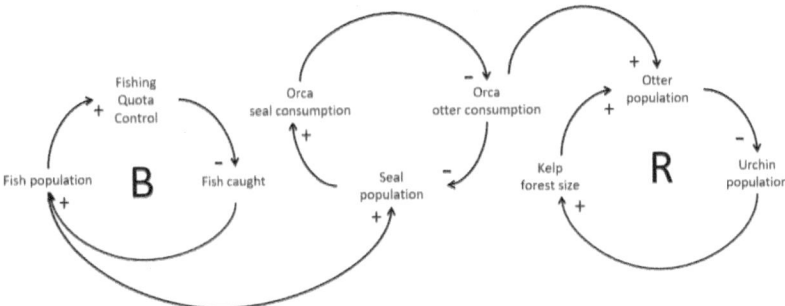

If you're starting to think about situations in your own life and workplace in terms of feedback loops, you're becoming a systems thinker!

ORGANISATIONS

Before we begin, it is necessary to point out that there are two perspectives we can take when dealing with an organisation as a system, (1) Inside-Out and, (2) Outside-In.

(1). Is a laboratory and, (2) Is the real world or the environment in which the laboratory exists.

This book is concerned with the laboratory – although even laboratories have environments.

The design of organisations has become somewhat of a template exercise, made up of ubiquitously named functions such as customer-services and finance, and terms that refer to processes like order-to-cash and procure-to-pay.

Performance improvement is generally regarded as a functional responsibility, dealt with in silos by departments individually, that gives little regard to the broader organisational system of which they are a part, let alone the external environment. This may sound somewhat harsh and to some may hint of a suggestion, that to improve requires the redesign of the whole organisation in one go. The point is only to surface that more than likely, the organisation wasn't designed with any conscious deliberation. And although plausible, hasn't been proven to be optimal.

We've already discussed that taking a system's view asserts that a whole system has properties of its own that don't exist within any of the constituent parts. This is a universal principle that applies to all systems, including organisations. This is what the expression "*the system is greater than the sum of its parts*" means, that the organisation although dependent on the properties of its departments, has properties of its own that are greater than the properties of the departments taken individually. Alternatively, when it is said that "*the system is less than the sum of its parts*", this can be taken as the system is operating at less than the total sum of the aggregated properties of its parts. Think about this for a moment. Imagine every department improves to a high level of performance, but they are not designed to communicate with each other effectively, it would create the same result as building a car using the best parts from every kind of car available – we would have a terrible system, because none of the parts have been designed to work together.

It is incredibly important to apply a social systems lens because they exert choice, and choice requires a conscious deliberation, not simply by individuals but by collectives.

Given the definition of systems states that the interconnectedness and configuration of the parts is what determines the behaviour of the whole, and it is the whole and the relationships of the parts that should be the focus for assessment, not merely the individual parts themselves, it would seem logical to assert that our focus should be placed primarily on the whole with a lead into functional design once that has been understood. However, as discussed, organisations aren't set up to operate in this way; to paraphrase Churchill, we become our buildings, so designing silos is not only what we get structurally it is what we become socially. Social silos can be tricky places to impart change because it's not the individuals we experience; it's the entire *social system*. What some pass off as cultural, meaning to change the behaviour [of a person], misunderstands some fundamental principles of social systems; social systems [as a whole], exert choice, and there are properties of the whole that don't exist in the parts [each person]. Systemic change is not achieved by trying to change the parts individually, a person; it is only achieved by changing the whole social system. Put simply, focusing solely on an individual does nothing to improve the performance of a team. The Greek football team in the 2004 European Championship are a testament to this.

The performance of an organisation is dependent on the flows of information and communication. These are the feedback loops between teams, department, functions and external partners. Managing the flows of information is not a reporting exercise, it is a systemic design task. The more people, especially managers, see information solely for the use of analysis and reports, used entirely as output control mechanisms, the more they run into performance dead-ends. Information flow is happening all the time in organisations, but it's not visible, and the necessary levels of integration just haven't been designed into the system. This means that the organisation as a whole also isn't visible. Of course, there are indicators, providing a snapshot of performance, but there is nothing that describes the nature of the organisation, it's lifestyle if you like. To use an analogy, I know several people with a high metabolic rate. They are slim, and they seem outwardly quite fit but take a closer examination, and you'll find an unhealthy resting heart rate, a higher than normal blood pressure and a troubling cholesterol level. I think organisations ran purely from financial reports are like this. On the surface, they seem healthy enough, but inside they're extremely laborious and inefficient. Designing for a better performing organisation requires a greater focus on the relationships in and between the social sub-systems, alignment of organisational and shared objectives, and above all, visibility of the feedback loops, that are required to make the organisation fitter and performing better.

Now, most people will agree with an earlier point I made, that it is very uncommon to see organisations that have turned their attention specifically to integration as a primary focus. Knowing where and how to start can be a difficult question to answer when we're sat in the middle of a well-established and firmly structured organisation. Two elements help us answer this question, demand and people. Notice I didn't say process. Process comes later.

Applying some focus here exposes social systems and their objectives and behaviours. Why do they exist and what choices are they making that influences the whole?

When organisations do take a systemic perspective, it is common for managers in those organisations to experience a fundamental difference in what they thought was happening to what is happening in reality. Deeper reflection starts to reinforce the reality that not only didn't the system invent itself, but its design was also done in pieces and brought together as a whole afterwards. The other thing that becomes obvious is that the organisation isn't static but moving and ever evolving beyond the original design. This movement is manifested in the emergence of informal networks that have outnumbered the formal structures. The troubling aspect of this is that those informal networks aren't visible. It starts to become clear that the thinking that created the original design is the reason for the emergence of these informal structures, and without them, the organisation would cease to operate. This lack of understanding of how the organisation is really working causes projects to falsely assume the framework of improvement is the formal structures and processes. In one organisation I worked for, the perception by the management team was that the IT systems responsible for resource and financial planning accounted for approximately eighty percent of the total effort. Their perception was centred on many assumptions such as their documented processes and the IT system in which the plan was stored, reviewed and approved. When we looked at the whole organisation, we gained an understanding of how each department completed the actual planning process and how information was flowing between them. It exposed that the IT systems were contributing to less than ten percent of the work, while the rest was being done offline by a small group of people (social system) they didn't even know existed.

How this and other organisations are typically shaped is based on a form of scientific reductionism. Reductionism is a vast subject and continues to be the subject of philosophical discussion with many facets. However, in its most primitive form it is analysis, the practice of trying to understand a whole by breaking it down into its constituent parts to determine their function and low-level interactions. Inside an organisation, it manifests itself in the disaggregation of functions to processes and tasks. These are then reassembled across other departments to create end to end processes. However, the integration between the different areas is treated as a secondary step, and in some cases as a neighbourly activity, rather than as a primary design consideration.

These principles of reductionism are applied to the whole organisation on the premise that the organisation is only the total sum of its functions. The English word reduce originates from the Latin word *reducere*, meaning, to bring back. By stating that the organisation is simply the sum of its functions, we are implying that the organisation can never be more than the sum of its functions. It also ignores that the whole organisation has properties that the individual functions and departments do not. Now, if this were said to most people in an organisation, we'd expect to get a fairly robust response, one that promotes a brand or customer value, but what I'm pointing out is that paradoxically, although these are probably true statements, it is not how people go about the task of designing organisational structures and processes.

A typical design implements the functions first and then the integration of functions. In one organisation, I worked with the Group Finance function saw themselves as a separate entity from the operating companies. The term *Group* in this organisation did not have a wholeness connotation, but a siloed one, and more importantly nowhere, in the organisation was there any sense of unity. I was once told that you can tell if people inside an organisation has a sense of unity, by whether they use the words *they* or *we,* to describe their organisation. If people talk about, *we* then they tend to feel a sense of belonging to a bigger purpose, but if they use the term, *they* to describe their organisation, it is a sign of fragmentation and disharmony. I'm not sure if this is a universal truth, but it is common to hear people use to the anonymous term *they* when referring to a broader entity.

Once each department has been established, the next step is to design the integration in what is commonly referred to these days as the end-to-end process. In some cases, these two events can be years apart. I never realised how stagnant organisations could be until one day I was invited to a meeting only to be presented with the minutes from the previous meeting held over five years before.

Because integration is not given a primary focus, we see gaps and spaces between functions and departments, and this we refer to as grey space. Areas that the organisation has little or no visibility of, and that no one manages or measures. In contrast to the Deming quote, the opposite is equally true, "*you don't get what you don't measure.*" I have heard many an argument against this view, but in the environment of organisational day to day life, if parts of an organisation are not owned and not managed, we see a new phenomenon, the emergence of social networks that come into existence to compensate for the lack of interconnectedness. In other words, they act as bridges over the gaps between areas of the organisation. They try and overcome the grey spaces between processes, but in doing so, they create their own, more significant grey space, as informal social networks are invisible in most organisations. For management, in general, it truly is a zero-sum situation.

The second and most important implication for designing the organisation in this way is that the customer's interests are lost within a purely internal and siloed centric focus. No one has the accountability, incentive or in most cases, the ability to move between functional boundaries to resolve the customer's problems formally. In one extreme case, I presented a senior manager with the whole system, of what I believed to be entirely under his control. I displayed it on a wall five meters wide by two meters tall. I was so proud of it. It showed, in the most explicit possible terms, the areas that were taking up to ten times longer to deliver certain types of customer demand, over the expected estimate. This was a good guy, I liked and respected him a lot, and he cared about the organisation. However, his response shocked me; in fact, it shocked me so much that it drove me to question my whole approach. After considering the wall for a few minutes and pacing up and down, he pointed at the wall and said, "*I don't own that bit, that bit or that bit.*" Moreover, although he was technically correct, I tried to explain how this was impacting the customer, but he wouldn't accept the areas he felt he wasn't responsible for or that didn't affect any of his performance measurements. Even more shocking was that all the other managers I later spoke with, that did own those areas he didn't, all said the same thing about their bits. In other words, no one owned the system, and even more disturbing, for all their pride in the company they had been for all their working lives, no one wanted to help fix the system or take the side of the customer.

When we take a step back and look at what's going on, people are surviving in a system, a system that doesn't allow for heroes. On reflection, what I was asking him to do was to take formal responsibility for areas his management neither considered his nor asked him to consider. Worse still, if he had taken the responsibility, he would have probably upset everyone around him, by 'stepping-on-toes', and exposing their problems to their managers.

The key for any organisation is not to focus on people individually but the social system as a whole and to question why people behave in the ways that they do. Weak organisational design is the main reason why we should assess the broader social systems, resulting in an understanding of how things are working. Not doing so leads to the fear of complexity resulting in a culture of cognitive dissonance, a culture where people convince themselves they're right to save themselves from the psychological anguish of realising they're wrong.

Even so, most organisations operate well enough, at least on the balance sheet, but this book isn't concerned with good or bad, it is concerned with how to make a systemic change that not only makes change systemic through normative intervention but creates results not previously thought possible.

Over time within organisations, there can become a detachment of the leadership team and managers from the day to day operations. This separation creates a division between what is intended or perceived to be happening and what is truly happening. To quote Peter Drucker.

"Management is doing things right; Leadership is doing the right things", Peter Drucker.

When there is a division between the perception of what is happening in the day to day operation and reality, conflict and tension are created between the leadership and the management. This conflict is created because there is a difference between what the leadership and the management perceive is the right thing. Also, because this goes unchallenged, we see people doing the wrong thing right. Not wrong necessarily in the sense of bad, but wrong in the sense of misalignment, and in conflict with the purpose of the organisation. Remember, the organisation has properties that don't exist in the functions taken individually. Only when the functions form the whole, do these properties emerge, so when departments change without considering the whole, these properties can be damaged or lost altogether. Misalignment is the most damaging cause of performance degradation inside organisations.

In very siloed and politically motivated organisations where an autocratic style imposes a command and control system for governing decisions, the ability for managers to do the right thing can often be impossible. *"A bad system will beat a good person every time"*, Deming.

Because this conflict is psychologically painful, it results in cognitive dissonance. Cognitive Dissonance is a psychological condition where we convince ourselves that what we're doing is correct, to mask a painful reality that we're probably not. So not only is management doing the wrong thing, they convince themselves they're doing the right thing. People generally want to do the right thing, so convince themselves they're not doing the wrong thing.

Doing the right thing is a leadership responsibility. When I was younger, I worked for GE. At that time, Jack Welch was the CEO, and he had decided to launch Six Sigma across the globe. All businesses in hundreds of countries. He explained that he believed variation was evil. What he meant by this was that when things go wrong not only does it cost the business money it also, and more importantly, hurts the customer. Five years later, I was walking through a very different kind of business in Sweden and there on the wall were precisely the same charts and style of statistical measurement we had in our business; totally aligned. What Jack Welch had done was to bring the shop floor to his boardroom so that he could see with as much clarity as was possible, how his system was performing. He mandated the methodology to such a degree that managers were asked to leave if they had not taken the training within the first year.

Now, most organisations aren't anywhere near the size of GE and don't have their financial reserves, but the principles of a whole organisation remain the same. For the organisation to be understood as a whole, there must be integration from top-to-bottom and left-to-right. In many leadership meetings across the years where the rollout of strategic change has been discussed the consideration of left-to-right integration is a common omission. The subject is almost always approached top-down because this is how leaders perceive themselves — above the management, propagating direction. Whereas, in a systems approach where the integration or relationship to management is paramount, then leadership becomes more of a supporting role that can be visualised as an inverted classic hierarchical pyramid, where the leadership is at the bottom, in a foundational sense, providing the ability for customer demand to flow across the organisation with as little disruption as possible.

System Conditions

It's easy to imagine how organisations can become misaligned due to individual functions changing their ways of working and establishing rules and policies to implement controls and governance. Every organisation is subject to law and regulation of some sort. The new General Data Protection Regulation, GDPR, has meant every organisation has had to look at how they handle and store personal data. Regardless, whatever conditions that are imposed on an organisation, at whatever level and however necessary, they create a constraint of some kind that results in a degree of overhead and ultimately an interruption to the flow of work. We call these 'system conditions', and it is critical to surface and validate them to gain a systemic understanding of the organisation.

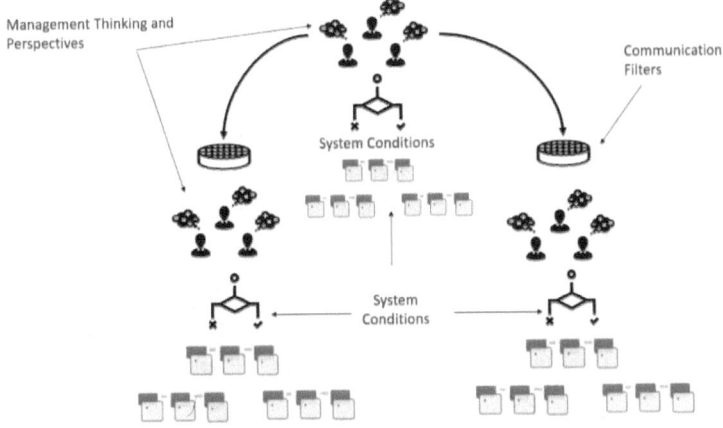

As these system conditions are exposed, it is typical to find that rather than being validated, most are found to be erroneous or at best superfluous to the real requirement. As conditions interrupt the work, and in many cases, create work, it is important to remove those that are not required.   With the increasing focus on risk and regulatory compliance, there is a strong temptation for organisations to view this as purely an implementation task (putting a policy in). But regulatory compliance should also be focused on appropriateness and be equally concerned with removing unnecessary policy as implementing it.

Beware of the *because*

When assessing a system condition, we need to be alert to the word *because*, because, *because* is a performance killer. As soon as someone uses it to explain the reason for a rule or policy, it should cause our spidey-senses to start tingling. In one very large financial services company, they had operated for many years under the *because* premise that the Financial Services Authority (FSA) had defined specific regulatory rules.   These rules introduced many rigorous operating controls (systems conditions) that placed a heavy burden on the organisation and was significantly impeding their ability to serve their customers. After a system-wide review that included a consultation with the

FSA, it turned out that over seventy percent of those rules served no purpose and were utterly spurious.

In very recent times with the introduction of GDPR, it is already becoming apparent that organisations don't understand the basic rules, and out of fear of breaching the new regulation, there is an overly bureaucratic *because* response that is imposing draconian measures on the use of data. The lack of understanding is always the reason why excessive and unnecessary policies are implemented inside organisations when understanding is replaced with conjecture and false assumption.

Information Flows

How information flows around an organisation is an essential indicator of how the organisation is operating. The weaker the flows, the weaker the organisation is as a whole. There are two types of information flow. First, is the formal information flows operated by software-enabled processes. Second, are the informal information flows that are typically a result of social networks that have emerged in the organisation.

Formal information flows have become a little confused over the last decade. My next point may not be universally popular, especially by those professionals in this area, but the term Business Intelligence has done more harm than good since Gartner introduced it in the early noughties. Before this BI, as it's known, was termed MI or Management Information in full. Management Information was made possible because of Management Information Systems, and this made good logical sense because from a systemic perspective a management information system is a sub-system of the management system, and this placed MIS firmly in the ownership of the management. In recent years those lines have become incredibly blurred, and in some companies, BI has become a purely IT-owned asset. The term BI has not only confused the industry it has transferred ownership of information from management to IT. More recently, terms such as *self-service*, and *agile BI* have become popular to promote a closer relationship to the business via a less invasive IT involvement. However, rather than correcting the situation these attempts have compounded the issue because they have kept the focus on technology, an IT domain, and not the root of the problem, which is information ownership, a business domain. Rather than face it, IT has avoided this question in the belief that business can't, and don't want to own IT, and out of a fear of losing control of it. As I mentioned earlier, there will be some that flatly disagree with this opinion and believes the role of the business is to purely consume information. I regularly hear that users don't care about technology. An analogy used in support of this argument is that of buying a car, "*I don't want to understand how the engine is constructed, I just want to drive it*". Although this opinion sounds plausible, it underestimates the need for managers to understand and appreciate technology. Holding them in a state of ignorance does nothing to build a relationship and solve problems together. It also, and more seriously, distances them from change decisions, and this creates a paradigm where it's always IT's fault. Finance learned this lesson in the 1980s. At that time, it was common for Finance to be purely a central department and be always under the spotlight. Finance was continually fighting with their Sales, Marketing and Operations colleagues, each blaming the other for lack of understanding and empathy. The answer was a redesign of the Finance function by introducing positions into each department while ensuring alignment to the mothership. This model is still the situation today and in fact, is an excellent model for MIS, or BI if you must.

In an organisation where managers jointly own MIS, we get a very different picture:

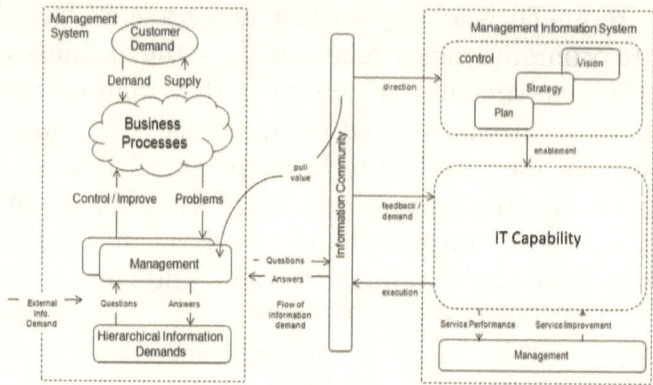

Here we see the information community acts as a bridge between the business functions and IT. Organising the information capability in this way creates synergies that reach every corner of the organisation and enables alignment. It also significantly improves the proliferation of know-how and consistent information.

As an illustration of the principle behind the community concept, we can consider an example presented by Eli Goldratt, the author of The Theory of Constraints.

Goldratt asked, which is the more complex system, System A or System B?

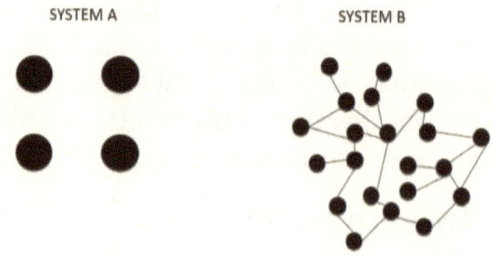

His answer was system A is the most complex. Because to introduce a change in system A would require four separate interventions, whereas system B would only require a single intervention, as all areas of that system are interconnected and therefore the intervention would propagate across all elements.

This is the essence of the Finance distributed operating model. More importantly, it is the most effective model for deploying change across an organisation.

The propagation of information should be built inherently into the design of the system. It shouldn't merely be an afterthought that is considered only once the individual components have been designed. It is a primary system property designed in from the beginning. There are barriers in the way of this propagation, usually in the form of conflicting or opposing objectives – more about this later.

Integration

If you managed to read the prologue, you'd remember that I mentioned I was working on a challenging project. Well, the reason that the project was so difficult was that during the integration phase, we were having lots of issues. The integration phase of a traditional software project, in this case implementing an ERP system, is where all the individual modules, such as taking orders, holding stock and receiving payments and financial accounting are all brought together and tested as a complete system. The phases of the entire project go something like this:

1. Design

2. Build

3. Integration Test

4. Acceptance Test

5. Implement.

As you can see, the Integration Test is step 3. You'd expect though looking at this that step 1 would consider the integration, especially when one of the outputs of this phase is a blueprint, describing the details of what is required to be implemented.

However, with this project and with the general industry, most issues come out in step 3. One reason for this is that the teams building the solution aren't integrated. Of course, they have integration meetings, but this isn't integration. Creating software solutions in modular or functional silos, and adding the integration later, to form a whole solution, is the primary reason why software projects fail. In one project, I was part of; there were over three thousand defects found in step 3.

Some years ago, I was working for a next day delivery business where the marketing team had decided to run a promotion on a large range of products that the Product Management department had decided to discontinue. The results were horrendous; lost sales, many customer complaints and damaged reputations.

Steve Jobs once provided a quote about the difference between a Dell installed with Windows and an Apple Mac with IOS. He said *"There's no other company that could make a MacBook Air and the reason why is that not only do we control the hardware, but we control the operating system. Moreover, it is the intimate interaction between the operating system and the hardware that allows us to do that. There is no intimate interaction between Windows and a Dell notebook."*

The expression, *intimate interaction,* is the subtlety that is lost when people think interaction simply means communication. *Intimate interaction* means to design.

In his book, Building Microservices by Sam Newman, he states *"Getting integration right is the single most important aspect of technology associated with microservices [the glue between modules in software applications]. Get it wrong, and disaster awaits"*.

So why then, when it's so evident that integration is such an intrinsic property in the design of a system, is it typically given secondary consideration? The reasons reside in our culture of reductionism, and most of that has been reinforced by our schooling that is broken down into subjects. Rarely are we taught how subjects overlap and complement each other and shown how they can be more effective when we apply them in combination into real-world situations. For example, why not teach statistics to children by involving them in a business setting, where statistics are brought to life. The children would not only learn experientially; they would also learn two subjects in one. I've met many production managers that don't understand basic statistics. We are taught as children that knowledge is gained from remembering facts, and intelligence is measured by how many facts can be recalled during an exam. We're also not taught how we think and how we learn; how habituation sets in, and when this is good and when it is bad; how social networks form, and how they breakdown; how to reflect and assess our beliefs and values; what self-awareness means and how our behaviour is contagious. We have an education system that is built purely on personal performance. Little wonder then that the workplace adopts the same principles.

When we enter the workplace, we're faced with imposed boundaries and demarcations that shape our thinking. We're placed within a team, within a department, within a function. The concept of segregating and reducing frames everything we do. It isn't surprising then that when we talk about large scale projects such as implementing an IT system, people find it difficult, almost impossible to consider an alternative approach that takes a system-wide perspective.

The concept of reductionism is so deeply ingrained in our psyche that undertaking an alternative way of thinking is extremely difficult. Unlearning or suspending knowledge on one subject is necessary if we are to understand something that seems to contradict it. Taking on a new mode of thinking is not to be underestimated. The physicist David Bohm developed a Socratic style method of communication called *Dialogue* that requires people to suspend their preconceptions, beliefs and prejudices so that the thoughts of others can move throughout the group enabling a psychological integration to take place, resulting in a collective understanding. Out of that, he proposed come new thoughts and ideas that produce results that are not possible of being created otherwise. He once said, "*Suppose we were able to share meanings freely without a compulsive urge to impose our view or conform to those of others and without distortion and self-deception. Would this not constitute a real revolution in culture?*". In other words, through better integration, the group will possess properties of thought not possible from a single individual.

If we take his words as he literally meant them, image how difficult this would be to achieve, but within his words is a fundamental truth that is so critical for guiding us through defining our organisation as a whole system, so it is essential that we self-consciously try to suspend our own beliefs until we have understood the larger picture at hand. It is ok not to do this perfectly, as long as we try. Improvement is about learning and direction, not perfection.

Understanding how we think first needs a self-reflective view of the beliefs we hold. Generally, we are not introspective enough, and we fail to review our current mode of thinking adequately enough to consciously determine whether what we're doing is correct or not. Two introspective questions that help us a great deal are; *assumption or fact?* And, *values or beliefs?* Assumptions are perceptions based on our perspective; *facts* are the reality-based on evidence. *Values* are those things we hold precious, like kindness, while *beliefs* are those things, we believe to be true like there is a God. Assessing our thoughts in this simple way removes a form of mental grey space, that unless cleared, can lead us blindly down an unnavigated path, in the form of unconscious sleep.

This traffic is a nightmare!

The term perspective refers to a vantage point, from which one position may make things look very different than from another.

Our role, position or even timing into a situation can skew our perspective. How many times have we entered a situation that isn't going so well and thought, *"how could the previous team have done something so crazy?"*. Unfortunately, our eagerness causes us to rush in and judge without considering the reasons for it first. Like the person who joins the traffic jam and criticises the number of cars on the road, without an elevated perspective, it isn't clear what the problem is or if we're even a contributing factor.

It also means that we often perceive a person's beliefs based on their actions, but that's not always the case. A person's view of the world may be entirely different from their current position. A person may decide to do or say something that is based purely on their perspective rather than their actual view of the world. For example, someone may say *"of course we would like to do that, but we need to be practical..."* or *"I'd like to help, but the rules say I can't."* A worldview is about the deeper values we hold, that can often feel compromised when we're forced to override them. This is quite common in organisations where people feel frustrated and lacking the ability to make the changes, they think are necessary. It is a very powerful exercise for both the individual and for teams to surface these perspectives and worldviews explicitly. Even simple questions like *"what's our purpose?"*, can get the conversation going for hours, even days. Doing so often surfaces many false assumptions, such as the FSA regulation example.

Surfacing false assumptions in a collective setting can result in a change to the group's perspective and consequently align them towards a common worldview. For example, several years ago, I was part of a small team tasked with implementing a new company-wide management operating model. When we first lobbied the executive team with our proposal, they rejected it immediately. We proposed to implement a quality management methodology supported by a new organisation structure that would consist of a left-to-right or end-to-end process management structure. We decided to perform an exercise of surfacing the perspectives and beliefs of each manager. The result was a broad consensus that the reason it couldn't be implemented was that the functional heads perceived it as a total replacement of their role and therefore as a personal threat to them. Even some of the executives struggled to see the practicality of it. After a few months, the answer that proved the most palatable was to overlay a process management structure over the functional structure, in effect the two working together with different perspectives, one functional and one process.

Although this created a systemic change in the organisation and was implemented systematically within each function and created value by exposing the grey space between them, the change was excruciating. The main reason why this was so difficult was that people found it very challenging to take a non-functional perspective. The conceptual boundaries that framed a function's existence were very real in the minds of all the managers. Supply Chain, Operations, Sales, Marketing, Product Management and so on all held a very firm view that these structures were what kept the company together and without them, chaos would ensue and result in collapse.

After a few months of relative harmony, things started to go wrong. What emerged was a biblical truth, "*No one can serve two masters.*", *Matthew 6:24.* A common flaw with matrix organisations. Conflicts grew between the process managers and functional managers. After some time and many reviews, we found the problem in the way each was measured, and the answer was to align these and to share objectives. A concept very alien to everyone, including HR.

The integration of objectives would never have been considered unless this conflict had arisen. However, had a full systemic review taken place beforehand it would have shown the causal conflicts that were inevitably going to happen. We had surfaced the assumptions and beliefs of the managers but not how they were operating. We had not considered the environment in which they operated. Because their management team above them had defined this environment, we had forgotten to understand the relationships or integration between them.

Contradicting or opposing metrics is something that needs to be fully sought out during an assessment of how the organisation is operating. Misaligned machine performance can lead to the overproduction of stockpiles, and marketing campaigns without a supply chain involvement can lead to disappointed customers. There are a plethora of opportunities for conflicts caused by the misalignment of objectives inside even small organisations.

Going back to the beginning of this example, the initial design work for the new organisation structure didn't start well. The problems lay in the way in which we approached it. We began with an analysis of the processes, and by creating roles for management across the new end-to-end processes while leaving the functional teams as they were. Equally troublesome, as mentioned above, we hadn't considered how the leadership team where imposing conditions on the functions, such as performance targets.

What this analytical approach to defining processes failed to recognise was how the organisation was currently working. Many of the people that were pivotal to the day to day operations were not invited to the initial workshops, generally because the management team did not regard them as senior enough. It wasn't until their names kept coming up time and again that they were eventually asked to attend. By this time, weeks had passed, and people had started to become frustrated and doubt whether the idea of a new solution was even doable. However, what eventually started to happen was some managers began to reset their worldviews as they began to recognise the value of the less senior people; you could say that they began to unlearn how they thought the organisation was really operating. Some people, but only a few, refused to accept the change, and it tended to be some of the more senior people that had established themselves as company *experts*. In their eyes, it wasn't right to suggest it was more junior people getting the job done. Pride took them over, and some even left the organisation altogether because of it.

Motives

The most significant challenge for any organisation wanting to make a substantial change is overcoming its very structure. To paraphrase Churchill again, 'changing ourselves needs us first to change our structures'. Change at scale is impossible without the CEO and his team onboard. Especially in siloed organisations where there are large divisions between departments, and where there is no formal visibility or controls between them. This truth is a bitter pill to swallow for any team trying to implement a change they want to become systemically adopted. Even so, there are many well-intentioned people I've worked with over the years that have failed, that had a senior mandate and took a top-down approach where they tried to influence the rest of the organisation by employing CEO sponsored change managers. The issue is not the change; it is the motive. Of course, everyone involved believes it to be the right approach and wants it to be successful, but when the underlying motive is idealistic, or worse, empire building, failure looms, and only success breeds success. It's not possible to focus on both ego and success. The history books are full of conquerors that have overreached and caused the fall of their empires. It is more important to develop than to grow. Success will bring its own reward. The only purpose is to improve so the customer benefits.

Are you sure you know where we're going?

Two terms that have become ubiquitous with change management are *plan* and *roadmap*. On the surface, they feel compatible if not essential for driving change into an organisation. However, they can become a real impediment to change if they become the focus. The first principle of defining a system is to get knowledge by studying it. The starting assumption from a study exercise is that we don't know what will be found and therefore we don't know what needs to be changed. The issue with the approach that most change initiatives take is that they stipulate the outcomes or deliverables upfront before any knowledge of the real situation has been gained. This fundamental flaw assumes that executives and managers know what problems need solving, such as, *"we need an ERP system!"*, leading immediately into the planning of these initiatives, that takes on an operational nature and begins an accounting exercise for the necessary resources of time, people and budget. It isn't uncommon to see a project plan thousands of lines long with countless interdependences, underpinned by an extremely paltry justification.

Alternatively, a common experience by those that practice a systems approach to change begins with an unconstrained study phase, whose purpose is to gain knowledge of what is currently happening. For clarification, unconstrained does not mean without a framework of resources; it means not constrained by a prescriptive outcome. When this approach is taken, the results are greater than what they first imagined, and they're always typically very different from what was first thought. In one conference I attended, a local authority that had adopted a systems approach for dealing with what they called 'problem families' that were regularly placing high levels of demand on over twenty of their local authority services. After a study phase and targeted intervention, they reported an eighty percent reduction in demand. They managed to achieve this through the introduction of multidisciplinary teams. The GP that presented their results said before they started, not only did she think it was a complete waste of her time, time she didn't have, it wouldn't even be practical – even if it did work, how could this approach scale? She'd concluded at the time that this issue was so systemic and so complex nothing was going to make any significant difference. It had been going on for so many years, and no change initiative had ever worked. At the end of her presentation, she said, *"no one ever imagined these results, not even me"*.

The temptation is to jump to conclusions about what is required and what can be achieved, but a study to gain knowledge of the reality is essential for identifying new opportunities. What the Doctor and her team uncovered were properties of the whole problem that were not visible by looking at the demand being placed on each service individually. These properties were what identified the real causes and consequently allowed the team to create a systemic solution.

The Roadmap

The prevailing view of a roadmap takes on a similar approach to a plan, in that it attempts to plot out beyond the current timeline what should be achieved over time. Again, this sounds plausible, even sensible, but the failure is to presume what direction the change should take. In my twenty years of IT, I can't recall a remotely accurate roadmap. It isn't just internal factors that destabilise the roadmap; external factors often do too, such as changes in technology trends and market conditions. The standard response is *"without a roadmap, how do we know where we're going?"*. The answer to this question is, we know better where we're going when we understand where we are, and what problem we're trying to solve. Gaining knowledge is always the next step. Having a roadmap without an understanding of the current situation is only a psychological comfort blanket. When I say, understanding the current situation, I don't mean a maturity model that most consulting firms present. I mean real knowledge of how information is flowing and how social systems are responding to the work.

Technology roadmaps have another consequence. Version chasing. As software vendors improve their products, they bring in newer versions and decommission the support of their older products. This incentivises customers to keep up to date, in fear of having systems that are not appropriately supported. As a result, many organisations find themselves in a perpetual planning cycle, forever trying to keep up. Those that slip and don't keep up find themselves with a much higher cost and impact later, as they are eventually forced to upgrade. Deciding this direction before implementing software is always much more preferable than realising it afterwards.

Studying

The purpose of a study phase is for the team to learn about what is happening and how the organisation is operating. Once learning occurs, the management team can adapt the system and collectively respond to the changing needs. Their goal is to develop a learning-adaptive Management System that can identify threats and opportunities, make collective decisions and create a culture of improvement. There must be a clear line-of-sight for all managers to observe how the overall organisation is performing and what level of contribution their teams are making. Information flow must be designed into the work to provide managers with the ability to make insightful and systemically balanced decisions while enabling them to remove grey space. However, this requires more than observation, no matter how accurate the information. It also requires an inquiry into the patterns and themes that are creating variations in performance; this is how to get real knowledge.

Feed me, Seymour. Feed me!

The term Key Performance Indicator or KPI is so generalised these days that the meaning of what they're trying to measure is often forgotten. I hear so many times people say, "*we need better KPI's*", without any idea of what *better* means. Jack Welch's statement variation is evil, implied improvement, and the lack of it resulting in a negative impact on the customer, but he also meant, that every small variance from what was expected or wanted, hurts the whole in some way. While KPI's seem to satisfy the appetite for measuring things, truly assessing performance needs an understanding of variation in the work, and this requires a statistical method, not a KPI. The report in the management pack may call it a KPI, and in general, there's no harm in that, but the damage happens when people in the organisation believe the focus of their attention should be on the KPI and not the variation.

Ackoff's model states that the journey from data to information to knowledge to understanding is what creates for informed decision making within the Management System. This journey, however, is a significant one that requires learning and adaptation to be realised within the Management System itself, and not as an implicit and undefined concept, but as an actual tangible activity so that managers know what learning means and can translate this onto their performance improvements for their organisation. The distance between information and understanding is significant. Big improvements come when the organisation can adapt quickly and know the difference between blindly tinkering and systemic change. Making changes in one department without the appropriate level of consideration given to the broader environment is blindly tinkering, however well-intentioned.

Adapt or die

To adapt is to respond to an internal or external change and still maintain or improve the overall performance. Adaptation is often confused with evolution. Many organisations believe they must evolve and even state that they have evolved. Whereas what they have actually done is to adapt. The distinction between the two is that evolution refers to an involuntary response to change, while adaptation requires a conscious choice; in other words, things don't choose to evolve. Learning and adaptation are also confused. Learning is to improve against a constant, whereas adaptation is to adjust to changing conditions. Learning and adaption are both required if performance is to be improved in both unchanging and changing times. Organisations that don't understand their systemic nature evolve. They evolve through the emergence of social networks that compensate for the lack of systemic management. There is no collective conscious choice taking place.

Charles Darwin, "It is not the strongest of the species that survives, nor the most intelligent that survives. It is the one that is most adaptable to change."

The key to understanding the effectiveness of any organisation is first to realise that the system as a whole can't learn and adapt unless its management can. After all, management is the control of a purposeful system. Therefore, the management system must be capable of learning and adapting. To do so requires a continual supply of information and that means the need for well-defined information, based on precise method, or in more succinct words, Method -> Measure -> Manage

Method -> Measure -> Manage

As managers begin to observe variation in their work, the demand for more information increases as the analysis starts to unpick the reasons for it. Often the source of the data is not present in any IT system, and this can be difficult to manage if the correct working practices are not in place that explains how to respond in these situations. It also sends IT into a spin because what they want to do is jump straight into a technology solution. Collecting data for analysis should be an obsession for all organisations; however, knowing what to collect is the key. Analysis performed on big data always starts with small questions. Big data for the sake of it, is not only a waste, but it also promotes a myth that insight can be found in data sets lacking in quality and structure. Therefore, it is critical that, big or small, data is collected and treated, in a way that is aligned to our starting question. It is very common to find non-systemised data in the grey space between formal structures and processes. These process steps in the grey space are often critical to performance because they disrupt or prevent the synergy across the organisation. However, these areas are usually the last places people look to get data from, and more often than not, if they do manage to obtain it, they will have usually stumbled across it by chance.

Another essential classification of failure that measuring variation, if done correctly identifies, is the types of demand passing through the processes. The simple formula, Capacity = Work + Waste is an important one because work should be defined as value-work and not simply work-to-be-done. If the work we're doing is wasteful, then it's work that we shouldn't be doing at all. By waste in this context I don't necessarily mean additional activities or inefficiencies, such as defined by Lean practices, I also mean demand that was generated because of not doing the work correctly in the first place. This differentiation of the different classifications of demand is critical. There are three types of demand; value-demand, demand-failure and failure-demand. Demand-failure is to fail to do something right the first time. Failure-demand is a demand that comes back because it wasn't done correctly in the first place. Value-demand is to add value to the customer by fulfilling their requirement in a manner that meets or exceeds their expectations. Essentially, supplying value-demand means that customers pull value from the organisation because it is their demands that are driving the need for improved performance. Therefore, by adopting this focus, management is also pulling value from the systemic approach they have developed and implemented. Call centres have been learning this lesson for several years now. Up until recently, it was a standard belief that the best practice for reducing cost in a call centre was to reduce the average call handling time, but this has now been utterly debunked. This simple truth can be found in our own experiences. How many times in the past have you had to chase an issue with your bank or even your internal help desk and found that the help desk doesn't help? Also, how many times have you experienced layers of IVR that make you press one for this, then two for that and after eventually getting to the end of it you're told, "*sorry we're closed, please call back later*". We all share this pain. What many call centres have realised, especially some banks, is that the number of calls received is not all of type value-demand. What those that have recognised this have found, is that most calls were failure-demand, resulting from demand-failure. Before this eureka moment, many organisations expanded their call centre capacity to accommodate all the incoming calls, rather than eradicating all their failure demand.

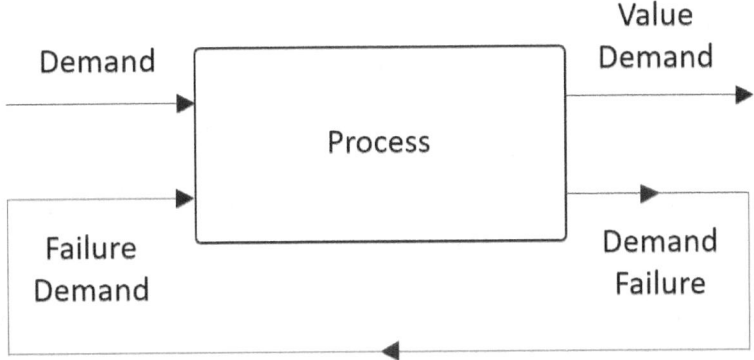

Another, possibly abstract, result of this kind of study is the concept of uncovering a property of the whole system called unintended consequence. Comparing the primary purpose of a system against what it actually does, begins to identify those things that happen that we don't want to happen, and they are another form of waste. Moreover, these negative things occur because of system design. By design, I don't necessarily mean consciously designed, often unintended consequences are found to be caused through evolved social practices, no explicit choice was made, but rather a chain of cause and effect that spreads through the network like the ripples on a pond. A straightforward example of this is conflicting measurements between departments or functions, resulting in opposing behaviours. Some unintended consequences, however, can result in much more severe situations than a conflicting measure.

An extreme example was the prohibition in the US. The banning of alcohol created an underground system of organised crime. In this case, the unintended consequence was much worse than the original problem.

The system says no

A significant insight because of understanding failure-demand is the realisation that it is the system causing the problem, not the people. It is worth re-reading the previous sentence, as it is a universal truth ignored by most HR policy regarding an individual's performance appraisal.

A culture shift in the call centre world has been to shift the focus from blaming people to listening to customer calls and designing the system to satisfy as much demand as possible by the receiving agent. This has resulted in many training front line staff to resolve up to eighty percent of demand. Deming commented about this; he said: "*The system that people work in and the interaction with people may account for 90% or 95% of performance*". However, for the majority that hold on to a cost accounting mindset, they believe that putting skilled people on the front line is too expensive and not scalable. This was the very thinking that brought about the introduction of the back-office concept invented by Richard Chase, and ironically most likely caused the high demand volumes in the first place.

FALSE PARADIGMS

The Back-Office and Shared-Services

The term Back Office was first introduced by Richard Chase from the Harvard Business School, although there were examples of separating the work going back to the 1930s. The Banque Nationale pour le Commerce et l'Industrie (BNCI) implemented a new way of operating on the views of Frederick Winslow Taylor as far back as 1932. Taylor had developed a popular method of management, known contemporarily as Taylorism, that looked to optimise work by breaking it down into individual units of repeatable tasks. Management back then was unrecognisable against today's definition; it was more dictatorship than anything else. Workers were asked to perform the tasks machines couldn't, either because it was cheaper to use labour than buy expensive machinery, or because the technology fell short of what skilled people could do. Skill, but no thinking was required, it was truly a labour market.

Chase had a simple idea that by separating front line services from the task of the actual work, the real work could then be done by different people without interruption, leaving front line people free to capture more customer demand. The whole idea was founded on the premise of activity costing; that is, it is the transaction that creates the cost. He described that to optimise the task of getting the transaction completed; work should be passed to a secondary function, the back office, where processes are standardised and tightly managed to reduce cost. Taylorism. Unfortunately for all those that have followed this path and implemented back offices, shared services and help desks that don't help, the truth is, the transaction does not create cost; instead the organisation produces it through the generation of failure demand. Most that implement these models don't question them at all. They simply follow the industry norms; however, empirically unproven they are.

It doesn't matter if the work is done wrong on the front line, in a back office or on the moon. Wrong is wrong; failure is failure and waste is cost. Moving the work to a back office and not defining how to stop doing the work wrong or from even doing the wrong work, is merely doing the wrong thing righter. Standardising processes that create failure demand is not improving quality. It is just regulating failure. Furthermore, adding inspection tasks to capture failure is not quality either because the failure has already occurred. In precisely the same manner as, ISO 9001 does, that is described as *"the international standard that specifies requirements for a quality management system (QMS)"*. ISO 9001 is concerned with standardising unquestioned procedures rather than eradicating failure. Efficiencies and cost reduction made possible because of back-office operations is a myth. It is demand-failure (getting it wrong first time) and the resulting failure-demand (having to correct it), that creates cost.

Outsourcing

Before continuing, I would like to emphasise that this is not a public flogging of outsourcing. Some outsourcing makes perfect sense, such as placing your IT infrastructure in the cloud and leveraging the expertise a modern data centre can offer. However, moving work that requires an intimate understanding of your organisation to a team on the other side of the planet makes no sense.

The main argument for doing so is predicated on cost accounting principles; person A is cheaper per day than person B. Once again, this fails to recognise failure-demand. The reason for failure in this setting is mostly due both to the lack of knowledge in the outsourced provider and the hand-off's required to pass clear instructions of the work to them. Knowledge loss during hand-offs is rarely considered during this kind of activity cost accounting.   Activity-based cost accounting (ABC) assigns an overhead cost, people, for example, to the product.   So, any unit of work needed to complete a task, such as operating machinery or answering calls, that consume resources is defined as a driver of cost or as it's known a *cost-driver*.   These cost-drivers are typically categorised in two ways, activity and duration, to calculate how long a specific task takes to complete.

An example of where it can go terribly wrong is when organisations enter into outsourcing contracts for IT projects. The process typically goes something like this: the organisation will define a set of high-level requirements, these will be written into a document called a Request-For-Proposal (RFP) in the form of a set of questions and sent to suppliers. The suppliers will then respond to this request and try to convince their new prospective client why they are the most suitable to do the work.   These responses typically propose as much work be completed as possible, in the least amount of time and for as little cost as possible.

As the RFP process continues, if the potential future suppliers have met the main acceptance criteria, there is a primary, if not sole, focus on cost as the procurement department takes a leading role.   Given the main drivers here are scope and people, and because the customer is reluctant to reduce scope because they want everything they've asked for, the attention turns to people and the cost per day of each person or as it's known in the industry, the *rate-card*. The focus then becomes one of reducing the rate-card to the lowest possible value, and to achieve this; the people located offshore are presented as the best possible option. The supplier then provides case studies and assurances that not only is the offshore model far more cost-effective, but it can also deliver the work as efficiently and to the same level of quality as an onshore model.   Of course, these claims are never substantiated by real data.

There are two fundamental problems with the way organisations assess the offshore model.   First is the work is defined as completing definitive tasks before the real problem is even remotely understood. The way these contracts are written is to include conditions based on assumptions. Moving beyond these conditions requires a request for a chargeable element of work to be raised, known as a change-request; in other words, new work not specified in the original contract. Because the knowledge of the task to be completed at this is stage is general and relatively high level, especially on larger projects; the accuracy of the assumptions is hit and miss. One supplier's account manager I was working with some years ago responded to my objection to a very low quotation by saying *"don't worry Mark; we'll change control them to death, they won't know what hits them"*. After the project, this same person introduced a policy titled 'Defend The Base', which meant the IT support team that was located in the same building as their customer, were not allowed to even speak to them, in case they asked for favours.

In addition to changes are risks. It is common on larger projects for risks to be assigned a cost. For example, 'IF, developer X can't get business involvement for n days THEN, the task would slip by n days AND, the cost of n days of developer X's time would be Y'. At the end of another project I was involved with, an organisation implementing an ERP solution paid for over a thousand changes and dozens of risks which totalled many times that of the original project estimate.

The second problem is that the tasks are costed by calculating the number of person-days of effort that are required to complete each task in the plan and then applying a daily cost to that total number of days. So, for example, a senior developer may be assigned to several tasks totalling a hundred days of work, and they have a daily chargeable rate, of say, £800, so their total cost for the project would be £80,000. Once all the roles, people and day rates are defined and calculated they are totalled to provide an overall estimate. This approach is remarkably like the basic principles of Taylorism. Moreover, it fails to recognise any significant limitations in the ability to predict a task in this way; namely, it assumes the problems to be solved are well enough understood, which is hardly ever the case especially in more complex situations. It also considers the work will be done right first time, on every task. Most project managers that understand this add some padding or slack, but this slack expects no significant issues will occur, after all the proposal needs to be as low as possible to win the work, so margins are squeezed as tightly as possible. Finally, it makes no allowance for the time lost in the increasing need for communication via meetings and email. The time lost on these activities can be huge. They are typically also extremely error-prone where misinterpretation and misunderstanding are commonplace. On a relatively small project I was involved with, done in a very siloed organisation, over a period of three months, the total number of lines written in emails was estimated at between seventy and eighty thousand. Even taking the lower end of this range, that comes to around three and a half months of work for one person – or ten average-sized novels. In larger projects using offshore teams, it isn't uncommon to have thousands of lines of emails written every day. None of this additional effort is built into the costing model. The consequences of waiting time between communication are also never understood. The collective waste of all these unrecognised and unaccounted for activities can be enormous.

A further unintended consequence of standard outsourcing working practises is that as timelines get squeezed tasks also begin to overlap and multi-tasking increases. Everyone these days works in a multi-tasking environment. We all must pause on one task, before that task is finished, to progress on another that has suddenly been given a higher priority. We do this so instinctively that we don't even realise that we're doing it, and everything just blends. We never stop to think if all this jumping around makes sense or whether it comes at a price, that could be a reduction in focus or efficiency or both. In a project where timelines become compressed because of missed deadlines, there is a very real and negative impact of multi-tasking, and this is compounded further in an outsourced arrangement were communication requires more effort and explicit attention.

Regardless of the impression the term multitasking portrays, our brain can only focus on one task at a time. Studies have shown that not only does it kill a person's performance, but it may also even be damaging to the brain. Research results by the London University showed that during multitasking activities, a person's IQ score reduced, and research by Sussex University, using fMRI brain scans, found that people who heavily multitask had less brain density in the anterior cingulate cortex, an area responsible for empathy, and cognitive and emotional control. When our brain receives more information than it is capable of processing in one go, it places it in a queue. However, if too much comes in too quickly, then it only holds the last two stimuli and loses the rest. This is a human condition and not unique to those working in a different part of the planet. The delay caused because of error, further compresses the work, and the more compressed the work, the more multi-tasking occurs. And, then weekend working is suggested. This reinforcing loop is only balanced by extra time or a reduction in scope. Outsourcing may have looked a good idea to the procurement department and the project accountants, but they are rarely made accountable for the failures that then ensue as a result of the unit cost-based decisions. Neither are they told they made the wrong decision, because only reality can teach them this, and the bureaucracy of the organisation rarely exposes them to that.

Economies of Scale

When most people talk about economies of scale what they're referring to is economies of large scale, a theory that is predicated on the premise that there is a correlation between the size of an organisation and its potential for efficiency. The bigger its size, the more potentially efficient it should be in reducing the unit cost of each item it produces. Two examples are typically used to describe it. The first example is based on purchasing power. The more an organisation can purchase the lower the unit purchase price should be because, in theory, the supplier is more likely to offer a higher discount based on a more substantial order. Whenever I hear the subject talked about this is the first example people bring up. In fact, in most cases, it's the only example they can think of. The second example is focused on exploiting fixed costs. Fixed costs are those that remain the same regardless of what is produced, such as salaries, rent, electricity, gas, and phones. Variable costs, in contrast, are those that change in proportion to the volume of work being carried out, such as temporary workers, raw materials, sales commission. To be able to exploit fixed costs, an organisation must increase production, for example, let's take a company that makes laptops and each laptop they make costs £200 to produce. If the unit cost of £200 is made up of £100 of fixed cost and £100 of variable cost, then making 10,000 laptops a year would result in a total cost of £2,000,000; £1,000,000 of fixed cost and £1,000,000 of variable cost. Increasing production to 20,000 laptops a year would mean the total variable cost would rise to £2,000,000, but the fixed cost would remain the same at £1,000,000, reducing the unit cost to £150. Because of this, managers calculate the projected reduction of cost based on these principles and are encouraged if not incentivised to expand production. This idea is also referred to as diminishing marginal cost.

Of course, looking at this situation, it's quite easy to see that the primary pitfall is overproduction and stockpiling if sales are not considered or have been overestimated. I have witnessed factories that have overproduced so much they had nowhere to hold the excess stock and have had to make or rent additional warehouse space to hold it. If this continues, this can become a critical mistake as it starts to hit cash flow. I've seen cases where the stock has become so old it was no longer sellable and had to be scrapped and even written off. It is also a self-defeating activity, what the economists would call diseconomies of scale.

Eli Goldratt's Theory of Constraints (TOC) tackles traditional cost accounting and criticises the focus on unit cost. Rather than focusing purely on production, TOC looks at the entire organisation-wide value stream, including sales to minimise excess stock and maximise profitability. Putting it differently, rather than attempting to optimise the output of machinery, if this is suboptimal for the whole organisation, TOC looks to reduce variable costs by increasing efficiency through the eradication of constraints and bottlenecks. It calls this throughput accounting, and it was designed to analyse the performance of an organisation. Now, it is essential to understand here that throughput accounting is very different from traditional accounting. Throughput accounting starts with the primary purpose of being profitable or if the organisation is a non-profit, then sustainable. For the purposes here let's assume we're trying to make a profit. The next step is to recognise the significant constraint preventing us from doing so. Again, we'll assume this is generating revenue. It takes all the items from the income statement, balance sheet and cash flow and places them into one of three categories that are easier to understand and make decisions from; Inventory, Operating Expenses and Throughput. The first is the inventory. To calculate this, we total up all our investments. By investment, I mean all the money that is tied up in the system, such as machines, tools, raw materials, and finished goods. The second is Operating Expense. Here we take the total cost of making the product, called operating expense, such as salaries, rent, energy. Notice how both Inventory and Operating Expense combine fixed and variable costs. The third and final category is Throughput. Throughput is the rate at which we generate money through sales. Going back to our laptop example, if we sell each unit for £200 and deduct the direct material cost, it comes to say £130. So, if we sell one laptop today, we would have £130 worth of throughput, and if we sell a thousand, then we'd have £130,000 worth of throughput. Using this much more straightforward accounting method allows us to see precisely where within the process our costs are being generated, but also, where the constraints in the system are, that are hurting throughput value, and where change would have the most positive impact to profitability. Managers focusing their teams in this way not only allow them to make the right changes, but it also links them directly to the overall purpose of the organisation – to make a profit.

In his book The Goal, Goldratt tells the story of a production manager Alex Rogo, that is under pressure to turn his plant's performance around, under a threat of closure. In his journey to increase quality and lower unit cost he discovers, with a little help, that what's killing his performance is a lack of throughput caused by bottlenecks. Overproduction in one area of the plant was choking another, increasing cost. The 'Goal' interestingly was regarded as essential reading by Jeff Bezos for Amazon management, and for Jim Whitehurst's, of Red Hat, it was his 'favourite book of all time'. The underlying principle of flow is the foundation on which all quality management concepts have been built. When Jack Welch talked about removing variation, there's no doubt it's an effectiveness point he was making, but underneath that is the concept of when a thing is done right first time it flows through the system more easily.

Cost accounting, on the other hand, is not a quality management methodology, and it has no interest in flow or variation at all, indirectly some may contend, but not in reality, and people that think this way are wishful thinkers. Cost Accounting is centred on the principles of economy of scale and unit cost. Whereas, throughput accounting is focused on the principles of economy of flow. Therefore, the economy of flow is deemed more aligned to customer's demand. Given today's society is very "*I want it now!*" centric, with an ever-increasing culture of self-gratification, speed is far more appealing for many organisations than lowering unit cost. However, the change in thinking towards quality and variation removal has been anything but ubiquitous, and even more so, the change towards flow in accounting practices has been almost non-existent.

When Taiichi Ohno, regarded as the father of all modern quality management systems, developed the Toyota Production System he did so by attributing total cost to how smoothly demand flowed through his system, even if this had a detrimental effect on unit cost. An important understanding of his approach is to realise he didn't focus on managing costs directly as cost accounting does. His focus or principle if you like, was that by focusing on flow, fewer things would be done wrong, resulting in better quality product and less cost.   In other words, cost reduction is a consequence of doing the right thing, and doing the right thing is a consequence of improving flow.   In a typical organisation that serves customers, doing things wrong tends to come back, so doing things right and only once is the reason for a focus on flow. When cost accounting predicts the unit cost or sets a standard cost, it does so, based on a set of educated assumptions, but it is not knowledge in the scientific sense. When the flow is calculated, as we'll show later, it is based on real empirically-based experience.

The concept of flow has been slow to catch on in western culture, but in Japanese culture, it is intrinsic to life, from psychology to architecture.   Maybe this is the only reason why a company like Toyota could have developed the concepts of flow in an organisational context. When the West tried to copy them, they failed because they misunderstood these deep routed principles and regarded their practices as mechanical tools to be deployed.

Aligning the subject of flow to IT and assessing it against methods like waterfall-based project management, identifies a stark contrast. Rather than with flow in mind, projects are planned on the principles of economy of scale and unit cost. Waterfall is a linear implementation method that sequences the delivery through phases, starting from the initial project setup to the ongoing support of the delivered solution.   Waterfall does not consider economies of flow at all. Consequently, Waterfall and its associated methodology Prince2 has been criticised for not focusing on speed or efficiency.   In response to this, the methodology Agile was born that has its roots in the principles of Lean. Although Agile has had a positive impact on the efficiency and effectiveness for delivering software, implementing IT using the Agile, or any flow-based methodology for that matter, is still doing the wrong thing faster when solutions are implemented before studying the system to determine what problem requires solving. Furthermore, in response to this criticism even more methodologies such as Design Thinking have come along to fill in the gap that has become so apparent in recent years, which is the need to design solutions that solve the real problem instead of a perceived one. The answer is not more methodologies; the answer is to study the flow of demand. Although, and without being in danger of contradicting myself, Design Thinking has some real merit and can be a powerful approach when implemented correctly.

Another norm in IT associated with economies of scale is to employ specialists that focus on specific activities. This is the Adam Smith thinking of division of labour or in more modern language the segregation of duties. The issue is not with having IT specialists, of course, this is necessary in a highly technical world, the problem is segregating them into different teams and in many cases, different locations based on a specific skill. I've witnessed, and on occasion, been pulled into horrible situations where the design of the operating model has created *factories* per technology discipline, where the segregated teams work in total isolation with little communication with the outside world, let alone the customer. Furthermore, the different factories significantly overlap, resulting in systemic integration issues and the duplication of work. In one example that I will explain in more detail later, a study uncovered four security teams under the same IT umbrella, contracted from different companies, with low levels of contact between each other and all overlapping to some degree.

To compound the cost associated with these practices, because the work is segregated, either by team or phase or worst both, organisations employ layers of project managers to pull the work together and attempt to report it holistically. In one very large organisation, they even employed a project management team to manage the project management teams. After a while and at great expense, it was scrapped because their perception that it is people that drive performance and not the system was proven to be utterly false.

Examples in IT seem endless. One of the most frustrating in my career has been the arguments over project infrastructure. No organisation I have ever worked for wants to pay for production sized non-production systems. The case is always based on unit cost and never the work. This is because only the unit cost is accounted for in the organisation's financial statements and never the wasteful reasons for the total cost. At the end of a project phase, even the *lessons learnt* exercises don't work to persuade the accountants, which means they're more *observations made* than anything learned. The issue is that in a large IT project, developers need to test their new configuration, the more realistic, the better. This also extends to the business. Without the right testing environment, things always get missed. Remember Stringer and his acorn analogy. On one very successful project, I was involved with we converted a corner of a warehouse to construct the new system; conveyor belts and all so that users could experience the solution first-hand in a safe and realistic environment. Without a correctly designed environment from which to test, it is not possible for IT professionals to develop solutions properly. What results is hundreds of hours lost in waiting, and many more defects found further into the project life cycle, if not in production. These defects are then fed back into the beginning of the delivery cycle as failure-demand to be corrected. The total cost is never calculated or analysed; it just disappears into the proverbial ether.

One last point on this subject before we close is the concept that some economists now believe that directly managing costs cause costs to increase. I know, this sounds wholly counterintuitive, but, when you think about it, this is precisely what Taiichi Ohno recognised. Furthermore, when you take a step back and think about our own experiences, it starts to make sense. In an everyday example, buying cheaper products usually ends up more expensive because their quality is generally not as good, and we must keep replacing them. I can hear my Dad now, "*buy a*

Boch Mark and you'll have it for years". However, more serious examples can be seen in cost-driven cultures. In an article from Mckinsey titled "*Five ways CFO's can make cost cuts stick*" they say "*Sometimes, managers lack deep enough insight into their operations to set useful cost reduction targets*", although I agree with this in principle it seems to conclude that managers are at fault.

They go on to say "*Amid a crisis, they look for easily available benchmarks, such as what similar companies have accomplished, rather than taking the time to conduct a bottom-up examination of which costs can—and should—be cut. In other cases, individual business unit heads try to meet targets with draconian measures that are unrealistic over the long term, such as across-the-board cuts that don't differentiate between those that add value or destroy it*".

In other words, under pressure managers that don't understand their system look outside their organisation for silver-spoons and quick fixes, and in doing so, they're likely to do the wrong things. Finally, they say "*While there's no single silver bullet to ensure that cost-management programs will stick, large, multi-business unit organisations can better their chances by improving accountability*". So, when all else fails, blame the people. My intention is not to openly criticise the author's intent, I agree with some of their points, however, assigning accountability and blame in an environment that fails to drive a culture of empiricist based study to determine the systemic drivers of cost, is shooting in the dark – and you may just kill some very good people. Rather, what this article demonstrates is that when we focus on cost directly, there's no easy answer; in fact, there's no answer at all for creating effective, sustainable change. The reason for this can be found in systems theory. When we look at things in isolation and only consider one property of it, in this case, cost, we fail to see all the other interconnected relationships and properties that thing has. So, changing one aspect of a system in isolation, without regard to the other components, damages the system.

The economy of scale does not consider the impact waste has on the whole system, and if the waste is reduced, whether this would change the basis of the initial decision. For example, by having help desks deal with requests immediately means the customer doesn't have to call back (failure demand). If failure demand is a large percentage of the total call volume, then an economy of scale argument is meaningless.

CONCLUSION

Organisations are a system. A complex system. Designing a system without understanding the whole will always result in suboptimal performance. Changing the parts of a system in isolation will, in all probability, also result in a detrimental effect on the performance of the whole. These principles are universal. So why then do we ignore them, fail to appreciate them or in some cases flatly reject them. I believe there are three core reasons.

Firstly, uncertainty causes anxiety-related stress, not fear. Unlike stress, fear is a response to an immediate threat or adverse situation. I don't believe it when I hear people say, "*people are frightened of change*". It's not fear, its uncertainty induced anxiety of something in the future. Uncertainty is the result of a perceived level of complexity that people hold. The greater the degree of complexity, the greater the uncertainty, leading to higher levels of anxiety and stress, resulting in the need for a neurological coping mechanism. The effects of uncertainty can be debilitating, causing severe levels of procrastination and maladaptation. It is a very powerful psychological protection mechanism. Our brains are designed to avoid stress, so our minds have techniques for resolving conflicts and calming the situation. We tell ourselves stories that rationalise inaction or a path of least resistance. It enables our brain to lower the flow of the harmful chemicals that make us sick and increases the production of chemicals that make us happy.

A second reason why I believe we don't change is that we get stuck in the way of thinking that perceives change as painful, mainly because it takes a great deal of mental energy, especially if the problem is complex and our capacity is low. I'm not implying people are lazy, on the contrary, many people I've met over the years are very motivated to change, but I also think that their primary beliefs rarely get questioned and if they do, not hardly ever rigorously enough.

Thirdly, and the most important, is motivation. Motivation, as obvious as it may sound, is directly linked to the difficulty of a task. The more difficult the generally less motivated we are to tackle it. However, although we assume motivation comes from our ability to reason and weigh up a situation, in an unbiased and logical manner, we are entirely wrong. If only this were true. Unfortunately, it couldn't be further from the truth. There are two kinds of motivation, intrinsic and extrinsic. Extrinsic motivation is conditional, an external incentive, for example, a bonus or something rewarding imposed on us. In these situations, it is typically only the reward that is pleasurable and not the task of achieving it. Intrinsic motivation is different; this is related to a person's values and beliefs, things that are personal to them. We all know the common expression, "*I was moved to do something!*". At the housing conference I mentioned earlier, I asked one of the panel members during the question and answer session, "*Why now?*", "*Why after all these years did the penny drop and caused you to do what you did?*". He'd been talking about the condition of social housing for the elderly and how after many years he realised the poor condition of it required a systemic solution. In answer to my question, he replied: "*the guys [the project team] took me to one of the properties and asked me if I'd be happy if my mother lived here*". Bingo!

The part of the brain that deals with reasoning and logic is behind your eyes. The part of the brain that deals with motivation or more accurately the part of the brain that produces the response for motivation is deep inside the brain. I believed for years that showing people data, that targets their pre-frontal cortex, should and would be enough to motivate them into action. When it didn't, which was regularly, I thought they were overly political or in some cases just difficult people. These concepts of how the brain works, at a basic level, are relatively easy and essential to understanding. I was going to write, it's not brain science, but of course, it is really.

I made the somewhat counterintuitive point earlier that focusing on cost has the effect of increasing cost. Well, in many ways, this same principle also applies to intrinsic motivation. For example, weight loss clubs are full of people whose weight regularly fluctuates up and down with no real consistency. The same is true for a gym membership, vegetarianism, reducing alcohol consumption or any goal where the outcome is the focus and not the means to achieve it. For example, one way to keep weight permanently under control is to play a sport we enjoy, or to become a vegetarian, is it probably more likely to last if the actual interest is animal welfare or nutrition. Whatever the outcome or goal, it should not be the focus. In other words, our intrinsic motivation can't be, mustn't be based on an outcome, however counterintuitive that may sound. It must be founded on the process of creating the outcome. Jack Welch once said, *"scrap the career plan, just be the best you can be today"*. In organisational terms, if the work isn't enjoyable and rewarding extrinsic incentives alone will never achieve success.

So, in the end, all organisations and more specifically, the people leading organisations and their managers must think differently about their system if they're going to make a systemic and sustainable improvement. Personally, the best way I've learned to deal with situations is through self and social reflection, what David Bohm called *dialogue*. To suspend your assumptions and beliefs and think, both individually and as a group, about the situation. Surface what is assumed and believed to be true and then aggressively attack them with everything you've got and see if they remain standing. I can personally testify that there's nothing like discovering the truth, especially when it's by the whole team.

CHAPTER 2

Me, Myself and I

"The ultimate value of life depends upon awareness and the power of contemplation rather than upon mere survival."

Aristotle

ME

It goes without question that as a society, we know we do better when we work together. It's how our race has managed to become so successful. In organisations, we talk about teams and how relationships matter. It has spawned a whole cottage industry for team building courses where we all learn to collaborate in building the best paper aeroplane or creating an egg protection system dropped from a second-story window. So, with all this focus on teams, is it sensible then only to measure individual performance or even measure it at all?

It's not the people – it's the system!

At my time at General Electric, personal performance was regarded as such a critical concept that they turned it into a policy called differentiation. The gist of it was that the bottom ten percent of the annual personal performance reviews were asked to leave the business. I think Jack Welch is one of the supermen of industry in the modern era, but his answer when challenged on this policy seemed very shallow and callous. He remarked that GE want the best people and it isn't fair to leave people in positions they aren't very good at, so by removing them from GE, it was doing itself and the employee a good turn, because the employee was then free to find a new job they were more suited to, and therefore happier doing. Many years later, I visited a very large insurance company practising systems thinking, and there I met a person that was extremely motivated, very enthusiastic and loved her job. During lunch, I asked her about her enthusiasm, and she told me that three years earlier, before their systems thinking initiative, she'd had a run of very poor annual appraisals and considered leaving regularly. This was a very smart person that was now adding high levels of value into her organisation. I couldn't help thinking at the time that Jack would have fired her. Shooting in the dark kills good people.

In my experience, the annual personal appraisal hasn't really achieved very much other than increasing bureaucracy and making employees feel inadequate. The number of organisations that follow-up and work closely with employees with their personal development plans and support them throughout the year is low. At best, I've seen the odd quarterly or half-yearly review.

In response to this criticism, many put the responsibility back onto the individual (a circular reference). I have also worked in organisations were it seems a job for life, where the environment is stagnant with a pungent aroma of *"we've tried it all before"* and *"some things may change, but mostly it stays the same"*, but just over the door is a sign saying *"We invest in people"*. Personal appraisals are not only dreaded by the employee but also by their managers. No one dare say it of course, in case of upsetting the establishment, but no one, other than HR, sees the real value in them.

The *personal performance* approach creates a form of ranking or league table of employees, where it takes losers to make winners. 'Employee of the month' for example, in a close and friendly environment, may be fun, but put it into a competitive and aggressive culture, and it can be toxic. It causes people not to share, to hold good ideas back in fear that their opportunity to shine might be lost. Collective performance has its roots in our social DNA – we are stronger in numbers. To make organisations successful, teams have to win not individuals.

Please don't misunderstand me here; it may seem as though I'm making a good impression of discrediting HR, but this is not my intention, all I'm interested in examining is the concept of personal attention organisations place on employees and their individualistic performance.

Who said what!?

In one article I read this was their response to personal 360 Degree reviews, a common tool for measuring personal effectiveness. If you're not familiar with it, this is where your subordinates, peers and superiors all provide feedback on you and in so doing you receive a rounded view of your performance. Here is what they said:

"The goal of 360-degree feedback isn't to punish. It is an opportunity to thoroughly examine and improve the performance of your team on an individual level to help the group succeed. These appraisals give employees ownership of their work and review. By working with employees on development plans, organisations hold their workers accountable for their performance."

So, let's quickly unpick this and apply some basic systems principles. Let's start with a positive; it's good that this is not a punishment. The next bit isn't so good. If we assume for a moment the team as a whole, then what they're purporting is that to measure and improve the performance of the (whole) team, then it is you (a part) that needs to improve. Carrying on; giving you ownership and responsibility of your work also sounds good but holding you (a part of the system) to account if you don't improve doesn't sound very systemic at all. No, this a totally false approach for improving team performance. In fact, it's anti-systemic.

These days many HR practices recommend continuous reviews, my question is, should they? Does it make sense to review a person's individual performance, even if that is combined with an overall team perspective? Probably yes, but it must start with a review of the whole team. Doing so will inevitably lead to a better understanding of any constraining system conditions impeding the team. And, understanding this will provide for a much better assessment of the individuals in that team.

I don't want to, and you can't make me!

I'm sure most people have heard managers say, *"we need to motivate our employees"*, but is this possible, really? The issue seems to be related to motivation, and that personal reviews reinforce the belief that motivation is engineered by setting objectives and targets, in a specific, measurable, attainable, relevant, time-based, SMART manner. However, we know from neuroscience, the study of the anatomy and physiology of the brain, and from psychology, the study of the human mind and human behaviour, that extrinsic motivation is generally not a pleasurable experience and that tasks are typically carried out reluctantly. However, this contradicts with the very premise of self-improvement put forward by all personal-appraisal strategies. Even when there is a real and tangible incentive, extrinsic motivation seems to struggle. It also totally contradicts the *"we need to motivate..."* statements many managers make. Extrinsic motivations aren't very effective. So, therefore, there is nothing a manager can do to motivate their employees directly. No, motivation comes from within. It is a very intimate and personal emotion. The question though is, can these internal feelings, beliefs and motivations be influenced and shaped?

John Shook, Lean Guru and former Toyota Manager - *"In my five years at Toyota City, I was never told what to do, yet neither was I free to do anything I wanted. I was given clear responsibility to propose countermeasures to problems I owned."* His manager at the time told him *"when you tell someone exactly what to do, you take the responsibility of that task away from them"*.

He proposes that this way of managing, the 'Toyota Way', solves the age-old problem of having the right mix of responsibility and supportive management. Where no one is telling anyone exactly what to do but is supporting them to solve problems and ensuring they are adding value to the customer. So, it is neither the command and control style of explicitly being told what to do or the new-age style of let's play pool for a few hours.

What Shook is saying is that the personal responsibility of an employee and a close relationship with his or her manager, who is responsible for defining these responsibilities, is the key to improvement.

In response to team performance, he goes on to talk about the Socratic method of dialogue between individuals to promote creative thinking and to bring out or surface presuppositions. He describes a dialectic approach were, although people who hold different views, the collective objective is to get to the truth, or in other words, to solve a problem by getting to its root. This is the approach David Bohm took with his Dialogue method. That ideas and improvement come from a collective mind rather than from an individual one. The difference Toyota placed on this was to focus it on the needs of the whole organisation. This is very similar to Goldratt's throughput accounting method that maps the profitability of the whole organisation across the entire value-stream.

However, there's still a big problem. These methods have been around for a very long time and have been studied by many. The practices at Toyota have been presented almost to exhaustion, but still, failure is far more commonplace than success. It is beyond empirical contradiction that large transformation programmes are prone to failure - disastrous failure. Our problem is not the misunderstanding of the empirical evidence. Our problem, as described by Daniel Kahneman, is due to our bias towards overconfidence. Overconfidence, he prescribes, is a manifestation of his model, WYSIATI (what you see is all there is), meaning that to form a meaningful estimate we take in information from the things we know about and construct a plausible story in our mind by filling in the gaps about what we don't know. He goes on to suggest that even if people are aware of their limitations of what they know, that will seriously impair their judgement, they would never admit to it out of pure social respectability. Saying, *"I'm guessing we will successfully deliver this project"*, or *"I've got no idea whether we can deliver it"*, in many organisations would result in ridicule. He quotes,

"Organisations that take the word of overconfident experts can expect costly consequences". Overconfidence is a result of social and economic pressures. Many organisations foster a culture of promoting the overconfident, presenting them as great charismatic leaders, while the person with the contradicting evidence is moved to one side. His research provided no evidence that the overconfident risk-takers had an abnormal appetite for high stake gambles; they were merely ignorant of the risks.

McKinsey report that 70% of transformation programmes fail. The cost to organisations is enormous. And I don't mean the triviality of money; I mean that a failed transformation programme decimates moral, breaks relationships, causes fatigue and increases mental health problems. When organisations talk about mitigating the risk of failure, they mainly regard it in terms of money, and concepts like sharing the financial risk with suppliers are tabled. However, the cost to the social organisation is much higher and lasts long after the money is forgotten. To have this amount of failure, something is seriously wrong. Something is missing in these explanations of how to make improvement and change happen in organisations that genuinely transforms the culture. Even though all the evidence and explanations of success seems plausible and necessary, there is still an intangible insufficiency that we can't grasp. There is a grey space where the truth of the failure sits. Toyota managed it, but for some reason, their success is not only difficult to replicate; it seems extremely difficult to articulate. There are clues, however. Taiichi Ohno once said, *"Data is, of course, important, but I place more emphasis on facts"*. The difference being facts are real, whereas data is not. Fujio Cho, honorary chairman of Toyota, provides three principles of improvement culture in leadership.

1. Go See: spend time on the front line. Stand in a central point and just observe.
2. Ask Why: every day ask why. Not merely about problems but about the way things work.

3. Show Respect: respect your employees by asking them to take responsibility and improve in real-time by getting to the root cause, and by not asking them to do non-value work.

Notice here he's talking about the leadership and not managers alone. How many executives do you know that regularly take the time to visit the floor, ask questions and be intimate with how their organisation is operating? So, what does Cho mean? Well clearly, he's talking about leaders taking an interest in the day to day life of the organisation, but even more profound than that he's talking about watching people and seeing how the work works. In Stringer's terms, he's observing the environment to see how it affects the work.

Concerning transformation programmes, Cho's words can also be taken as *Go See* the reality of transformation programmes that sit outside the boundary of your organisation. When organisations decide to enter into a large IT transformation, they typically use three rationales:

1. They build the case for change by comparing their organisation to the anecdotal construct of a corporation, probably of the type that the decision-makers have previously worked in, and thus conclude this is the correct answer.

2. They overlay the software sales pitch into this construct and determine one isn't valid without the other.

3. They ask the software companies for examples of successful case studies from other organisations (that are usually pure conjecture that require imagination more than intellect).

An alternative empiricist approach would look like this:

1. Study the organisation to determine what constraints are causing costs to be higher than they need to be, impeding the ability for information to flow, and impacting the customer's demand to be met.

2. Design solutions that pull IT into a specific problem to be solved or an opportunity to be realised

3. Analyse failed implementations of the software to determine parallels to what is being proposed. These will be harder to compile but much more valuable than the success stories.

Standardise everything!

In today's corporate world, we seem to be transfixed with standards. They are the things that we believe will solve all our problems. We need to implement them, that's the secret, we say. Most organisations convince themselves that standardisation is a correct assertion by asking the following question, "*how different can our organisation be?*". Meaning, if other companies can be standardised, then why can't we? The irony is, everyone is thinking the same way, even though none of them has standardised. However, ingrained this way of thinking is in our modern culture; it is missing the proverbial elephant-in-the-room – people. It doesn't question what makes people do what they do or recognise that motivation is a property of the brain. That people and social systems have and do, exercise choice. So, using basic deduction; because there is no such thing as a standard social system, and an organisation is a social system, there is no such thing as a standard organisation – and yet, everyone is trying to do it. To turn people into standard objects that fit into standard processes, operated by standard software, requires no thinking. Now to be absolutely clear. I'm not saying defined ways of thinking are wrong; I'm saying that blindly imposing ways of working from a different environment onto a workforce doesn't work.

Get your tanks off my lawn

Psychologist Daniel Amen in his TED talk "*The most important lesson from 83,000 brain scans*", made the observation that in

all other areas of the medical profession they look and see to diagnose, but in psychiatry it is only in the last decade with the introduction of fMRI and PET scans that neuroscience and psychology have started to come together to provide a single unified, physical and psychological, diagnosis.

Human behaviour is complex, but in comparison, social motivation is relatively simple. Our most basic need is to be loved. When someone does something against us, we care more about the person than what they've done.

The desire to hurt another person and revenge is not a natural behaviour. In Hollywood maybe, but not in reality. Knowing that someone lied about us, for instance, to protect their interests means we can rationalise their motive and understand it, even if we don't like it. Human motivation is simple; by getting underneath what a person has done and exposing why they did what they did, provides a formula for building a positive relationship.

Friend or foe?

At the most basic level, our subconscious mind is assessing whether something is a threat or safe. The amygdala, located near the base of the brain and directly correlated to the brain stem, reacts to the perceived threat. The hypothalamus then activates the processes that release adrenaline and cortisol to keep us alert.

As a result, there's a motivation in the conscious mind to do something based on the result of this fight or flight assessment. The key to understanding this is to recognise that the criteria for this assessment are not taught but learnt through experience and show us what a threat is and what is not. These mechanisms drive us away from what we perceive hurts us and move us towards those things that help us and comfort us.

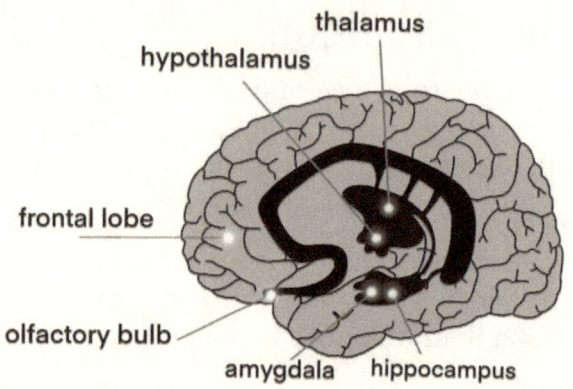

How we perceive the world is based on these experiences. We analyse everyone in every situation all the time, trying to read their intentions, consciously but more often subconsciously. For example, when people try to give "*positive and constructive feedback*", as the HR handbook tells us to do, such as "*why did you come to that conclusion?*", how we receive that message can be the difference between friendship and all-out war. "*Don't park your tanks on my lawn*", one American colleague once accused me of, when I asked him a similar question.

In response to this, the HR handbook tells us to 'assume positive intent', meaning assume the other person is being friendly and is asking with the right intention. The problem is that this requires the reasoning part of our brain to be on full focus, and our prefrontal cortex takes up a great deal of energy. Steve Jobs once described how he would test if someone were thinking hard about a problem by walking them around the building perimeter when he asked them a question. He said, "*If they stop walking, then I know they're thinking hard*". You can try it for yourself. An easier example is to try doing simple mental math while doing some vigorous exercise. Our pre-frontal cortex needs a lot of energy to function properly. Think about lying in bed at night and how problems in our lives can seem much worse. This is due to the reasoning part of our brain being at rest and not providing a balanced assessment. When people are fatigued at work, it is unwise to expect them to apply thorough logic and reasoning.

Expectations

How we receive a person is based on an initial expectation of their intent. I've been audited many times in my career, and I can say with absolute certainty, that I never received them as a friend, even though my prefrontal cortex was reasoning *"they're only doing their job"*. Expectation setting feels deep-rooted, and this is backed up by research into identifying the brain regions associated with expectation violation. Participants in a study demonstrated higher degrees of memory recollection when they were offered proposals different to their expectations. These studies also showed that different brain regions were involved in responding to lower and higher expectation experiences. If our beliefs set our expectations, then our experiences must also shape those expectations. If a group held the same expectations, then that group should respond to a given situation in a similar way. In different words, their brains should process the expectation violation in the same way.

Moreover, this seems to be at the centre of Toyota's success. From the leadership team, they defined the goals of the organisation and then explained how those would be achieved. In their simple mantra, 'through flow, we win!', they set the expectation in every employee that they had a responsibility for improving that flow. Leaders, managers and factory workers all experienced the flow of the work first-hand. In other words, Toyota's achievements, whether deliberate or not, were not due to method alone, but psychology. A point that has been misunderstood for decades – and still is. Leaders defined the system while managers and workers worked on improving flow in their areas, and this provided both a systemic and reductionist strategy for improvement. Framing it this way, it is easy to see that pure instruction from the leadership wouldn't have been enough. They set the expectation through example. While the leadership's lens was broad and shallow, and the managers' lens was narrow and deep, both shared the same simple expectation, that everything they did needed to increase flow. Of course, they still had departmental silos, the human brain isn't so expansive it can consider the whole company in one go – not even in Japan, but they understood that whatever changes they made had to be compatible with the environment around them. So, although their organisation was siloed, their thinking wasn't.

Although flow and waste reduction at Toyota was the success that is always cited and led to the Lean movement, their ability to unify their workforce was, in many ways, by far a greater success. It does them a disservice to attribute everything to their method, even though it was so instrumental. The beauty of their approach was how it recognised how people behave and respond. Their monumental achievement, at that time, feels similar to how people refer to the Egyptians building the pyramids with no heavy machinery. Toyota did what they did without science, just human respect and a recognition that people have a brain, and that what's vital is respecting in every employee and creating a sense of oneness to the cause. Jonny Wilkinson, talking about the England Rugby team, said in one interview *"the secret is for the manager to work with the players to focus only on what we want and what we need to do to achieve it. Nothing else matters. He [the manager] can't push each player mentally too hard, but he must work with each of them to instil this focus"*.

EXPERIENTIAL LEARNING

William James, an American philosopher and psychologist, was born in 1842. He developed an idea called radical empiricism, that was a combination of knowledge based on experience acquired through the senses and rational thought.

Everything we know to be true comes from experience and is validated or reinforced from our experiences. He founded, with his colleague Charles Sanders Peirce, an American mathematician turned philosopher, a theory they called 'The philosophical school of pragmatism'. It essentially describes how our thinking drives our actions and behaviour, and that *truth* is to be determined by assessing the consequences of these actions. James theorised that happiness was a state of mind, based on free will and that happiness is not created but discovered. He said that happiness is found during moments of reflection on memory. We have all had times after the heat of the moment when we've thought about our actions and initially felt remorse but later relief once we've apologised.

Many of us, have learnt in those similar situations not to react to save ourselves the pain afterwards, and in that choice, there's a sense of contentment, of having done the right thing. James wrote that it's too easy to fall into a pessimistic attitude that creates anxiety, caused by the paradoxical conflict between what we experience and what we want to believe is behind a more optimistic world, such as people that suffer chronic cognitive dissonance over the toxicity of the culture in their organisation and the externally perceived excellence of the brand.

James provides two explanations, which he goes on to reject as ineffective behaviour, of what we convince ourselves is true. Firstly, that we accept the status quo, driven out of science or more likely in today's world a great deal of pseudoscience, such as believing in the best practices myth that has no empirical basis. Secondly, to be convinced there's an unseen order, a force that will eventually get us to a brighter future – an unfounded optimism. James's wisdom in this thinking was profound. To overcome a pessimistic state, he said we should adopt a more optimistic perspective of life based on faith and to believe in possibility, trusting in a *maybe* way of acting. He described that in the act of moving forward in a *maybe* frame of mind, events unfold that deny our rational thought, and in the moment when reality surprises us, happiness is found.

When we study an organisation in the right way, we can discover things that are not possible to find any other way, problem-solving can be truly a happiness generator because we find things we never imagined.

David Kolb, an American educational theorist, developed a model called the 'Experiential Learning Cycle'. The cycle consists of four phases:

Concrete Experience. Begins with something new we encounter that changes or adjusts our beliefs and forces us to reinterpret a previous experience. For example, we have judged a person on a negative first impression and later gone on to re-evaluate our view of them based on a new experience in a different setting.

Reflective Observation. When having a new experience that conflicts with our current understanding, it causes us to pause and reflect.

Abstract Conceptualisation. From this reflection comes a new understanding, having learnt something from our unique experience.

Active Experimentation. Our new learning turns into a new behaviour or action, where we try out our new understanding to determine what will happen.

This model presents some important ways of thinking about learning. Firstly, that it is based on experience, secondly, that it goes through phases, thirdly, that it is ongoing and iterative and fourthly, that it requires self-reflection. Without self-reflection, the cycle can't complete. There is an important differentiation between this, and learning based on memorising facts.

The process of self-reflection is a form of meditation. Not in a psycho-religious sense but a mindful contemplation, where we are consciously aware of our surroundings and how they are affecting us both physically and psychologically, enabling us to respond, adjust and adapt. It also enables us to experiment with our new-found knowledge.

Our ability to think past a situation is at the heart of learning. In everyday life, in every situation, we make snap judgements about almost everything. It takes practice to self-reflect properly, and Ackoff was right, they should teach it in schools.

People are different and prefer to learn in different ways. Kolb recognised this. He presented learning styles as two pairs of choices that we all make, one is perception, and the other is processing. Perception is our emotional response to a task, how we feel about it if you like. Processing is how we go about the task.

He presented these as axes on his cyclical model, creating two sets of choices, both styles having one *thinking* and one *feeling*.

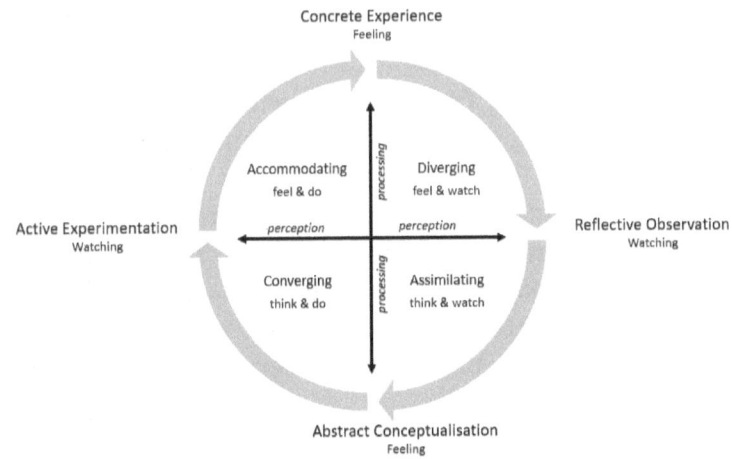

These learning styles enable us to think about our style as well as the people we're working alongside.

Accommodating. Jump in. These people have hunches and rely on experience or intuition more than logic, so will try and gain the required knowledge from others. They want to get stuck in from the get-go.

Diverging. Watch and reflect. These people are observers and prefer to weigh-up rather than weigh-in. Kolb referred to them as *diverging* because they tend to be creative and look at situations from different perspectives.

Converging. Design and Build. These people are technical in their thinking and like to engineer and experiment with ideas. They are less concerned with the social aspects of learning and want to determine practical applications for their ideas.

Assimilating. Logical. These people want an explanation, not a demonstration. They assimilate information exceptionally well and can draw coherent patterns and conclusions from data.

Whatever style people take there is active participation in the learning process. Experiential learning is about thinking about and feeling a situation to understand it properly. It is a form of learning that sticks. It enters our long-term memory and stays there as knowledge.

Learning by memorising facts has its benefits, of course, but learning through experience tends to have a higher retention rate. Some even say that the person that learns the most in the classroom, for instance, is the teacher because they are both transmitting and receiving the information they're teaching at the same time, and hearing themselves acts as a form of confirmation, causing them to reflect and either reaffirm or question what they had previously understood. It is a truly fascinating phenomenon.

As an aside, if you wish to spot all the grammatical errors in a document or presentation that you've written, don't mind read it in silence, read it out aloud. You may feel awkward, but you will spot almost everything.

Promulgate to accumulate

Learning individually is one thing, but we want learnings to be contagious, for experiences to spread. We want transformation.

"The active ingredient to large-scale behaviour change is facilitating insight in social situations over time. Research points to the importance of a three-step process: seeing something different in a social setting, having an insight about that behaviour, and making these types of connections over time. Insight to action causes change. If you have those insights and discuss them in a social setting, you are more likely to want to change." Neuroscientist, Dr David Rock.

Experiences in the workplace must be positive for us to learn. We are not receptive to constant negativity. Our senses are working all the time and storing memories, both consciously and subconsciously. When organisations punish failure, they literally stop creative thinking and create toxic neurological chemicals in our brain. Toxic environments don't learn, and they don't improve.

Neuroscientist Gretchen Schmelzer describes how our short term or working memory transitions into long term memory. He says that there are only three ways that this can happen; urgency, repetition and association.

Experiential information comes in through our senses, and that information comes in either through the emergency response amygdala or the hippocampus-cortex, a pathway from the hippocampus in the limbic system responsible for spatial navigation and long-term memory. Typically to remember something for a long time takes practice, but a single sudden jolt to the system that triggers the emotional memory pathways from the amygdala can create a memory that lasts a lifetime. The problem is the retrieval of that memory, as it's triggered and stored by emotion rather than a narrative. This is what Schmelzer refers to as urgency.

Repetition is with what we're all familiar. The expression 'practice makes perfect', is very apt because repetitive learning creates the longest lasting memories and the most effective learning.

Schmelzer comments that therefore, deeply ingrained behaviour is so hard to change because the new behaviour needs a great deal of dislodging and repetition to replace it. Instructing people to remove an ingrained behaviour, and to replace it with something new is likely to be ineffective, yet this is our standard approach to change management.

Association is where we connect a new experience in our working (short term) memory with an existing one in our long-term memory. Like when we use word association to remember a new word or phrase by associating it to things that are already familiar to us.

So, when we consider learning, both psychologically and neurologically, it seems that repetition is the only real way of making something truly stick. Being taught something and mastering a subject are two very different things. Even though we're taught the rules and techniques of a sport, relatively quickly, it still then takes us much longer, and lots of practice to get good at it. Why then do we think management and improvement can be mastered in a classroom or out of a book and without practice?

When we learn a sport, we fail all the time; when we fail at work, we're punished. If we were punished every time we failed at a hobby, we would give it up immediately. There is no difference. It's the same brain regions that are used to memorise the rules and techniques of a sport as it is to learn how to improve what we do at work. The same.

Punishing failure is so damaging to both the organisation and the individual, and it's both a lazy response and incredibly ignorant of the way our brain works.

Deming was quoted as saying that "*no one comes to work to do a bad job*". It is far more rewarding and enjoyable to feel like we're contributing and participating in something worthwhile. Leaders of people have an obligation to create a positive environment that promotes problem-solving and improvement.

I see it all the time in many companies. The dreaded project culture and the weekly management meeting. Everyone sharpening and smoothing their messages. Green traffic lights are good, amber suggests we're behind but still in control, but red is to be avoided at all cost. Red is when all the difficult questions come in, and the blame starts. People may not literally have erythrophobia (the fear of red), but it can and does cause low levels of anxiety, which causes people to be defensive. The truth seldom gets surfaced because people are frightened. Anxiety causes cortisol and adrenaline to start flowing through our system. We can't help ourselves from not telling the truth and from not putting everything on the table. Failure is punished in most organisations because blame is usually the game. In my view, not addressing how to respond to failure, at all levels in the organisation is one of the most critical failings in organisations today. To be clear by "*not addressing failure*", I don't mean controlling an emotional response and being nicer to employees, I mean a less emotional mechanistic response, a method. Without method, we're left with opinion and the personal style of the individual. It is without structure, and it's not scientific.

Without a methodological approach, human behaviour kicks in, and in times of trouble, this is usually a threat response, better known as fight, flight, freeze or faint response. All of which cause anxiety and stress if experienced over a prolonged period. It also means the wrong brain regions are triggered. We want the logical part of our brain to be solving problems and not the areas designed for survival. It isn't just the subordinate that experiences these emotions, even leaders are answerable to someone, so the larger the failure, the more likely they are to experience these feelings too, which in many cases invokes the fight response, that results in them cascading blame in a downwards direction – the delegation of blame, as one COO put it.

Furthermore, when people leave an organisation, it can very often be due to a flight response. This is the thing about method; it saves everyone.

STRESS

Stress can often be a misused term. To start with we talk about it as a thing or as an event, whereas it is more of a process were, physical, mental and social overlap. For example, sitting in an uncomfortable position for long periods (physical), debt (mental) and family feuds (social), are all different forms of stress that overlap.

Our perception of stress is typically a negative one, but it's important to differentiate between stress and strain. Straining to achieve something may well cause us stresses both physically and mentally, like running a marathon or putting a late shift in at work to complete a proposal, causing us to feel exhausted and drained. However, these aren't necessarily negative. In many ways, they can be extremely positive.

The medical profession describes our response to stress as 'stress response mechanisms', and there are three categories. Firstly, a biological response, how our bodies react, with the production of chemicals such as cortisol and adrenaline. Secondly, an emotional response, how we feel about it, for example, does it wash over us, or do we lay awake at night worrying about it. Thirdly, cognitive response, what we do about it? Do we struggle and fight against it or accept it and adapt? All of these are happening at the same time in a cause-effect-cause-effect chain of events. Of course, there's a price to be paid, even if we're not conscious of it, whether this is pure physical exhaustion or more serious mental health issues. The problem is the price we pay isn't all paid up immediately. We can suddenly find ourselves with some of this debt to pay in the form of mood swings, anxiety and even depression many weeks after the event. At the time, there is a defensive responsive, so we seem ok, and the debt stays dormant. Then as time passes and we think we're back to normal, wham! The debt needs paying. Most organisations misunderstand this point. After the end of a prolonged period of hard work and sustained effort, where people have been putting in long hours and sacrificing personal and family time, organisations assume that after a few days people are back into a normal pattern. Nothing could be further from the truth. Studies have shown, for instance, that stress response can occur up to twenty weeks later for certain types of major stressful events such as bereavement (Surtees and Wainwright 1999).

It all happens in the brain. As Professor Joe Herbert, from the University of Cambridge, put it, 'Stress is a brain event'. He describes it as having multiple levels or layers, starting with the cortex that analyses the current situation. It doesn't attribute meaning or value to it, only an assessment of the what, for example, I see a gun. Further down is the amygdala that evaluates if it's dangerous or not. Then the hypothalamus sends a chemical signal to the pituitary gland, and this sends another chemical signal to the adrenal glands that are located in the abdomen, just above the kidneys. The adrenals then produce large amounts of cortisol.

In association with the brain in our head, we also have a second brain in our gut. *The Second Brain*, the title of the 1998 book by Dr Michael Gershon, an expert in the field of neurogastroenterology, describes how, as well as controlling gut behaviour, the neurons embedded in the walls of the alimentary canal, also influences our state of mind. So, while some may think that butterflies in the stomach are an old wives' tale, it is actually a physiological stress response.

The stress hormone

Cortisol is a powerful, steroid hormone. It is essential for life as it regulates many processes in the body from blood sugar levels, metabolism, immune responses and of course, it has a crucial role in helping the body deal with stress. Without it, we would die.

The consequences of stressful situations are why it is very important for organisations to understand stress and its effects. When people in stressful situations are secreting large amounts of cortisol, it prioritises all resources and energy to be diverted to addressing the dangerous situation. Cortisol affects conscious memory recall; remember those blank moments in the exam, well now you can rest easy that it wasn't a stupid moment but a neurological condition. Research has found that adults with higher levels of cortisol perform worse on memory tasks than their peers of a similar age with normal cortisol levels. Higher cortisol in the blood is also associated with smaller brain volumes, according to the study, published in *Neurology* in October 2018, the medical journal of the American Academy of Neurology. Because cortisol reinforces bad memories that help in the future during threatening situations, the formation of new nerve cells in the brain is inhibited.

The illustration below shows a distressing image of two brain scans from two three-year-old children. The smaller brain is from a child that has suffered from a high degree of neglect and stress.

3 year old child

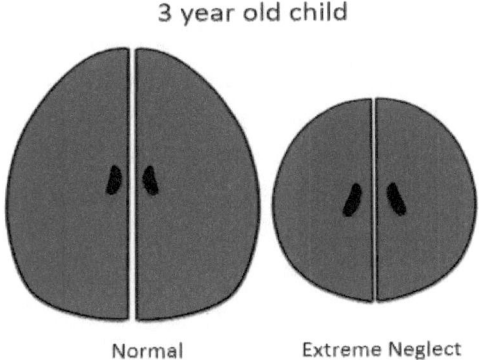

Normal   Extreme Neglect

Original image by Bruce D Perry/The Child Trauma Academy can be found at:
https://childtrauma.org/wp-content/uploads/2013/12/PerryPollard_SocNeuro.pdf

The field of epigenetics has very recently suggested that due to external or environmental events, such as neglect or punishment, a chemical process called methylation actuals stops certain genes from working, an effect that can last a lifetime.

One of the effects of long-term chronic stress is the suppression of the immune system. Adults who experienced parents constantly arguing as a child are likely to have some degree of immune system suppression.

Physician Vincent Felitti developed a model called Adverse Child Experiences (ACE). Through thousands of case studies, he claims his data demonstrates that most patients in the American health system, suffering from many kinds of ailments, from asthma to arthritis, is due to exposure of varying degrees of ACE's. In one experiment he performed, involved putting patients through resilience-based treatments. The results were staggering. In just the following year, doctor appointments had reduced by thirty-five percent.

The resistance of organisations in dealing with this knowledge of stress and its impact on their workforce is enormous. Whether this be a conscious decision or not, it would seem the wrong one. Research shows that resilience practices to treat stress and anxiety really work, be it for low levels of stress like losing a file on your computer or higher degrees of stress like turning up to the management meeting with a red traffic light or even the risk of being fired. It is totally inadequate to measure the resilience of a person in terms of social standing, such as 'they're good at their job' and 'they have an excellent reputation'. Resilience education should be an objective for all organisations.

CONCLUSION

In the end, attention to personal performance and rewarding purely on what is entered onto appraisal forms becomes a winner-takes-all situation, in an overall organisational zero-sum game. Because it is always the perceived best that succeed, in fact, it's more likely to be the lucky or worse the cocky that gets promoted. When a bright, enthusiastic individual that works for, in the words of Jack Welch, a horse's ass, that is more interested in their ego than their team or simply doesn't know any better, the system fails the silent heroes. This is another perennial problem with HR appraisals; how to spot talent and develop talent? Many people feel that the only way to progress a career is to leave their existing organisation and seek higher, more responsible, better-paid roles elsewhere. But not before they've gone through mental agonising to determine what course of action to take. Some poor souls that are too frightened to leave their jobs because of security concerns find themselves beaten by the system in which they work and are left in this torturous situation for years and years.

Football clubs for decades have been developing extensive networks across the globe to seek out talent at smaller clubs and even at the grassroots level. With these networks, world-class players have been discovered, let alone the thousands of other players from impoverished beginnings, that have managed to find a better life for themselves and their families. It seems that

HR would benefit significantly from understanding where talent already exists, buried in the informal networks, and many managed by the kind of managers that are also just surviving.

Talent can't rise to the surface when it's buried under layers of a broken system. The only answer is to study and change the system.

By not understanding how our brain works grey space is created across our grey matter. It is important because, although I talk a lot about method in this book as being necessary for systemic improvement, it isn't sufficient. It also takes a systemic approach to our thinking.

CHAPTER 3

Our Social Brain

"I realised if you can change a classroom, you can change a community, and if you change enough communities, you can change the world."

Erin Gruwell

TRIBES

Socially wired

We crave for social interaction, and it shapes us in so many ways. We all belong to many different kinds of groups, whether these be our family, sports teams, religious groups, charities and even work. Loneliness is painful and not just psychologically but also physically. Scientists now know that social separation triggers similar brain regions as physical pain. We are inherently aware that there's both safety in numbers and essential for getting things done. We need it so intrinsically that it's how we define the meaning of life.

Neuroscientist Matthew Lieberman, in his book *Social*, explains how the brain's default network comes on when other tasks have finished. This region of the brain supports social cognition that makes sense of other people and us. Anytime we have free mental time this region is activated. Babies show activity in this default network almost immediately after birth. It's why we feel lonely when we're less busy. In one study, adults were each given math tests to complete with only short gaps between each exercise; during these gaps, their brain activated the default social network. People that have experienced grief talk about the pain coming in waves, suddenly. One moment they're fine and the next they're in pieces.

Circle the wagons

We're precious about our social connections, and we know that social groups can become very protective and will defend themselves against external influences that threaten their beliefs and core values.

As a consultant for many years, I have been shocked at times to witness how defensive certain teams are and how aggressive the situation can be when people feel even slightly exposed. It's not uncommon for a passive-aggressive default position, just in case they feel threatened – in a kind of, *offence is the best kind of defence*, strategy.

The word *tribal* to explain the behaviour of a social group sounds primitive, but, psychologically, we are probably almost identical to people thousands of years ago. The good part is that we build friendships and trust, and those relationships allow us to develop collectively. The bad part is that a tribe creates a them-and-us mentality, a separation where we're usually correct, and they're not, and in some way, we're better than them. It may not sit very well with the elevated view we hold about ourselves, but the reality is we make judgements about other groups every day that are wrong more often than they're correct. Separation is sometimes harmless, but in many organisations, it can be extremely damaging to the cohesion of the whole. How can the roots of improvement establish a hold when the cultural soil is so divisive?

Over the years, I've experienced four typical types of social groups, or tribes if you like, inside organisations. This list is in order of the worst behaviour and lowest happiness:

1. **Dysfunctional.** In this group, you find people that are generally miserable. They exist in their job, but they don't like it. They have lots of sick days and in some cases, plan them. They generally don't like the company, but paradoxically they can be very proud of the brand. They tend to distrust others, and their general performance is low. They are also very cynical and resistant to change. Apathy is the norm, resulting in good people that want to make a difference continually coming and going.

2. **Arrogant.** A highly politicised environment where people think they and their tribe is more superior than the others. They act robotically and struggle with empathy. Failure is punished, and members tend 'not to suffer fools'. Long hours in the office is perceived to be

necessary, and individual personal performance is of primary concern. People in this group tend to hate their job when they hit forty to fifty years of age. They feel they don't belong to anything meaningful and seek desperately to get into the next (creative) group. Some even start their own business for this reason alone.

3. **Creative**. This group has a team ethic where there is more emphasis on getting work done together than on individuals. This group feel socially connected and tend to enjoy their jobs. External people that encounter this group feel welcomed and energised by their enthusiasm.

4. **Purposeful** In my twenty- or so-year career, I have only experienced a few groups in this category. The whole organisation and the individual teams were indistinguishable in terms of purpose. To clarify, I don't mean they were religious in some way; in fact, I've experienced religious groups that are in categories 1 and 2. I mean that they genuinely believed in their cause or purpose, from top to bottom, and were fully aligned to a common set of goals.

Of course, there are flavours and extremes, but unfortunately, these four groups form a pyramid-like structure of commonality, with groups 1 and 2 being far more common than 3, and certainly 4.

The negativity in groups 1 and 2 creates a downward spiral of emotion in its members that causes real pain, especially when there are serious personal issues at play. Our brains won't tolerate this conflict because it's neurologically damaging, so people rationalise their negativity by believing it to be normal or 'it must be them and not me'. Many do suffer, and stress is commonplace. The number of times I've heard external people (usually consultants) refer to parts of an organisation that are seemingly obstructive to change as dinosaurs and classify them as hopeless, in an attempt to cognitively wash away their distress.

Leaving these situations unchecked for long periods, years in some cases can be disastrous. One terrible example of how rotten cultures can break people happened several years ago in a company I was working for; I was sitting at my desk when someone from outside my project team approached me and asked me if they could speak with me urgently. It looked serious, and she was visibly upset, so we grabbed a small room. She told me there were six people involved with the project that she was worried about. One had gone on sick leave the day before with chest pains, one had left the site with stress-related symptoms that morning, two others had to be separated from fighting, one had started being aggressive towards her, and another had confessed to drinking heavily. The project wasn't particularly stressful; in fact, it was quite relaxed. It was the culture. It was absolutely toxic. The smallest mistakes resulted in people blaming each other and openly lying about things. One person even admitted they lied all the time, "*it's fun*", he told me – this was a person that had been off work with stress at least three times before. They were well and truly in group 1. The saddest thing is that all these people belonged to the same organisation – or did they?

Coordination and Consistency

In 2016, West Ham football club made headline news after their fans turned on each other and fighting broke out in the homestand. It happened again in 2018. We see less physical examples everywhere, especially in politics, where infighting is commonplace. The US Republican party seems to be in all-out warfare since Donald Trump became president, and the UK Conservative party aren't any better over Brexit, finally ousting Theresa May.

Consistency is described by Klaus Grawe, in his book *Neuropsychotherapy: How the Neurosciences Inform Effective Psychotherapy* as "*compatibility of many simultaneously transpiring mental processes*". What Grawe is saying is that we need congruence, a harmony between how we interact in our environment and our most basic motivational goals. In an incongruent state, where our needs are constantly violated, we create avoidance tactics that result in feelings of insecurity, anxiety and sometimes aggression.

People seek cognitive consistency and as such, tend to gravitate towards people that hold similar views and behaviours. There are times when we find something we like and gravitate to that, such as a particular phrase someone says that we adopt for ourselves. I've even known people to start smoking just to join the smokers' social group.

Consistency is created when each person in the group aligns towards these social attributes and normalises them. They form a kind of social signature that coordinates the group around a set of common behaviours. It is this combination of coordination and consistency against a set of social norms that enables the members of a group to cooperate and collaborate effectively with each other.

Think of an orchestra and how it's made up of different sections; strings, woodwind, brass and percussion. Now imagine each section playing their piece beautifully in total harmony with each other. Now also imagine if all those sections were just a few seconds out of alignment, where each one is slightly ahead or behind the others. It would be a musical disaster.

Even in a small but disharmonious orchestra, should the discoordination continue then, cognitive inconsistency will build and eventually each section will likely blame the others. Each musician wanting to play beautiful music, only to be spoilt by other less capable sections.

Organisations that struggle with coordination and consistency find it difficult, if not impossible, to operate with any degree of effectiveness or efficiency. They find themselves with many disconnected factions that are unable to learn, develop and improve. They have 'economic backwardness' as Kenneth Arrow put it.

An attribute of this discord is a lack of personal trust. Trust in this context comes down to everyday interactions, such as fearing what someone will say in a meeting about you or being blamed for a particular situation. It is common for a person to hold a positive view of someone, simply because they didn't expose them in a meeting. Research by Ron Inglehart shows that trust even correlates with a nation's GDP, with Scandinavian countries at the highest end and certain African countries at the lower end of the scale.

As we've discussed, how people feel about a social norm governs their behaviour. These things can be simple everyday things, that when held collectively form a group's behaviour. Here are a few examples:

- Should you read all your emails every day?
- Do you believe working from home is acceptable?
- Should contract staff manage permanent staff?
- Is it ok to regularly turn up late for meetings?
- Does it matter if people regularly take a longer lunch?
- Does a formal dress code matter?
- Is bad language ever acceptable in the office?
- Is it ok for people to turn up to work when they like?
- Should people be punished for poor performance?
- Does standardising working practices help?
- Are zero-hour contracts acceptable?
- Is regularly working late a sign of commitment?
- Is it ok to have open laptops in meetings?
- Is it ok to outsource certain jobs?
- Are personal appraisals important?
- Should IT work alongside the business?
- Should business leaders regularly visit each department?
- Is it ok for managers to get a bonus but not their staff?
- Does a degree matter?
- Should alcohol be allowed in the office?

Answering yes or no to questions like these places your views into a category, along with other people that share those views. Some of these you may hold to a higher degree of importance; for example, you may say, bad language is never acceptable, while someone else may say it is okay, or you may say, a suit and tie is important, when some may think that shorts and t-shirts are perfectly fine. Some may even take a neutral position and not care either way.

The view that an organisation has a single culture is an overgeneralised myth. Because culture is based on a set of accepted social norms, an organisation can have many sub-cultures. For example, the twenty questions above shape how people coordinate. In this simple example, there are only two possible answers, yes and no, but even this results in over a million different combinations. So, the answer to why cultures differ is, paradoxically, because people try to coordinate with likeminded people that causes separation between groups. This is why leadership is so essential, because leading by example drives up coordination in the workforce towards the leaders' behaviour, that in turn creates alignment and collective consistency. I believe this is what Toyota achieved at all levels of their organisation, with their daily mantra of 'through flow, we win!'.

A lack of visible and demonstrable leadership can lead to the emergence of informal social networks inside organisations because people with similar views from different departments want to socialise and work together. If our neighbours are not like us, we tend not to interact with them, and this can happen even within departments. This is another reason why formal structure, like departments, is an abstraction from how work is really getting done. The benefits of effective leadership on social structures is enormous because creating universal social norms is more likely to reduce the separation between groups and create a reduced set of sub-cultures.

Programmed to transmit

One interesting discovery by Matthew Lieberman is that our social brain is triggered when we learn something; it's like our brain is geared to tell someone else — switching us from being information consumers to information broadcasters. Just think about how we communicate online today. The online revolution has placed a mechanism in our hands that enable us to do what our very nature is programmed to do — transmit. I have four daughters that transmit a lot.

Division equals conflict

By dividing an organisation into sections and by not understanding the critical importance of the interfaces between them (grey space), we create a mechanistic construct that places a conflict in the social system, resulting in social separation and tribalism. Not knowing the value of social is our most significant barrier to success. In other words, the way we design our organisations, in silos without a shared purpose acting as a sociological glue, is the primary reason for reduced performance. These structural constructs create harmful systemic conditions that hinder the ability to make behavioural or cultural change sustainable.

Siloed structures not only divide people, they make it much harder for leaders to lead.

Rebels without a cause

People within informal social networks break the formal rules every day. The risks can be high, but they do it regardless, motivated by cognitive consistency and the need to get the work done, and they do all this without being recognised. Now if you're reading this as an HR manager or change manager, ask yourself this question:

why do people take risks to get work done against the formal structures with no extrinsic incentive, and without any known cause (in so much as no manager is asking them to do it), and with the risk of getting into trouble?

Whereas, on the other hand, formal change programmes seem to have the opposite effect on these people. But why?

The answer is because when change is imposed on people, their choice is removed, and they are forced into situations that often contradicts their existing social norms, in one form or another. Pulling people out of their current working environment into a foreign project landscape to implement change needs some time for them to adjust and coordinate to re-establish an acceptable level of consistency. In other words, large scale projects and programmes do not promote a normative learning style; instead, they prescribe treatment and are imposed with retrospective change management techniques used to get something implemented. They are coercive in nature.

A sense of agency

A famous experiment by Stanley Milgram in 1961, showed that people would do things under orders that they would normally find abhorrent. The experiment involved volunteers given painful electric shocks to an unknown person in the next room. All the volunteers could hear were the pretend screams by a professional actor. The disturbing results of the experiment showed that almost two-thirds of the volunteers were willing to continue to lethal doses when told to do so. Since then, many other experiments have been run, but it is still unclear why people do what they do in these situations. Psychologists use the term 'sense of agency' to describe the feeling of being in control of our actions and behaviour. It turns out to be hard to assess because people tend to view personal responsibility as a reflection on them rather than the impact on an outcome. In experiments where people are given a free choice whether to proceed with a specific course of action, the results are very different. It seems that when people are given a choice, they reflect much more on the outcome than they would if they were simply instructed to do so. The answer seems to be centred around who's responsible for the outcome. When people have a choice, it places the responsibility on them, so they are far more thoughtful about the consequences, whereas when they are told to do something, the responsibility shifts to the instructor. Some psychologists have described this as a kind of damper that's placed on the brain when under coercive conditions. Interestingly, the management practice at Toyota aligned to this phenomenon, in that managers were never told what to do, only the outcome that was required.

Boundary disputes

Changing boundaries and demarcations between groups can destroy a community; you only have to understand the history of the Middle East over the last hundred and fifty years to realise this. However, even at a local level, the law courts are riddled with examples of neighbours fighting over as little as ten centimetres of land. Building a sustainable culture is a journey in which a group must travel through several phases.

The 11 C's Culture Cycle below describes how conditions can create consequences in an environment that can lead to people communicating with each other about their concerns, and if this increases then a consensus can form that leads to some commitment to act. The need to act drives an increase in the level of cooperation to form an agreed plan and coordinating behaviours that eventually results in people wanting to collaborate and work together. With focus and consistency, a community can begin to form, where the group's shared beliefs shape a culture of social norms. However, introduce a disruptive enough condition, and this can change behaviours in the community that results in some individuals not participating or even refusing to collaborate at all, and the cooperation begins to weaken. If the conflict is not resolved at this point, then all commitment can be lost, and there is no longer a consensus on which agreement can stand. Communication becomes destructive, and that has hugely negative consequences to the sustainability of the community. Coal mining communities in the UK experienced this reversal so severely as a result of the union strikes in the 1980s that they were literally torn apart, with families that are split even to this day.

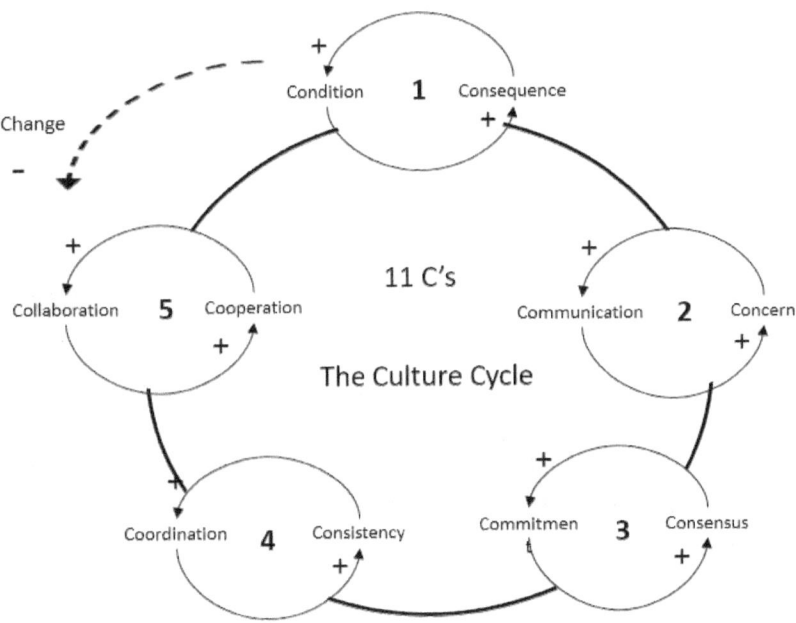

CONCLUSION

We take for granted the way organisations are structured to such a degree that any alternative seems impossible, but ironically, people that work in siloed organisations realise the damage that they cause.

Silo's place arbitrary boundaries around people that drive precisely the opposite behaviour organisations want to promote. They not only inhibit communication and drive up costly hand-offs; they also create conflict.   For individuals to function effectively as a group, they must possess similarities within (Lionel Trilling – 1955), and resolve any internal conflict.

Think of our social tendencies as a two-sided coin. On the one hand, we care about other people and want to help them when we can, and on the other, we fight like dogs over ten centimetres of land.   It is the totality of these mental and physical interactions that shape a person to their environment and others (Franz Boas 1911).

Collaboration is the result of a journey that involves building relationship and trust, based on a shared set of values and beliefs. It doesn't happen instantaneously, as the 11 C's model demonstrates, there is a substantial distance between a group forming and them being effective.

The role of management is to look carefully not just at the people and their profile but at the boundaries that set them apart.

Simply providing people with new tools and methods does nothing to change their behaviour because they value different things.   The perspective of a shared goal can shift these behaviours, but it must be consistent, extremely clear and be built on a foundation of trust.

When organisations introduce large transformation projects that bring in significant numbers of external people, they can easily find themselves in a *them* and *us* position, as the internal and external people don't share a common set of social norms.

Organisations that use social network analysis techniques can identify cliques and communities that are working across the boundaries of formal processes and structures. These groups will very likely be multidisciplinary in nature and made up of people that have established a degree of coordination to help them achieve a particular task that would otherwise have been more difficult through the formal routes. In other words, people seek out likeminded people to get the job done in the easiest way possible.

In the last chapter, I'll talk about how the organisation of the future is structured around a formal approach to the multidisciplinary team concept, and how this can satisfy both the need for growth and social development.

Finally, what we learn from the experiences of Toyota and psychology, is that giving people explicit instruction about how to go about specific tasks, switches off their consequential thinking. They no longer feel responsible for the outcome. The way we operate needs to change completely. Imposed standards and governance has the effect of numbing the minds of people, rather than energising their intellectual curiosity. Of course, there needs to be controls and safeguards, but the ability to continually drive up improvement requires thoughtful adaption, not unquestioned repetition.

CHAPTER 4

The Naturist

NATURISTS MAKE TERRIBLE SPELUNKERS

"If you begin to understand what you are without trying to change it, then what you are undergoes a transformation." – Jiddu Krishnamurti

The purpose of this section isn't to criticise. It is to highlight a habitual behaviour that some find themselves. On the surface, it seems effective, professional even, but a deeper assessment exposes a fruitless existence, where effectiveness and natural curiosity is neutralised by sophophobia.

True improvement requires both a personal ownership of the problem and an intellectually inquisitive mind. It is common for people to get stuck in a perspective of methodological dogma, a black hole that sucks the life out of curiosity, a tedious place where complexity is mentally debilitating. The only relief is to hand the exploration reins over to someone they feel is more qualified.

Before anyone can lead improvement, it is essential that they not just understand their environment, but that they first understand themselves.

The naturist is the kind of manager that goes through life in blissful ignorance, running from one crisis to another, while convincing themselves that they're correct and everyone else is to blame. They belong to *the* organisation, and *we* only extends to their immediate team.

There are two kinds of naturist. The narcissist and the sloth. Both seem, on face value, to be the antithesis of each other. However, a more in-depth examination identifies they share the same DNA.

The naturist doesn't read (apart from the odd blog and the self-help, 5-minute-manager book). This lack of intellectual curiosity impedes their logical faculty and the ability to help themselves. Their decision to bring in *experts* is often a way of parading their peacock plume and improving their self-esteem. They hold firm opinions, but they never reflect. Their degree of introspection stretches as far as looking in the mirror each morning. It causes them to have self-awareness blindness and creates conflict with other naturistic managers, also exhibiting the same behaviours.

They believe everything the expert tells them (they have to because they don't read anything), significantly increasing their risk of being led astray, and if they are a budget holder, it is highly probable money will flow – outwards. Just like feeling poor requires a presence among the rich, when they socialise with experts, they feel dumb. To ease this psychological pain, they give themselves the persona of smartness by inviting the expert to all those meetings were the complicated questions will be asked, but at the same time not recognising the difference between a clever answer and an intelligent one. Not wanting to be caught out by their archenemy, the naturist manager from the opposing department, they convince themselves that this asymmetry is of value. Meanwhile, the expert is rubbing their grubby hands together, as they 'land and expand' their agenda. The naturist is amused by technology but struggles to apply it to their job, which is why they need the expert – who because of this, holds them in friendly disdain believing them to be some prehistoric dinosaur.

They rarely wander out of their native habitat – their department. Their unwillingness to explore new opportunities and discover areas of improvement creates a mundane stale culture. They confuse projects funded by a sales pitch, created by the expert, with real informed knowledge and creativity. Confused by the ineffectiveness of these projects, they blame the project team.

They occasionally extend beyond the reach of their departmental boundary to partake in meetings (which they regard as work).

Their tenure is far greater than their experience, and they regard management to be more about managing people, rather than an interest in how the work itself gets done. Consequently, they believe the clock governs performance and is more a personal attribute, than anything collective, of which they have little understanding. They practice the allocation of blame as their primary method of problem-management when things go wrong, while paradoxically they think they understand people, that causes them, in times of trouble, to micro-manage – an emotionally exhausting experience for their team. Picking low-hanging-fruit is their favourite past time. Not only does it provide those above them with a sense of effectiveness (who may also be naturists), it reinforces their self-belief that they are truly smart. They have lots of reports and keep changing their mind about what they want, believing that drilling down into data provides them with answers, (they believe this because this is what the expert tells them).   To compensate for their lack of knowledge, they over-simplify everything and want reality presented on a nicely polished silver spoon. Not knowing in one person is power in the heads of the knowledgeable, but naturists march through life spouting soundbites that they use to attempt to extricate clarity from uncertainty, producing more confusion in their wake. They genuinely are grey space makers.

The narcissist and the sloth; the ego and the lazy. On the face it, they seem to other naturists to be at odds with each other, separated on a spectrum of wit and pride, where position and size of salary are the only measures of success. However, a much closer look exposes that they are, in fact, the same person, each wearing the emperor's new psychotic clothes. The only genuine antithetical relationship is between the naturist and the practitioner. The practitioner is the combination of the builder and the erudite. The phronesis versus the injudicious. The only thing stopping the practitioner from calling out the intellectual nakedness of the naturist is their seniority and a fear of being fired.   The expert loathes the practitioner for their gung-ho style, and the practitioner finds the epistemological snobbery of the expert immensely irritating.   Occasionally the naturist must intercede and resolve disputes between the two. This causes the naturist to exhibit cognitive dissonance; they need both, but both are fighting. They try and address the issue with logic, not recognising that the problem is more about fundamental beliefs and philosophy of life than it is about the work. More often than not, the naturists, when pushed, will side with the expert, deeming them more reputationally valuable than the practitioner. Reputation is defined based on perception, and the naturist has an underlying feeling of inadequacy that only the expert can soothe (this is because the naturist regards persona more valuable than work - even the sloth variety – both the narcissist and the sloth operate on a backdrop of fear).

The naturist apologetic

Some may be offended by these views, but please do not misunderstand my intention. Most naturists are very decent human beings, some of which I would regard as personal friends. However, we mustn't get confused. This is a set of candid observations about how some managers regard work; it is not a direct castigation of any one individual's character.

The truth is, I've experienced the naturist manager in many organisations, at all levels. The procrastination they cause is debilitating and destructive, and their poor decisions can be extremely costly. All of which causes pain and stress.

The goal is to turn every naturist into a practitioner and allow every expert the opportunity to have skin in the game. People must be taught a new way. Systemic learning is normative, meaning that sticking a silver spoon in someone's mouth every day does nothing to improve them or the environment in which they exist. Consultants are for times when we don't know what we're doing but recognise we need to know. But when they're gone, the know-how must remain, and the doing must continue.

Method is the only antidote. Its absence is the primary cause of mismanagement, misinformation, poor performance and mental health issues. There is no other substitute. Without it, we are left with emotion and personal judgement and all the biases that we are not even aware we possess.

SECTION 2

LOST

CHAPTER 5

The Complexity Syndrome

DON'T PANIC MR MANNERING

The thing I will talk about here will beat you every day if you let it.   It has immense power, and it can destroy progress and productivity in a heartbeat.   It is no respecter of persons or authority. It immobilises both the weak and the powerful. It is enemy number one. The poem at the start of this book is talking about this. It has to be addressed by giving it our full focus and bringing it to the front and centre of our minds. If you do, and most don't, you will find it is the Wizard of Oz.   It has no real power. It is all a show. A fear projecting machine behind a screen. The perception of complexity.

The definition of complexity on Wikipedia sums it up perfectly,

'characterises the behaviour of a system or model whose components interact in multiple ways and follow local rules, meaning there is no reasonable higher instruction to define the various possible interactions.'   – in other words, parts of a system that aren't visible – grey space

We're designed to believe what we perceive.   We read situations, listen to the people we have trust in, scrutinise those we don't and base our opinions on our previous experiences, as far back as our childhood – we are riddled with bias.   All these shapes our thinking, and we tend to believe we're right most of the time. Talking to one social worker several years ago, she told me that one twelve-year-old she was working with passed out at the smell of talcum powder. They'd had her in their care from two years old, so whatever trauma that caused this was before that. Our brains start to develop our sensory pathways from three months before we're born.

From a very early age, we're taught that failure is bad. We have an education system that is intrinsically designed to punish failure more often than not. Knowledge is regarded as recalling facts rather than exploiting it to solve problems.

This chapter is not concerned with learning, but it is relevant that we're not taught how to learn. We're not asked to solve problems by applying the multiple disciplines we are taught. We're not taught how to join the dots, or even how fantastic it feels when something, however innocuous, dawns on us. Moreover, we're not taught how to deal with complexity or ambiguity.

It saddens me when I hear teenagers say, "*why am I learning this, I'm never going to need it*". We specialise and segregate subjects so much that they become islands in our young people's minds that seem to have little or no real relevance and without practical value in the real world. Little wonder then that we tend to think in silos and design our organisations to be a collection of specialist subjects. More understandable then that we regard systemic thinking as alien to the reductionist mental models that consequently places us in a state of uncertainty.

Humans are not designed to cope well with uncertainty; we regard it as stressful. We worry about future events and take a pessimistic position imaging the worst will happen. The phrase "*we are creatures of habit*" outlines our need for familiarity.

In 1994 a team of researchers in Quebec developed a model for measuring the scale of uncertainty, called the 'Intolerance of Uncertainty Scale (IUS). It assessed how much people prefer and move towards situations more predictable, including procrastination, and how they respond to ambiguity.

When presented with ambiguity, the brain seeks out clues about the situation. The part of the brain that has been associated with this assessment is the amygdala. In combination with the prefrontal cortex that applies logic to regulate raw emotion, research has shown the amygdala manages our emotional memories.

The amygdala is located on each side of the brain and found in the temporal lobe, located lower down in the brain and part of the limbic system.

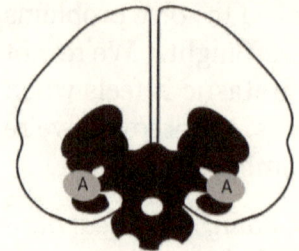

The fear of uncertainty has been well understood for over sixty years. The term 'Fear, Uncertainty and Doubt (FUD)' has been a prominent sales and marketing strategy since the seventies. It focuses on messages that are designed to generate an adverse reaction in its target audience. It has been used as a strategy to prevent the competition from encroaching on a particular patch. The famous example I experienced, especially in the early nineties, was the fear of not buying IBM products. Rather than positively promoting their products, IBM salespeople would present the risks of not buying their reliable products. It was so effective that the axiom 'nobody ever got fired for buying IBM' became ubiquitous in most IT departments.

The perception of complexity creates powerful levels of uncertainty in our minds. The effects can be, and often are, extremely crippling. This presents a burden on the organisation. The organisation as a system is built upon a set of conditions. These system conditions are brought about because of our previous experiences, as discussed earlier.

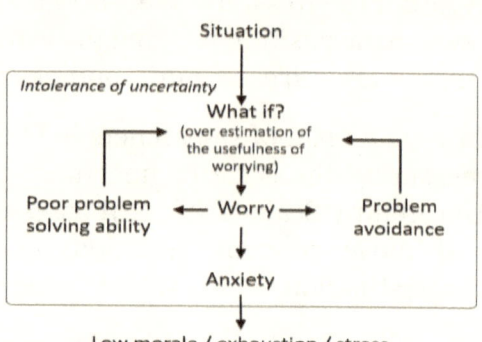

They manifest themselves into big assumptions about what is right and wrong.

The definition of *right* in our mental models is the foundation of how we build our organisations. For example, would anyone today challenge the siloed departmental configuration present in virtually all organisations going back to the post-war era?

The key for defeating this foe is to expose it. Seeing the system as a whole, by mapping the routes the demand flows take and observing the social networks that are doing the actual work removes the uncertainty that is a major cause of procrastination. The challenge, however, is that we need to move past our uncertainty induced anxiety to allow us to start this work of mapping the system in the first place. Unless we consciously bring the fear into full focus our brain operates on autopilot. It's as if a little person in our head is making all the decisions for us.

CONCLUSION

Fear induced procrastination is a condition that has been researched and studied for many years. Some that have approached a solution have done so by suggesting playing mind games with the FUD tactics and even applying reverse psychology.

Habituation occurs when we don't allow our thoughts to influence the way we respond to a situation. Regularly exposing ourselves to a fearful situation and trying to not react to it, dissipates our negativity towards it. The practice of mindfulness has a central theme of observing our thoughts rather than trying to control them. A nice expression I heard once from a mindfulness practitioner when asked how she stays so objectively balanced, was *"My thoughts don't bother me, so I don't bother them"*.

In the closing scene of the film 'A Beautiful Mind', an aged John Nash played by Russell Crowe, has just given a speech after having been awarded a Nobel Prize. In the lobby with his wife, as they're about to leave, he sees three people he has known for forty years, looking directly at him. One is a young child. They are a mental product of his paranoid schizophrenia. Although he sees them, he is aware that they're not real and to live a normal life; he must choose to ignore them. The secret to overcoming complexity syndrome is similar to this. What we see and perceive isn't always real and to overcome it all we have to do is to observe it, and not mentally engage with it. Not judge it. Not respond to it. Just let it be. This counterintuitive approach brings real objectivity to a situation that would otherwise, with an engaged response, create negative thoughts of uncertainty and doubt in our minds that cause us into inaction.

Observation without reaction is a choice. By bringing complexity into full focus and bringing it to the front and centre of our mind, we are free to see past it and move on.

As a simple illustration of the power of attention; we've discussed the neurons in our stomach and that during times of anxiety and stress our second brain can cause us to feel a nauseous sensation, we call *butterflies*. The next time you have this feeling, such as before a presentation to a large or unknown audience, rather than trying to dismiss it or fight it, spend a moment to focus and observe it. Describe how it feels in your mind, in an unemotive logical sense. What you will find is that it quickly dissipates, and the feelings of anxiety disappear altogether.

When we're faced with a large complex organisational problem the first thought that pops into the minds of most is that this is too big to tackle, we don't have enough time and resources, or it's not our responsibility. These are the first signs of fear-induced complexity syndrome. These first negative thoughts need to be observed, acknowledged and pushed to one side. If a person can master the practice of controlling their thoughts in this way, they can move mountains.

CHAPTER 6

Methodology Dogma

"Simple can be harder than complex: You have to work hard to get your thinking clean to make it simple. But it's worth it in the end because once you get there, you can move mountains."

Steve Jobs

NECESSARY BUT NOT SUFFICIENT

The Emperor's new clothes

This chapter isn't a methodology bashing session, in fact, quite the opposite. As I mentioned earlier, having the appropriate method is what moves a company forward more than anything else. The keyword, however, is *appropriate*. Less most certainly means more when it comes to methodologies.

Methodology with no purpose is learned ignorance, and knowledge for its own sake is meaningless folly. There is more value in creative activity than in learning methodologies (value meaning to do something useful). There is zero intrinsic value in a methodology, the knowledge of it, or even the practice of it. There is only extrinsic value if and only if something emerges that results in a change for the better. However, without method, there is a void, a grey space in which it's impossible to work out what needs to be achieved.

Organisations that have no method find every day is a brand-new day and full of surprises. On the other end of the scale are those organisations that apply methodologies religiously and to the letter, with little connection to real-world value, get bogged down in needless policy and bureaucracy with little demonstrable progress. In some organisations, they won't even give you an interview unless you have a formal qualification in a given methodology.

The other thing that is very prominent is the concept of best practices. It's extremely common to hear people talk about particular methods as being best practice, that must be adopted and followed without question. Most methods come with tools, and they too also fall into the same unconditional thinking dilemma. People stuck in this mode of thinking about best practices don't generally ask 'what task was this tool designed to complete and is it appropriate here?'. In addition to the best practice people, there are the methodology pretenders. The people that use the terms but don't carry out the method as it was designed to be. Software delivery methodologies are a classic case for this. Suddenly everyone is *doing* Agile and DevOps, but when you look, it is generally anything but, and worse still they've ignored or abandoned the very principles in which the methods were built on in the first place.

Methodologies have an essential place in every organisation, but they must be applied on a foundation of a principled understanding of purpose and appropriateness, and they must not be regarded as a homocentric approach or a sacred cow. One-size definitely does not fit all. Or, as my father used to say, *"everything in moderation"*.

More waste, bigger waist

In one UK national organisation, I had just started working as an analytics consultant. I was walking down a corridor one morning when I saw something on the wall that stopped me in my tracks. It was a statistical process control (SPC) chart. I made some enquiries about its origin and discovered a team of around forty Six Sigma black-belts and master black-belts (experts). I approached them about my project, and they invited me to talk at their next monthly meeting. I jumped at the chance. After I'd finished presenting, I took the opportunity to ask a few questions of my own. After all, I had the *quality elite* all in one place. What they told me left my jaw wide open.

The team had been established about five years earlier, and in that time, they'd grown from two or three to over forty. They were all very well trained, and they made me feel a little intimidated – a lowly Green Belt – a truly uneducated peasant. Then I asked what financial benefit they had achieved in the last couple of years. Silence. After a couple of uncomfortable moments, one of the more senior people at the front said, *"well we don't actually run improvement projects, we measure performance"*. So, what they told me was that they had effectively removed the 'I' from DMAIC. They were doing DMAC. They were Defining, Measuring, Analysing and Controlling but not Improving. They could see I was shocked (I think I nervously laughed a little). They too looked a little embarrassed and more than a little irritated with my question. Embarrassment can often invoke anger in the beholder. A few folded arms occurred – not a smile to be had. What they had done for five years, and they knew it – and realised I knew it too, was to generate waste; the very thing their methodology was supposed to eradicate – the irony was beyond belief. They had grown into a large team and got fat on generating worthless charts. There was a clear abandonment of purpose as they were practising Six Sigma for no valid reason at all. Their error was that empiricism isn't about measurement or even cause and effect. It is about making a difference through intervention. Output (a thing) is not the same as an outcome (a difference).

This was an extreme case, but I see this behaviour everywhere with project managers that follow Prince2 religiously, IT architects that preach TOGAF all day long with no demonstrable benefit, data specialist that promote DAMA and Agile guys that are about as agile as my house (my house is not a caravan).

Another quality methodology that is often misunderstood is Deming's PDCA. I once sat in a presentation by a project manager endorsing Prince2 based on the Deming method, Plan-Do-Check-Act. He was suggesting that the *Plan* stage was aligned with building a project plan. I looked around the room, and people were listening intently and a few nodding in agreement. Although he was an experienced project manager, he knew nothing about PDCA. Deming didn't mean plan in the sense that Prince2 prescribes it, of course, he meant to get the right resources in place and organise them but what he really meant was hypothesise about the problem that needs resolving, theorise, define success and think about how to study the problem. He was not talking about building charters, controlling tasks and managing risks; his focus was on knowledge and improvement.

It is so critical that we question every so-called, industry-standard-best-practice. Of course, I see some value in all these methods because they were designed to solve specific problems, but many people that practice them have gone too far (or not far enough) and have lost sight of the core principle of improvement, to *think* about the problem they're trying to solve, not just react with plans, methods and tools.   If some smart person has developed a useful tool, and it makes sense to use it, then this is a good idea, but not to question it and assume it is right for the problem we're trying to solve because some expert said so, is not correct.

The inability to think is not a disability; it's a choice.   The environment around us conditions us to think in a particular way, to the point where we don't question things as we should.   In many organisations, we're not supposed to.   It is a paradigm that must not be challenged.

A box of bananas

Although there is some doubt to its authenticity, the Five Monkeys experiment is at least a good analogy for what I see in organisations all the time.   The experiment involves five monkeys, a ladder and a box of bananas. Five monkeys are placed in a room and in the centre of the room is a ladder. On top of that ladder is a box of bananas.   When any one of the five monkeys attempts to climb the ladder to get the bananas, the remaining four get showered with cold water. As the experiment continues, the monkeys get wise to this and grab any of the group that attempts to go up the ladder for the bananas, in fear of being showered.   Then the experimenters start swapping the existing monkeys in the room for new naïve monkeys that have never experienced the cold water treatment. When each new monkey enters the room, they spot the bananas and head for the ladder, at which point the other monkey's jump them. This goes on until all five original monkeys have been replaced, and all the monkeys now in the room have never experienced the cold water. But still, anytime a monkey tries for the bananas, the other monkeys stop them.

If we could ask one of the current monkeys why did you stop one of the group from going up the ladder, they'd probably say "*I don't know, we've always done that*".

As I say, this is just an anecdote, but it has some truth in it. When the rest of the social group behaves in a particular way, more often than not, we follow too, without question. If you doubt this, ask yourself what empirical evidence of success you have for a best-practice method or tool that you've previously adopted.

In the opening chapter, I talked about false paradigms; a whole bunch of bananas. There is one other box of bananas. It's one that is so ingrained in our corporate culture that no one would deny it. Project Planning. In IT we have Prince2. Prince2 was made popular in the mid-1990s, and it is the prominent methodology for managing change. In some organisations, it's mandatory to be a certified practitioner. Its goal is to base change on a business case, to define a project team and work breakdown structures, a scoped set of sequenced activities to carry out the work needed to be done. The plan is divided into phases with milestones, approvals and stage gates that explain the *success criteria*. To make all this work requires a project management office (PMO) that is made up of people managing and updating the plan, creating risk assessments, escalating problems, providing reports that are coloured coded red-amber-green, to represent status, and chasing project teams members over progress updates and delays – with the ubiquitous question 'when will you be finished?', hold regular steering group meetings with senior people, and finally, organise *lessons learnt* sessions that somehow propose that learnings will improve the next phase. There are layers on layers of plans, from the programme to the project, to the stages and the teams. In most educational literature, they even state, 'Even planning needs a plan'.

All of this requires a significant management overhead that does nothing to solve problems. Prince2 and methodologies like it miss one critical ingredient, the ability to get knowledge and understanding. They assume that it is already taken care of but do nothing to contribute to it. It presumes a business case must be written and stakeholders must *buy-in*. It uses techniques like charters and case-studies as a persuasive lever to provide credibility and to demonstrate a return on the required investment.

Ditch the tele's!

When we put traditional project planning in the dock and give it a thorough cross-examination, the evidence against it is overwhelming. It is widely reported that seventy percent of all transformation initiatives fail and now we're moving into the digital age. The Prince2 zealots will respond by saying, it's not the method's fault the programme failed, but this is like the old Egyptian joke, they're in 'de-Nile'. It is absolutely the fault of the method. When a Prince2 project manager is asked by their boss or the client to put a plan together consisting of definitive delivery dates, they have three basic choices:

1. They can put a plan together by asking the team to estimate (guess) how long each task will take.

2. They can put a high-level plan together, which truly is a finger in the air (a wild guess) before spending time in workshops and detailed work to get to better estimates, before putting the detailed plan together.

3. They can get the project sub-team leads to create their mini-plan, and then aggregate and summarise into a collective plan.

All these options are fundamentally flawed for three reasons:

1. It's all guesswork

2. It's not based on real problems backed up with empirical evidence, and does not ask questions such as, what specific problem are we trying to solve? (which couldn't be answered anyway because there isn't any data)

3. The integration of tasks is a secondary step, or as they call them, dependencies, and whole solutions (systems) are planned retrospectively once all the tasks (parts) have been defined. In other words, it's not a systemic approach.

None of it has anything to do with encouraging change, removing waste, resolving problems or innovation. And, those that say, 'of course not, this is a management tool', are missing the point, that if something is not directly contributing to the change, it is a waste. Prince2 is a way of holding people to account by pushing them to meet deadlines and milestones, that have all been estimated through guesswork. Milestones are used as a kind of subversive and extrinsic psychological incentive because missing them causes anxiety and stress. Once met, the pressure is off. When the project team is placed under extreme pressure to hit deadlines two things happen: firstly, the temptation to cheat and cut corners, leaving tasks incomplete or not done at all, and secondly, they ditch scope by throwing the tele's (scope) out of the project van as they try and escape the project management office (PMO) police, to arrive at the milestone before the steering committee report is published. Delay is always met with pain, even if that was the correct decision. Most project managers talk about managing risk, but it's typically a masquerade and put under pressure, they'll take the short cuts just like everyone else. The reasons for denying the enormous body evidence for failure can only be psychological – because the method doesn't work, and the data proves it.

Agile was the answer and still is to many people that have come through the Prince2 era with a bloody nose and want a better way of delivering IT change. But many of these people are desperate and will grab hold of anything that looks less cumbersome and more dynamic than Prince2.

In contrast to popular belief, except for those that properly understand it, Agile is not a replacement for Prince2. Prince2 is not a software delivery methodology. It is a project management methodology for controlling change programmes. It often fails because it is intrinsically detached from the problem as Agile is but Agile and Prince2 are not alternatives or opposites; they are simply different methodologies, designed for solving different problems.

Agile promised a lot because, in many ways, it seemed to be based on the thinking behind Lean and the principles of flow. It used Kanban and words like *continuous*. It had daily stand-ups and Scrum that looks and feels like a kaizen event. However, it too has received fervent criticism for not bringing people on the change journey, not measuring and promoting quality and not taking a whole systems perspective. The problem with Agile isn't that it doesn't work; it is that it can't work, not in isolation. It fails for the same reasons Lean does in most organisations that try and implement it. It fails because it does not fundamentally understand the change it is implementing. It takes no responsibility for understanding the systemic nature of the failure and the opportunity.

Critics of Lean regularly talk about the *buy-in* problem. That leaders want *someone* in their organisation to *do* Lean for them, treating sponsorship and management of Lean initiatives as a delegatory task. Systemic change involves the whole system and Agile and Lean do nothing to address that. For change to be systemic and sustainable, the initiative must be based on thinking at the whole system level by everyone involved. Instead of focusing on solving problems, management in organisations spends enormous amounts of time creating frameworks, selecting methodologies, choosing technologies, preparing and presenting proposals and lobbying potential sponsors, all in an attempt to persuade their leadership team to *buy-in* and fund their initiative. Doubling-down, their leadership team, expect them to do this, after all, they have delegated this responsibility, and they expect to be presented with solutions, not problems. This behaviour places a barrier between the leadership and the systemic problems in the organisation, and it turns managers into salesman rather than problem solvers.

The lack of recognition that our thinking is what creates the conditions that become properties of the systems we design, and that these properties ultimately determine its performance, is at the heart of why methodologies fail to deliver. It is our very thought patterns that shape our future, not the methods. When managers delegate, they detach themselves from this responsibility. They are no longer engaged in the design of the system, and their leadership is superficial and ineffective. Of course, we don't expect everyone to be skilled in the methodology as some Lean gurus propose, but we do need them to be directly involved with the problems that their team is attempting to solve.

All methodologies can be necessary to some degree, but none of them is sufficient to deal with systemic change alone. Methodological pluralism is required not methodology dogma; using many methods together to form different perspectives and opportunities for solving problems, wrapped up in an approach where the leadership is involved in understanding the systemic problems that need to be addressed inside the organisation.

Methodologies and tools are essential for getting specific tasks done. However, it is about the task, not the methodology and not the tools. Methodologies and tools should be pulled into a problem when required not pushed onto the problem, and they should be designed in from the beginning. Many Six Sigma projects I was involved with at GE made sure the majority of the tools had been used, not merely as a training exercise but for completeness. It is unsurprising then that during my time there, the average Six Sigma project took around six months. Methodologies should never be the focus or the outcome, but the journey of solving problems and pulling in the appropriate methods and tools when required. Using tools for the sake of using them generates waste that is not visible, and this grey space, because of an expert's endorsement, goes unchallenged.

It can seem at times that breaking through the years of engrained dogma and tradition can be like cutting through rhino skin with a plastic spoon. People get wedded to their ways of working, especially if it was their idea or if they've invested many years in it. It's important, however, to take an ontological position rather than make epistemic assumptions. Jumping in with methodological knowledge without an understanding of the *what* and *why's* of the environment is a paradoxical mistake. We need to know what problem we're trying to solve. Some designers may say that innovation is found in the grey space of uncertainty, and to a point, this is true, but it can't be without purpose.

When considering a methodology, it's important not to throw the proverbial baby out with the bathwater. Every methodology I've worked with has come with a unique perspective or purpose. Of course, there are overlaps with other methodologies, but each one has a specific focus. Each of these selectively focused on problems at different times can add a potent mix, a super toolbox if you like. But please, for those of you that like tools, remember this is about the problem, not the tools. And, the rule of keeping it simple means a little knowledge can go a very long way. Less is most definitely more.

ALIGNMENT OF THE PLANETS

Several methodologies are commonplace in organisations today. Some are relatively new, and some have been around for decades. Each has its focus and merits. You could say that each tries to fill a gap, to compensate for something missing in other methodologies. Placing Systems Thinking in the centre pulls in the value from each of these by creating a systemic agenda. None has to be implemented in full to gain value but taken as a collective; they form a much more systemic model of how change can be more systematically implemented.

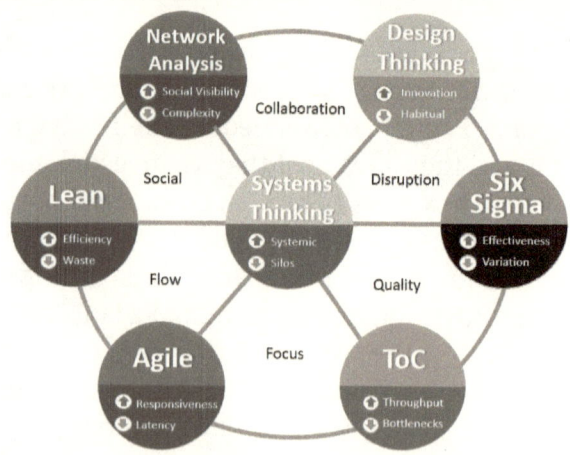

Some may look at this and say, *"my goodness! we struggled with one or two now we're being presented with seven!"*

The point is that only a central part of each has to be extracted to gain a powerful mix of improvement capabilities. In the model above, I've paired them to show how each can add value to another, but of course, this model can be mixed again and again. For example, using statistical process control, a primary tool in Six Sigma would certainly add value to an Agile software delivery approach for looking at the variation across sprints of similar size and complexity, making future estimates far more predictable.

I've also paired them in such a way as to address common criticisms when each is taken individually.

Design Thinking brings a disruptive nature to Six Sigma for which 'Continuous Improvement' has been a long-time mantra. However, often, what is required is not a continual improvement but the discontinuation of whatever isn't working. Discontinuous improvement is at the heart of Design Thinking because it is about taking a very different lens to any given situation by using experimental and experiential techniques to uncover radically new solutions.

Social Network Analysis drives out the complexity that typically stops the design of a new solution in its tracks. It uncovers those embedded communities that contain vital knowledge of what currently happens and why. Design Thinking has nothing in its kitbag to drive out this knowledge from a complex organisation. Neither does Lean or Agile. As Ackoff said 'doing the wrong thing right is still doing the wrong thing'. Without exposing the grey space of social interaction, the likelihood of doing the right thing is extremely low. Knowing who is doing what and why is the first step in defining the right thing. Design Thinkers may believe this is simply about involving the right people and running workshops, but people aren't normally aware of the broader social context in which they exist, and therefore aren't able to provide a truly accurate picture of what is happening. The other issue is that until we see the social network, we don't always know who the right people are. Remember, most people of centrality (in the hub) aren't usually the most prominent.

Lean and Agile share a common bond, especially in the latest version, Agile 2.0. Both are heavily focused on flow. Both struggle with the social aspect of organisations to determine where and how their changes can have the most significant impact, and they also both share the principles of Theory of Constraints. Kanban, a traditionally Lean tool, is used extensively in Agile and is a very powerful visualisation aid for identifying bottlenecks and blockages in the flow. Because Agile is focused on short, concentrated periods for developing smaller solutions, flow is essential, and visibility of that flow is required almost real-time (which has the up-side of removing the need for project managers continually asking the team, "*when will it be finished?*"). The capacity of the team becomes another critical aspect of delivery. The formula, Capacity = Work + Waste pulls in the need to eradicate those things that add no value and even constrain flow. Lean principles can help here. Notice I didn't say Lean method. The types of waste in vehicle manufacturing are not the same as in software or service delivery.

Theory of Constraints identifies the weakest link in a given process, such as a step in an Agile delivery process. These can often lead to blockages and build-ups. TOC enforces the principle that when a bottleneck occurs all resources where possible should be deployed to clear it. This emphasises a focus on promoting throughput or flow above everything else. It has the concept of 'Process of Ongoing Improvement' or POOGI. Still, with a focus on throughput, Theory of Constraints can often become a victim of quality, and other methodologies in combination can help.

Six Sigma and its focus on variation and parts per million failure provides for a very robust and simplistic way of assessing the quality of a system. Lean, TOC and Six Sigma provide a powerful mix of waste reduction, quality assessment and throughput. Agile sat in between these three methods benefits from an elevation of throughput and quality. Using the Six Sigma score has become very unpopular over the years because of its association with the heavy-duty framework of Design, Measure, Analyse, Improve, Control (DMAIC), but it is a very powerful way of quickly identifying the quality of a process. Something that has a score of 6 Sigma is defective 3.4 times per million iterations. A score of 1 sigma has a defect rate of 690,000 per million iterations. So regardless of what process we're looking at, it's easy to see that a process operating at 5 sigmas is far more effective than a process performing at 2 sigmas. At my time at GE, this is how people thought, whether it was in a financial services call centre or a light bulb manufacturing plant.

Systems Thinking pulls it all together to look at a range of properties that the whole system through improvement should develop. A socially collaborative workforce that is applying creative thinking to produce quality and throughput with a constant focus on the flow of demand and the systemic performance of the whole organisation. No method as an individual component can make this happen, but combining the golden nuggets from each of these does.

When we look at software delivery, the development of DevOps based on the principles of Theory of Constraints has been its saviour. Before DevOps, the IT functions, delivery and operations were very separate, not just organisationally but also culturally. It made overall delivery very siloed and waterfall centric, where it was more about approvals, stage gates and handovers than about flow. As well as making the processes between delivery and operations more flow enabled DevOps has provided the opportunity to develop new ways of working such as Continuous Integration and Continuous Deployment. Amazon now deploys over twenty thousand small IT changes to its production system every day.

CONCLUSION

The point about all these methodologies is that they're all based on the founding principles that Taiichi Ohno and Edward Deming developed over sixty years ago. The people that have taken the essence of these principles and adapted them over the years to solve their problems have been the ones that have largely succeeded. The ones that have merely copied a *best practice* are more likely to be the ones that have and will continue to fail. When I look at some of the more recent descriptions of DevOps, and even the job descriptions, that have now become popular such as *DevOps Engineers* I worry that they miss the point of it altogether and because DevOps is the *new way* it cannot be questioned. All 'models are wrong; some are useful' is a mantra that all IT people should hold onto.

No methodology is complete, and some are just plainly inappropriate. It isn't about learning new tools; it's about solving problems creatively, sometimes the tools help but often, used inappropriately, they can hinder. Anyone that says the *"methodology must be followed"* is losing sight of the objective. Also, organisations that insist on certification fundamentally misunderstand the purpose of methodologies and tools. Whole methods do not have to be learnt, and you certainly do not need to be a Six Sigma Black Belt to make improvements. Learning is normative and is achieved through experience. Tools make the job easier at times, so it's essential to learn how to use some of them properly. Focusing too heavily on one way of working isn't healthy. It creates a very narrowed mindset that over time, becomes the 'only way', and the proverbial sledgehammer to crack a nut.

The purpose of this chapter isn't to create a new model; it is to show that no one methodology is complete and that following any of them blindly and to the letter, is applying a wrong focus. Understanding the properties of the system enables us to address them directly. Ignoring those properties as every one of those methodologies does in some way, makes for an incomplete system, and therefore, the change that is being implemented is unlikely to become systemic - and stick.

CHAPTER 7

Social Networks

EMERGENCE

Social networks are more commonly associated with social media these days, but here I'd like to discuss them as a component within an organisational system. In this context, there are three main types of social network that I have come across.

1. **Structural** These are formally or consciously designed. They have hierarchy, process, roles and responsibilities.

2. **Fixed** These are informal. They are permanently in place to achieve a task because the formal arrangements do not satisfy the requirements of whatever is being asked.

3. **Temporal** These come and go, needed only for a short period while a specific task is completed, and they are informally created.

Category 1 is consciously designed and adapted over time. It does not evolve but adapts to situations based on experience.

Only categories 2 and the informal variant of category 3 have emergent properties and have unconsciously, without design or structure or even general awareness, evolved from the formal structure to provide something new, necessary to do something previously not designed into the formal organisational constructs of category 1.

In scientific terms, we theorise that emergence, the appearance of new structures, as a result of interactions, occurs to adapt the system and to make the whole stronger; but in what way? To understand the different properties associated with emergent social networks within an organisation, we can take three perspectives:

Structure They form new relationships between people; relationships not part of any formal hierarchy or process in the current set up.

Knowledge They create greater levels of shared awareness within this structure from different areas of the organisation and nurture new thinking to stimulate ideas within the network.

Effectiveness They get work done that would not be possible otherwise. They also make people happier in their work for reasons such as social connection, job satisfaction, recognition (from within the new network).

An emergent social network within an organisation has the same construct as any social structure; people, physical objects and cultural behaviours, even if they are extremely temporal.

One challenge with this concept is that some people deny emergence and the existence of informal social networks within organisations. They put it down to people just doing their job. The problem with this opinion is that seeing is believing, and those that generally hold this belief don't look and don't study (and they spend a lot of time with experts).

The second criticism is that even if informal networks are emerging, then they shouldn't. *"As an organisation, we mustn't be moving away from our standard processes, and if we are, then this should be stopped"*. The problem with this thinking is that it underestimates the real nature of the work and doesn't try to determine if what is happening is necessary. Non-standard is not necessarily wrong if it is getting a job done that wouldn't otherwise. However, in many situations, the completion of the job is not the focus, but the lack of compliance to the standard, for which criticism and blame are levelled at the perpetrators, instead of empathy and a willingness to understand why a person did what they did.

The main point that is missed by those that deny the existence of social networks inside organisations is that social networks don't form as a result of conscious thought from a single human mind. They form because of a collective, or systemic need.

So the question is; why do social networks emerge within organisations? The answer is because of formal constraints.

Constraints in the higher order of the organisation. These constraints then generate multiple constraints down in the lower orders; for example, some important customer may place an unusual demand on the organisation via an executive mandate. In one very large organisation, I asked one of the main production managers how he managed this particular situation on his [production] line. His answer was *"I just tell them to p*** off"*. Unfortunately, not everyone has the luxury of this liberty. These constraints surface themselves very quickly. Not understanding the complexity of the lower systems, more senior people simplify the task in their mind, while down at the operational level the realities of the formal structures begin to materialise themselves into constraints. This is one reason Cho from Toyota advised leaders to *"Go see"* the work actually being done.

I've heard some commentators propose the idea of predicting the growth of social networks, but I think this is folly. Social systems are not deterministic and can't be predicted as such. The change over time of social systems is perpetrated by the interaction of many events within thousands of grey spaces, both internal and external to the organisation, such that, trying to predict their future existence is futile. The value is in understanding the effects that brought them into being and what they are currently doing.

SEEING

I was once asked to implement a new financial planning system for a national utilities organisation. They had been running for years without any conscious or mindful design of how annual financial planning and monthly reporting was being done. There was a general perception of the process, in that people thought they knew how things were working but were dissatisfied with its heavy manual nature, lack of visibility and general slowness. Their conclusion was they needed a new financial planning software system and a new business intelligence capability. Prior attempts had been made at developing a so-called 'Enterprise Performance Management Strategy', but the proposed concepts were perceived too high level and abstract, and it didn't get the right level of support, both in terms of the leadership's understanding or the buy-in from the management.

Before proposing any solution to their unknown problems (which is what had been done before), I initiated a study phase based on the principles of systems thinking, that would require collecting data through interview and other means. This lasted for approximately two weeks. We then compiled the data into a systemic picture and what we uncovered both surprised us and the business. Consequently, it resulted in a very different intervention than had been initially perceived.

During the work, we effectively covered two main subjects. (1) What is the purpose of your department, and how does it align with the purpose of the whole organisation? (2) How does information come into, through and out of your department, especially data related to financial planning?

During the study, we uncovered the following findings:

> **IT less than 10%:** Financial planning was mostly done off-line, even though the perception before the work began was that the IT systems supported most of the work. In fact, when we took a holistic view, the IT systems were

contributing less than ten percent of all planning activities, including asset management planning. Also, ninety-five percent of all data flows were manual with literally hundreds of spreadsheets being managed and shared off-line. Most of which were centrally invisible.

Go-to People: We discovered two *go-to* people that were at the centre of all this activity. Both were young and regarded as junior. If either one of them left the organisation, it would have caused significant disruption to the financial month-end and year-end processes. In general, the emphasis placed on the importance of the formal hierarchy was blind to the vulnerability these two young people presented. To the degree, that if one, or worse both, had left the organisation in quick succession, then the lights on the financial processes would have temporarily gone out. Whereas, if one or more of the senior managers had left the organisation, then there would have been little or no impact. Just to repeat – for emphasis. Two junior members of staff were more critical to the continuity of their operational financé processes than any of the managers.

Not Finance: Financial planning was not the most important issue to solve. Through interviews with the asset management team, we discovered that the asset management plan (AMP), was not correctly accounting for the costs of certain assets. The reason was that only the larger, more costly assets were being maintained and inspected in the field. This was due to their higher balance sheet value. However, the fault's data showed eighty percent of the cost was against smaller value assets that fell outside of the maintenance and inspection procedures and that they were failing regularly, not just incurring a high cost but disrupting services to customers.

Before presenting our feedback to the management team, the message we'd had behind the scenes was that they were expecting us to be true consultants and tell them what they already knew. The internal IT director that had worked directly with us and knew what we'd found held a very different view. He was very interested in their response.

When we presented our findings back to the management team, we made four points. Firstly, we reemphasised the purpose of the company. Secondly, we identified and recognised the two-junior go-to people. Thirdly, we described our three key findings, and finally, we showed the organisation as a whole by describing how, where, and why the information was flowing.

We showed how each department was contributing to the whole, and for effect, we presented an animated graphic in the form of a jigsaw (below) that slowly uncovered the whole organisation.

After the presentation, people were talking in groups, pointing at the diagrams and thanking us of the *"interesting feedback"*. The best feedback was from the HR director; she said *"You've shown us our organisation like we've never seen it before and recognised key people that weren't on anyone's radar. What you've given us is amazing"*.

The thing about this exercise is that we did all in two weeks. The whole organisation. Also, although we got plenty of compliments, the study was relatively easy to do, and more importantly, we only showed them their reality. We didn't present them with clever methods and technologies. We simply showed them how they operate. For the first time, we enabled them to cut through their false perceptions and beliefs and allowed them to see.

One person said to me afterwards that the most fantastic thing about their response is that people were genuinely excited, not about a new solution, but about having the ability to see for themselves the overall complexity in a digestible format.

This is the key to normative learning and improvement. By allowing people to see their reality, there is a kind of awakening, a form of realisation that they are intrinsically interested in understanding more about, and out of this comes a type of transformation that doesn't require any extrinsic change management, no hard sell, no stakeholder forcefield analysis – just reality. To quote Jiddu Krishnamurti again:

"If you begin to understand what you are without trying to change it, then what you are undergoes a transformation."

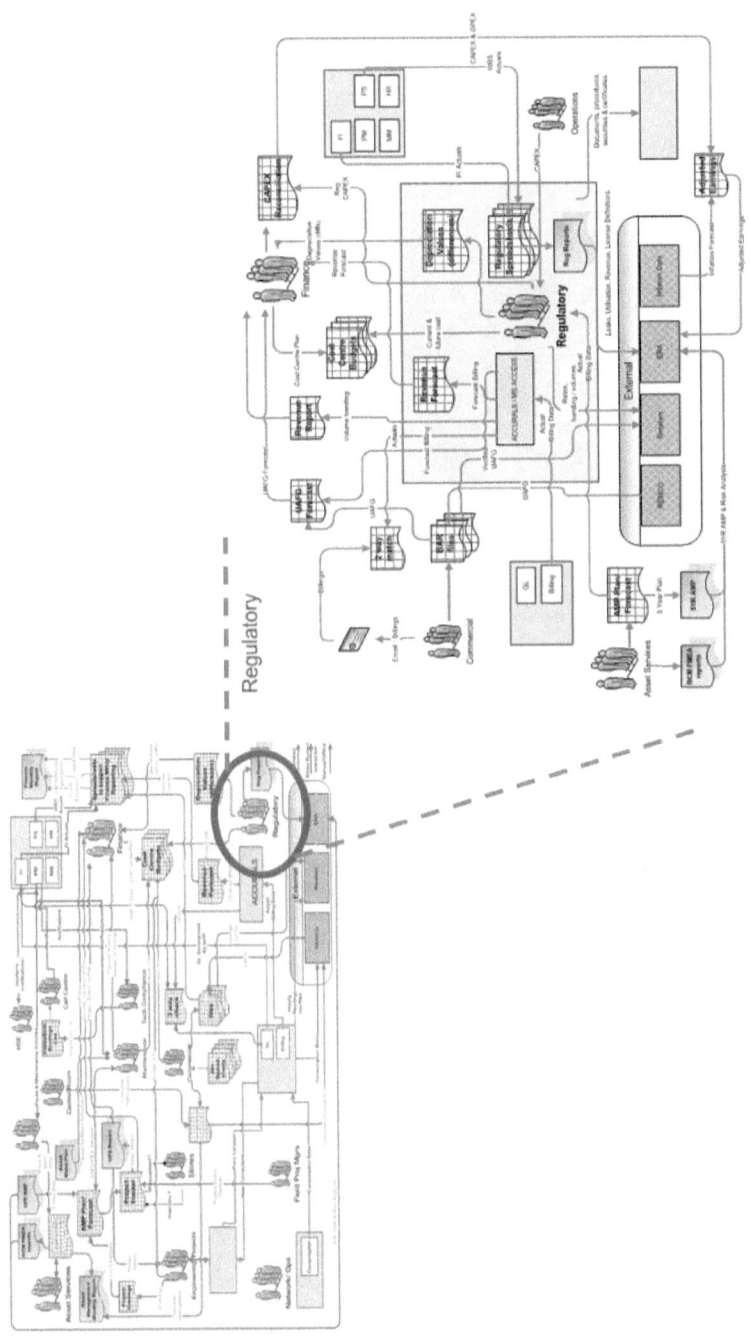

Regulatory

% contribution	
> 90%	Business Activity (sharing of information and completing processes)
< 10%	IT Technical Architecture (complex / disparate)

CONCLUSION

Every social network I have come across has hubs (or people) of centrality. Studies, like the one above shows us that the network is a reality, whereas the formal organisation structures and the formal processes are at best ways of segregating people into largely abstract constructs that pertained little to the actual work that is taking place. But most importantly, they identify that there was a tremendous amount of waste that is neither visible nor understood – grey space.

The people that we observed at the centre of the activity, people we called the *go-to people*, were not on the management's radar - not even close. The management team saw them as average and people that ran around a lot. People that were good for sorting basic problems but not for things needing higher levels of experience and responsibility. However, to their peers, they were highly regarded. As a result, because they felt personal satisfaction from the gratitude received from their peers, they passed off the lack of attention from management as a normal hierarchical protocol. When, in fact, they were the most productive people in the whole network and added more value than anyone else.

Finally, the contribution of the IT systems in many organisations is hugely exaggerated. They are perceived to be largely running the processes with some manual effort, whereas in actual fact they are contributing but a small percentage, less than ten percent in the earlier example. The social networks, on the other hand, had emerged out of the void to respond to these structural, process and technical deficiencies to address over ninety percent of the work. They are the silent heroes.

SECTION 3

METHOD

Studying the organisation as a system

FOR ALL THE TOOL-HEADS

Before starting to write this book, I was very unsure whether to include this section or not. The purpose of the book is to get knowledge about how the organisation is really working, to take a systemic view, but essentially to think differently about the work and the environmental factors impacting the ability to improve. The anti-systemic (experts) love methods and tools-especially those sold by other experts that they admire. Without tools, part of them is missing. It is the purpose of their whole life.

 And unfortunately, it creates pseudo-experts that know enough to be dangerous but not enough to be effective. Instead of introducing a method to augment the work and improve how it can be done, these people have brought disruption and stagnation to many organisations with stifled layers of dogmatic procedures, practices and policies. They are what I call 'tool-heads'.

If you've picked up this book, read the contents and jumped straight to this section, you're most likely to be a tool-head. But don't worry, it's never too late to change, we're not old dogs. However, please do one of two things for me, either turn back the pages and start from the beginning and tell yourself you need to change (and ditch the black belt, if you have one, it only impresses naturists and fellow experts anyway) or put the book down and go read something else. Remember it wasn't people like you that developed the tools in the first place but creative problem solvers.

There is an irony behind the ego that makes someone project they are an expert. A need to be respected and assert authority; probably born out of some deep-rooted feeling of inadequacy brought about by an overbearing parent or some other adverse childhood experience. The irony is that the more a person exerts their so-called expertise, the more arrogant they become, and the less respected by others (especially by practitioners). The only way to genuinely gain respect is to understand the work. This allows you to help others and to put self-interest aside. Applying expertise in this way adds a tremendous amount of value. The more we focus on ourselves, the less effective we become. The job is an honest one, a practical application to get enough knowledge to implement solutions that improve the current situation. By honest in this context I'm not suggesting tools-heads are deliberately dishonest people, I'm saying they are overly principled about methods and tools that are not empirically proven to add real-world value.

Life is about doing and achieving. Those that get in the way of this and won't change should be kicked out of organisations. Anyone that doesn't want skin in the game should also be kicked out of organisations.

Interestingly, as an aside, social networks do this filtering inherently through natural selection. It's only the formal structures that keep the criminals inside.

The next section is about direction and focus rather than an exhaustive education on tools, so the tool-heads would probably get bored anyway, or say that they've heard it all before.

For the rest of us that journeyed here through the previous chapters and believe the organisation's problems are more socially complex than methods and tools alone can solve, let's continue with a few simple reminders; less is most definitely more, all models are wrong, but some are useful, methodologies and tools need to be fit for purpose. *"It's all about the freekin darda"* – as my old American COO used to say.

CHAPTER 8

Method Measure Manage

"Oh, you can't help that," said the Cat: "we're all mad here. I'm mad. You're mad." "How do you know I'm mad?" said Alice. "You must be," said the Cat, or you wouldn't have come here."

Alice In Wonderland - Lewis Carol

METHOD

Carrying out tasks without a defined way of working is madness, a hit and hope strategy. Analysing data without knowing how and expecting insight is fantasy.

Business Intelligence and spreadsheets are software tools (a what), not a method (a how). Only *how* can get insights.

Whatever task we're performing requires some degree of method. A method (the way of working) is tailored to the specific task, and so when we're managing the organisation, we need to select the right method for getting the results we want. Only then can we select tools.

Whatever task we decide to undertake, it's essential to know why. Managers that bring in consultants and ask them to help define the problem are naturists and need to do this for themselves. Jack Welch once answered the question *"should we use management consultants?"*, with, *"only if you don't know what you're doing"*. Before starting anything, we must get knowledge of the current situation. *"Go see"*, as Cho put it. Find out what they're struggling with and what the biggest problems are. Then think through how these problems hurt performance and cost, but more importantly, how this hurts the customer. Remember that stress causes real tangible pain and emotions, and it's contagious, not just to colleagues but to their families. So, when you observe the big problems in your organisation, and you will, those people involved will have anxiety and stress, so it is also your collective responsibility to prevent that. There is no 'them and us – only we'.

The mantra, when we're talking about operational performance, is to *'serve the customer'*. Some may say there are other aims for operational performance, such as making a process improvement, operating ethically, meeting legal and regulatory requirements, and so on, but these are all means to an end. For the purposes of understanding how to improve the systemic nature of operational performance inside the organisation, I'm establishing the premise that anything that detracts away from the customer being able to buy and receive products or services as efficiently as possible, is a constraint that needs to be understood and addressed.

To satisfy the customer's demand involves the whole organisation to some level being connected, but to understand how the organisation is responding to these demands requires us to achieve three fundamental objectives. First, understand the nature of the demand. Second, to understand how this demand flows through the organisation, to describe where it goes, who touches it and why, if it gets stuck along its journey and how much time is being consumed. Thirdly, how variable is the flow, is it up and down like a fiddler's elbow or constant and smooth.

The nature of demand: We are extremely interested to understand if this is a demand that has been received for the first time, such as an enquiry or an order, or whether it is a demand that we've seen before, such as a customer chasing progress or a returning a product. We divide demand into three categories; value-demand, failure-demand, and demand-failure. We'll discuss these later in more detail.

Where it goes: Here, we want to know who gets directly involved and why. In one extreme case, I studied a service delivery process consisting of eighty-nine steps and found thirty-seven approval steps. We want to map the process flows. However, it's extremely common for the data to run dry in the main IT systems. This is because of incomplete processes and grey space between departments. Social Network Analysis covered in the next chapter can be an extremely powerful method in these situations. For this chapter though, we'll assume we have visible processes.

Variability of the process: The customer experiences the variability in the internal processes. We call this process variation. The cause of incorrect or incomplete quality and throughput performance measurement is often because organisations take purely a silo or functional view that ignores the grey space between departments. To obtain a more balanced view requires a perspective that considers the end to end process.

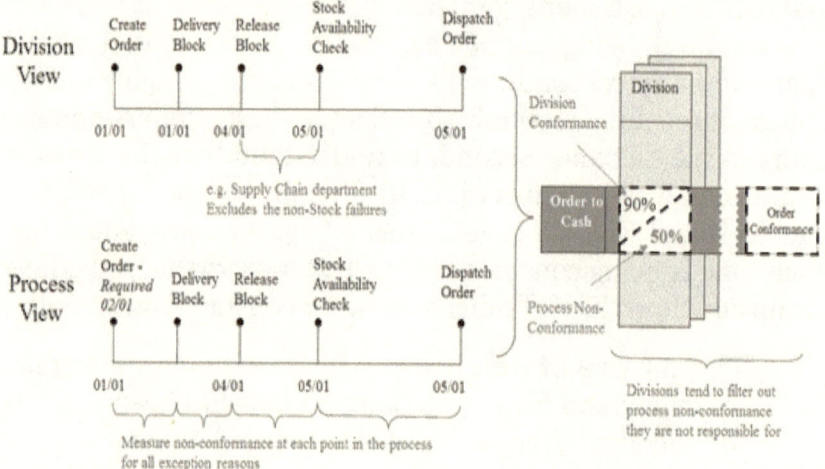

The diagram above shows an example of the different perspectives between the way divisions (or functions) and process teams (or value-streams) taken when measuring their areas.

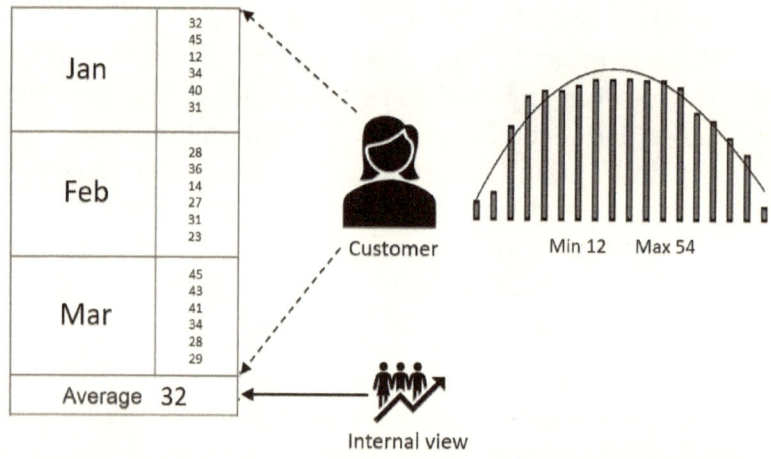

Measuring performance using averages is a fundamental flaw because customers experience reality, not averages.

In one operating company I was involved with based in France, we performed a study and found that their reported ninety-eight percent delivery performance KPI was actually only fifty-six percent. The reason for the enormous err was because they only accounted for the process up to handling the delivery to the despatch or outbound area in the warehouse. Once we included the journey from the warehouse to the customer into the measurement, their performance was terrible. It meant all the hard work done internally was being completely wasted, and even worse, this delusion had been going on for years – everyone, including the Managing Director, thought they were operating at ninety-eight percent.

How we define what to measure and what to improve is based on a customer's demand. We must understand what it is and what they want from us. Listening to the customer is essential for understanding what we need to measure. We can assume their demand is what they require, or we can ask them.

The critical difference here to the method Six Sigma and the DMAIC framework (Define, Measure, Analyse, Improve, Control), is that we want to observe the end to end flow first. Before anything else. In this approach, we are taking the primary principles from Goldratt's Theory of Constraints (ToC). He described how the flow is interrupted by bottlenecks, what he called constraints. So first, we want to understand what and where our most significant constraints (bottlenecks) are. This is not a deterministic root-cause analysis; it is an observation of the synergies.

We need a starting point. We can assume we know what this is by merely implying that from the customer's demand, whatever it is. It can sometimes be useful, though to perform a quick exercise of collecting customer feedback. The reason for this, as one example shows; several years ago, we assumed that the first step was when the customer placed the order. It turned out that for this particular service, it started with a visit from the salesman. Another reason to take the customers feedback into account is to clarify a perceived purpose over an actual one of the system, or in other words, does the customer want something different to what we perceive they do. We won't know unless we ask them.

However, it's not always necessary to do this, but if it is, then there's a quick way of doing it.

There are a couple of simple tools we can adopt from Six Sigma here. The first is the Voice of the Customer or VoC. This is a simple data capture mechanism. Let's take a mail-order example:

Service Experience Description	1	2	3
I want to get through quickly and reliably at all times of the day and night.	Customer Call Centre	Abandoned calls to order lines	Greater than 5 secs pick-up time to orderlines
I want to talk to a person who is able to handle my requirements without the need to transfer me. Where a transfer is unavoidable, this should be only once, to the right person and "seamless" for me.	Customer Call Centre	Calls transferred	Outbound calls to customers related to order capture

From here, we can easily see what matters to the customer. The initial step is to compare this to the purpose of the organisation. They should align. If they don't, then there must be a conversation with the manager involved, about the perceived problem they are trying to solve.

Once we have this list, we then need to consider what is important to the customer; in this example, they are clearly saying they don't want to wait on hold for long periods and they would like the person answering their call to satisfy their request. We can then go further and map these to the process to give them a more precise definition. Columns 2 and 3 are measures that will help us understand whether the customer's needs are being met. In this case, we may be able to obtain the data from the telephony system. If not, we may have to capture the data manually for a period. Remember though we're only observing and not analysing. This is an important point. The temptation is to jump straight in and to get into the details pulling huge amounts of data. We don't need it. What we're interested in is simply observing the system. We're interested in synergies not analysis, in other words, what is the nature of demand and how well does it flow through the system?

The important thing is to first understand the start and end of the customer's experience. It can often be the case that although the data may be in some database or other, there is no process map to reference it against. We must understand the process in steps, so it is necessary to map them out. Again, one common mistake at this stage is to go too deep and apply too much detail. We need to keep it simple. We only need enough to understand what's happening to the flow of information at a high level. Like a traffic helicopter. A detailed analysis will come later. For now, we just need to understand the performance of flow. We only need to go down to level two of a traditional process map. So, if this was an order taking process, then it might look something like this:

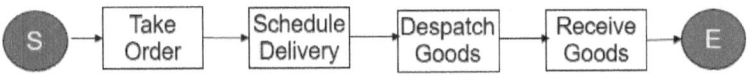

At this point, you might start to feel a little anxiety. We're programmed with a reductionist mindset, and I don't mean we have a tendency towards reductionism, I mean our neural networks and memory have been configured from childhood to want to break things down into parts. Many psychologists believe this to be there from birth. But it's important we resist the temptation.

VoC feedback may not be easily plotted against the map, for example, "I want to get through first time" is clearly in the 'Take Order' box somewhere but it's not possible to plot it exactly. That's ok for now. During the next stage, we'll cover how to study at a lower level of detail. For now, we're only interested in understanding the general flow.

Now we can classify our metrics. The two types we'll need are volumes and percentages. In our example, we want to know how many customer orders start the journey for a given period. At this stage, we need to categorise the types of demand. Mixing them can produce meaningless, ambiguous results. For example, the same product could be based on different delivery charges. One fast and one not so fast.

Once we have our categories, we need some data. Hopefully, because at this stage, we're only dealing with the start and the end, the data will be in a database somewhere. The period is essential. Taking as wide a range as possible is better because we can normalise any noise that is caused by things like seasonality.

Measure twice, cut once

Now we have our customer's input, our start and end of the process, and our few years of data; it's time to measure.

Knowing how to measure is so critical. The enormous amount of meaningless, backwards-looking KPI's I've seen over the years is horrendous, that not only cost a fortune to produce they can be misleading.

Russel Ackoff said that process measurement to managers was like a formula to a scientist. In the beginning, there may be many variables about an observed phenomenon that they need to study, but over time as they understand more, those variables get whittled down until they end up with something refined and even elegant. Managers in the same light that have a large number of reports don't understand their processes well enough.

We have to learn to read signs and patterns rather than explicit indicators. The movement of a process from one state of variability to another over time is not conclusive evidence something is abnormal. Depending on our perspective (an example being the period we've observed) we could be experiencing a recalibration from a period of abnormality.

Assuming something is up, is a mistake, the reality could be, something was up, and now normality is resuming, and this isn't always good news. Something abnormal could be a sudden spike in demand. It's quite common for organisations to set new targets based on spikes.

With measurement alone, it isn't enough to assume we understand the situation. For that, we need a method. Over the last twenty or so years analytics software has been telling us we need to drill down to get answers. However, in most cases, this isn't true. Not only is the cause generally in a very different time and place than the effect it also doesn't get to the nature of the thing we're measuring; is it normal or an exception? A person's heart doesn't beat perfectly even in top athletes, and neither does your data hit perfect averages every time, but this doesn't mean it's an exception. People that chase data points, such as daily sales, are fundamentally misunderstanding the nature of systems. Let me explain.

Variation

We measure variation for two primary purposes. First, is to determine whether something we make in a factory is being made to the acceptable tolerances. Second, is to determine whether a service process is being completed consistently. Each can use the same method, but the reasons are very different.

The later, measuring the variation within processes is what we're focused on here. Using variation to determine the rate at which something, say a customer order, passes through the organisation without getting stuck. Flow and variation are therefore intrinsically linked – which is interesting when many that practice DevOps, for example, only monitor flow. When the Lean guys talk about eliminating waste, they're talking about systematically making improvements to stop variability in a process that is generating the waste. When the Six Sigma guys talk about improving sigma, they're talking about reducing error by reducing variation.

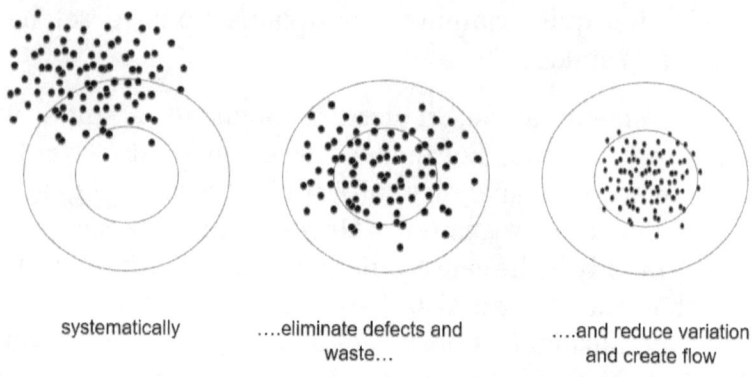

| systematically | ....eliminate defects and waste... | ....and reduce variation and create flow |

Unnecessary necessities

When we respond to individual data points, we react to noise in our data. It's like trying to hear through the interference of an analogue radio signal; its effect is to increase our confusion and inhibit our ability to hear the real message.

It's a form of neurotic hypochondria that believes the answer is in the data; that every downturn is a problem and every uplift is a Willy Wonka golden ticket. The true meaning of the data is a property only present in the collective, over time. Even then, the true meaning may be in a very different time and place. The true use of data is to provide better questions, not answers. Over-intervention is harmful. It causes people to tinker, not in a good experimental way, but in a bad naive way. Their tinkering, however well-intentioned, causes harm to the system. Neither do they fully understand why they're applying intervention or have any idea as to the unintended consequences it may cause. Their efforts to improve, can and often does, make the situation worse, known in the world of medicine as iatrogenic (illness caused by treatment). To quote Oscar Wild, *"We live in an age when unnecessary things are among our necessities"*.

The answer is to only look at large changes in the data, not small ones. If, for example, you manage sales daily, you are exposing your organisation to iatrogenesis and removing the ability to implement sustainable change. This brings me to real-time analytics, the favourite pastime for all those analytical software vendors, presenting it as a *finger on the pulse* capability all managers should have. Real-time analytics is excellent for alerting people to intervene in a particular situation, such as to prevent an error or a break-down, or to improve a process flow by removing blockages – like approving an invoice. If organisations use it for any other reason than a pre-defined intervention, they are causing potential harm. Real-time analytics outside of prescribed intervention causes an over-emotional reaction and does not let the naturalistic nature of the system balance itself out through homeostasis. At best the waste is time lost navel-gazing at meaningless data, worse is false-intervention that interrupts the natural flow, or heartbeat if you like, of the process and causes and an imbalance. It is like applying the defibrillator to someone with harmless arrhythmia.

Where's my freekin darda!

At a time in our history where more data is the norm, and big data is the goal, the antidote to too much noise is method. Big data is often misunderstood. Its purpose is to cover as many unknown angles as possible when presented with *small* questions. Only method can remove the noise that distracts so many analysts and managers and causes them to intervene in damaging iatrogenic ways. Method reduces the data an analyst or manager receives by reducing the noise and enhancing signals. Put another way; an analyst or manager doesn't receive big data, the analytical model does. Data is not information and information is not knowledge, but large amounts of data in the forms or reports, however meaningless and unhelpful, gives people hubristic tendencies. Pride in the printed report or the slick graphical dashboard that are paraded out like a lipstick-smeared pig wearing the 'so what?' printed t-shirt. The answer to all this isn't new; it's actually rather old.

Please show us the way, Mr Shewhart

The Shewhart Chart [AKA Control Chart or Capability Chart]

The way to measure variation is to use a Shewhart Chart. Walter Shewhart has been referred to as the father of statistical quality control. Born in 1891, he developed two fundamental principles:

1. Data have no meaning apart from their context.
2. Data contain both signal and noise. To be able to extract information, the signals must be separated from the noise.

The capability chart plots the data across a timeline (X-Axis) against a measure (Y-Axis) and calculates 'control limits' placed at plus and minus three standard deviations from the mean. This allows us to categorise the data into two buckets (1) Normal (2) Special Cause.

Data within the control limits is regarded as normal. This means that it is normal for the system in question to have data between these two limits.

For example, my heart beats normally around sixty times a minute while I'm at rest and up to eighty times while I'm walking in the stairs at work. If I'm not feeling well and my heart rate increases above these levels, then this would not be normal. On a capability chart plotting my resting heart rate, this would show as an exception or a special cause.

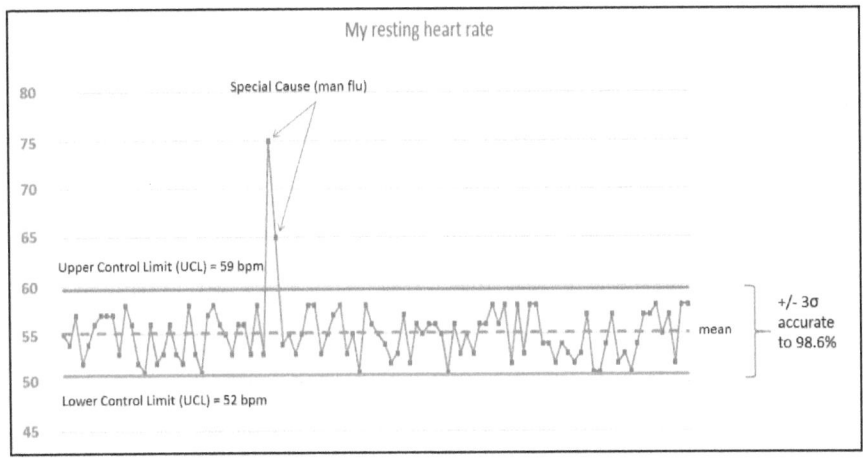

So, normal variation is the variability we expect to see; it's a result of the way the process has been designed and the way it is being managed, or as I like to refer to it, the health of the process.

Special cause variation, on the other hand, is something we don't expect to see; something has changed in our process and is having an unexpected and unwanted impact.

How we respond to what the data is telling us is what drives both effectiveness and efficiency. What this means, is that if the system is designed in a particular way that makes it perform within a given level of normal variation then chasing data points above or below a mean is, well, meaningless. For example, organisations that track daily anything are wasting their time. Yes, they may make a minor impact, but it's not sustainable. Only systemic change can achieve sustainability. And, this involves the systematic reduction in variation. Every manager would do well to remember Jack's Welch's quote *"variation is evil"*.

Failure is valuable

Failure in most organisations, because it is regarded as bad and results in blame, disappears into the grey space of our memories never to be seen again, especially if we work in a toxic environment. Measurement and analysis in many organisations aren't typically scientific, not merely because method is loosely applied or because of the fallacy that drilling down into data actually tells us anything; it's not scientific because it aims to prove and not disprove. Not finding evidence for a phenomenon in business is regarded as a failure, in the laboratory its value, and as a result, organisations never record them. What we're left with is not an empirical record of past research and experiments but abstract anecdotes of 'we've tried it all before', created by our unreliable, fragmented memory, one that struggles to handle non-linearity. Managers that rely on purely intuition regularly find themselves in situations bereft of empirical evidence and can only rely on sensory feedback to guide them. It can be a desolate and confusing place where the only explanation is that it must be someone's or something's fault.

MANAGEMENT

A little history

Some regard that the beginning of economics and capitalism started with Adam Smith, as far back as the mid-1700s. If you look at a United Kingdom twenty-pound note, you'll see Adam Smith and the quote *"The division of labour in pin manufacturing: (and the great increase in the quality of work that results)"*. His book 'An Inquiry into The Nature And Causes Of The Wealth of Nations', opens up in chapter one, with 'Of the Division of Labour'. Where he describes that the economic growth is predicated on dividing work into specialist tasks. He used the example of pin manufacturing that can be divided into eighteen different steps to increase productivity by making each person an expert on one or two steps in the process.

The industrial revolution took the UK from a nation of farmers and cottage industries to mass production of goods using machines in factories. It took us from a population, were in the 1820s, less than twenty percent were dependent on a wage income, to over ninety percent by 1950.

In 1911 Frederick Winslow Taylor published his book 'The Principles of Scientific Management' in which he introduced to the world, management as a science. He advocated the accountability of managers to cost efficiency and emphasised the need for the effectiveness of labour by specialising the work into repetitive tasks.

In 1913 Henry Ford took those concepts and implemented them in his Ford-T factory. He made massive improvements in efficiency and cost reduction by dividing the labour into specialists' workers and keeping those workers static by moving the product, the black Ford-T, through stages from start to finish, what became known as the production line. His methods were so effective that he became extremely profitable. To prevent his skilled workers leaving, he bucked a labour culture by increasing wages.

In the 1950s Taiichi Ohno started to develop the Toyota Production system by implementing parallel production lines, operated by multi-specialised skilled workers. In 1959 he implemented the Kanban system (a visualisation aid of cards on a board that move through stages from left to right) to control workflow through the factory. From this became his principles on the flow of work; "*Let the flow manage the process, not the managers administer the flow*". He also became famous for his categories of waste. In his 1950s book, Walter Shewhart developed the PDCA (Plan, Do, Check, Action) or 'Shewhart Cycle' and statistical process control (SPC) or 'Shewhart Chart'. Both were made famous by Edward Deming, who himself later went on to write his classic management book 'Out of The Crisis' published in 1986.

In 1990, James Womack, Daniel T. Jones, Daniel Roos published the book 'The Machine That Changed The World'. It was this book that first introduced the term 'Lean Production' to the world, and it was based on the automotive industry. The term 'Lean' is reported to have been coined by a young John Krafcik who now works in the automated car industry. The authors Womack and Jones followed up with a second book 'Lean Thinking' that methodised and codified the concepts described in their first book, that was born out of a study of the Toyota Production System. Over the years, 'Lean Thinking' has been criticised for codifying what Toyota embedded in their culture. When you consider the comment from Toyota employees, "*we were never told what to do....*", it's easy to see the perceived paradox when organisations train and *tell* their employees to do Lean. And as a result, most have not replicated what Toyota managed to achieve.

Six Sigma was developed in 1980 by Motorola and became popular because of the global adoption of it in GE by Jack Welch. Six Sigma is focused around reducing variation, and as I've mentioned already, Jack Welch was famous for once saying "*variation is evil*". The method at the heart of measuring variation is the Shewhart Chart or as Six Sigma called it the control chart because it is the main component in the Control phase of its DMAIC (Define, Measure, Analyse, Improve, Control) framework.

In 1984 Eliyahu M. Goldratt published his book 'The Goal' and introduced the concept of Theory of Constraints. His premise is that flow and throughput is what drives performance and reduces cost. Therefore the `focus should be on identifying bottlenecks by reporting variation using the Shewhart chart.

In 2001 the concept of combining Lean and Six Sigma into a unified framework called 'Leaning into Six Sigma: The Path to Integration of Lean Enterprise and Six Sigma', what has now become simply known as Lean Sigma.

In the last decade, John Seddon been a major critic of Lean. His main points being that TPS was designed to make cars, so what has that got to do with service organisations.

In more recent years, the concepts of flow have found their way into IT in the form of Agile and more recently, as mentioned, DevOps.

How effective quality management has been over the years; no one knows or will ever know. Taking a specific observation, such as Toyota or GE, does nothing to improve the estimate. All that can be said is that when single organisations get it right, then, significant improvement is observable, but success has been the exception and not the norm.

The problem is that people have been arguing over the right way to *do* quality management for decades. It is possible to place the population of improvement advocates into one of two categories. 1. Those that are genuinely trying to solve their problems 2. Those that rely entirely on outside help and bring in methods and tools. The organisations in category 1 will always outperform those that are in category 2.

History? - Oh darling, that's so yesterday

The reason for highlighting a little history is not to provide a history lesson for its own sake but to show that at each stage in our recent past an idea has led to more ideas as each generation adopts, adapts and extends the ideas of the generation gone before it. It is a foolish mistake to assume we know more than they did and that we're in some way superior because of our technological advancements. They were solving problems that existed in the environment in which they lived. Many of those problems don't exist anymore, but many still do.

A nice quote from Georg Hegel, a German Philosopher, "*What we learn from history, is that we do not learn from history*". It's important to read between fairly broad lines of this lineage because it shows us that there are two approaches to quality management; Study versus imitate.

The Ford and Toyota Way clearly laid the path. Taiichi Ohno building on Henry Ford's genius. He realised that everything isn't black. If you remember Henry Ford's famous expression, *"they can have whatever they want, as long as it is black"*. Ford standardised his work and reduced waste to levels that revolutionised production methods. He recognised Taylor's point, that people and time are the most valuable asset in the production process, so reducing time wasted by moving the product and not the people, and specialising those people, so they become skilled, transforms production. There's a little bit of neuroscience here. Malcolm Gladwell, in his book Outliers, talks about the ten-thousand-hour rule, and this is what you need to become an expert. Depending on how you calculate it, it's about five years of daily practice. As we practice something, the synapses between our neural connections strengthen, allowing information to pass between them more efficiently. Like an insulated copper cable allows electricity to flow better. This insulation is called myelin, and the process of creating it is called myelination. In his book 'Black Box Thinking' Matthew Syed, ex-world table tennis champion, challenges the concept of talent by describing how, on his small street, several top ten world-class table tennis players all grew up, and all belonged to a small table tennis club. Myelination develops with practise so the more you practice, the better you get because the information in the brain is flowing very efficiently between neurons, to a point where we become classed as an expert, or in other words, our behaviour is so habitual we don't even know we're doing it. In Syed's book, he talks about how psychologists have discovered that experts at racket sports don't look at the ball directly because it's moving too fast. Instead, their brain with hours of practice has learnt to calculate velocity and trajectory to anticipate where and when the ball will arrive. In other words, their brains haven't become expert reactors, they've become expert calculator predictors. So how often you practice determines how much myelination occurs, which affects our mastery of a subject or activity. Now I don't know if it takes five years or ten years to become a true master at something, but it is clear that Ford recognised the value in those people that had become very good at their jobs. By increasing their pay, he secured those people for life, and everyone wanted to work for Ford at that time. Taiichi Ohno also recognised the value of people, but he had a different problem, his vehicles weren't all black. He had many different specifications to deal with, and he realised that to increase production and lower cost, as Ford did, he had to keep things moving but also absorb variety into the production line without creating waste. He was famous for coming up with his seven classifications of waste, and he and his employees tirelessly pursued increasing the flow of production by reducing waste.

As we move through the years, all the attempts to improve quality and performance have their heritage in what Ford and Toyota did. In some instance, they simply copied their methods and tools; in others, they developed their own. Rightly or wrongly, it was all based on the same theme, increase flow and reduce waste. In today's service-oriented world, many of the methods and tools for producing cars just aren't relevant. Even still, I still hear some Lean experts talking about takt time, which is the average time between the start of production of one unit and the start of production of the next unit, which has nothing to do with providing services. It is not correct to blindly imitate. Best practices are a modern version of this. I realise in today's contemporary corporate society this sounds contradictory and counter-intuitive, but our problems are ours to solve, and not someone else's.

A correct approach begins by thinking through our problem and studying our system, to determine what our organisation needs. Now, it may well be that what someone else has done might well fit our situation perfectly, but this is a conclusion we must come to consciously, and mustn't be a de facto response. The now-famous example of a Lean initiative by the civil service for staff to keep their desks clean, with reports of staff being asked if a banana was "*active or inactive*" (active meaning – is it about to be eaten), and if it wasn't to be eaten immediately then it must be cleared from the desk. The estimated cost of this initiative was seven million. I had a similar experience many years ago; a Lean zealot made my team take a picture of the inside of a cupboard in our office (I had to; part of my bonus was based on meeting his quality objectives), We then had to place the photograph on the outside of the door, showing what the inside should look like. I was managing a team of twenty software developers at the time, running the company's supply chain systems, and the cupboard contained our stationary. Idiot.

When we're in the practice of measuring flow and using a capability chart to do it, we achieve too basic but fundamental things. Firstly, we understand normal systemic behaviour, and secondly, we're able to predict with ninety-eight percent accuracy what future performance will be unless we make a systemic change.

Before we continue, just a word of caution about the term prediction. The past is a narrative, one that is prone to an anecdotal assertion. History must never be treated with absolute certainty. This is the trap of 'this year versus last year' analysis. It comes from the psychological need to have certainty and context. In other words, the same problem with the prediction of future performance also applies to the treatment of the past. They are both unknown, and history simply provides us with markers.

Moving on, let's explore prediction in the sense of statistical norms a little further. In most organisations, we have an abundance of KPI's. In many companies I've worked with, their month-end finance pack contained over a hundred pages. All were either measures based on historical events or predictions based on the best guess. If we manage like this, then every event is a surprise, waiting to see the next period's results. The other reporting method is the bar and runs charts. Plotting data over time historically. Again, this shows a trend, but they do not identify what is normal and what is an exception. Over a short period of time, they show us absolutely nothing, and over longer periods, their output is too subjective to extract any meaningful insight from them. Yet I can search Google now and be presented with an abundance of Business Intelligence solutions, all presenting status (not statistically based) metrics and graphs of all shapes sizes and colours, but with no insightful meaning.

This is important. Imagine you are managing a team that processes invoice payments and you have set a daily target of 200 per day and 1000 for the week. On Monday the team achieves 250 payments. You're pleased, and you congratulate the team. On Tuesday they achieve 180. Not on target but not bad, and anyway on average they're still ahead for the weekly target. Wednesday, they process 160, *"mmm"*, you say to yourself, *"now we're below target"*, so you need to intervene. First, you run a BI report you had the IT department create for you a couple of weeks back. It shows the number of invoices processed per person. The report shows Anna is way down – some fifty percent short of her quota. You pull a meeting that takes an hour. You ask the team why, but you're told it's just taking some time to deal with issues and questions coming into the department. You tell them they're doing a good job but ask them to involve you if anything comes in that needs escalating, and that it's important, they hit the weekly target. Your tone gnarls their emotions because they already felt under pressure without your intervention. Now the team's cortisol levels start to increase, their heart rates speed up, and they start to feel a little anxious, after all, they're trying really hard, and you seem to be criticising them. After the meeting, you pull Anna into your office. When you show her your report, she flushes with anger a little and then explains how many problems she's had to deal with because the Finance department has been blocking payments. She seems emotional, so you calm the situation by saying *"I know, but just try and involve me"*. As she walks out, she mutters something under her breath that you don't quite catch, *"toss..."* something.

Thursday comes, and they hit one hundred and twenty-five. *"What's going on, didn't they listen properly yesterday?"* you ask yourself, so you pull another meeting that takes another hour, and the same stories come out. You're frustrated now because it looks like you're going to miss your target this week and this goes into the monthly operations report. This week was a particularly important one because it's the end of the quarter and these results are used in the board pack, and this will probably result in a series of irritating questions coming from above.

You look at the team from your office, and the mood seems low. You're now on Friday, and the team manages one hundred and eight. Better, but they missed their target again and more importantly, the weekly target is short by ten percent. You hold another team meeting and tell them, "*We must hit the target, it's not acceptable to miss by ten percent. We have vendors complaining that we're breaching their payment terms – and on top of that, this poor performance will be visible from the highest level in the company*". The team disappears for the weekend deflated. There a couple of offers to work the weekend to try and catch up.

Monday morning comes, and you start all over again.

Over the weekend, you read this book. The first thing you do is create a simple capability chart, and you populate it with the last twelve months of invoice payments and set the timeline to weekly. You immediately see that there's a normal variation ranging from one hundred and twenty to two hundred and twenty, with a mean line at one hundred and seventy. You think to yourself, "*wow, that's a big range, hey? This is normal? Last week I gave the team a hard time, and they actually performed above average*". You now know that this is correct because the capability chart that is predicting a range of between one hundred and twenty and two hundred and twenty is ninety-eight point six percent accurate. You also notice a regular exception (special cause); seemingly occurring once a month on or around the last couple of days. Last month seems crazy, three hundred and fifty processed invoices in one day, "*wow the team were on it then, but hold on this is not normal, so it's wrong to assume this is repeatable*". You pull some more detailed data, and it tells the same story. However, nothing in your data analysis is giving you any clues as to the reasons for the wide variation or the special causes, but you do recognise that it has given you much better questions.

So, you run a meeting with the team and explain the capability chart. One of the supervisors announces that the three hundred and fifty was achieved because *"We had the whole team in which is a first for years"*. She explains, *"that the shifts got mixed up and we had everyone in by mistake"*. Another team member looks at the lower values that trend around the start of the month, and he says, *"it's tough then because we get a lot of distractions from procurement that are getting chased by vendors that want to close their month-end."* She also adds *"we also get quite a few payments we have to hold because there's a difference between what we've been invoiced and what we received. Once we understand the reason for the difference, we then have to raise a credit note, and that all takes time. In many cases, we have to actually chase them so we can meet our quota because they are counted in the KPI"*. *"How do you do that?"* you ask. The team goes on to explain how this all happens by mail, phone calls and favours. They show you a circulated email confirming many people involved from across the company clarifying, approving and processing. You had no idea this was going on. You knew there was the odd emergency, after all, that's normal, but this, this is a cottage industry!

You begin to realise there are clearly some systemic issues causing the variation. Moreover, it's not correct for you to be assessing the team against a daily target or to be focusing on individuals. You see now that the target you set is completely arbitrarily and meaningless and that it is actually doing more harm than good. In fact, the definition of the KPI is actually creating more problems. So, what to do about the activities outside of your department that are disrupting your department? And what to do about agreeing on a new KPI definition presented in the Board pack? The important realisation you have is that every day is a surprise and that the demand coming in is both value and failure demand. To improve performance, you need to reduce waste and increase flow. To smooth the flow of demand requires a systemic approach to reducing variation. To reduce waste, at least in the first instance, requires a reduction in failure demand. Smoothing the flow will require an understanding of both the periods were value demand increases and the root cause of the errors causing rework. You conclude, *"This cottage industry is full of grey space, and it needs to be exposed"*.

Seeing the system in this way makes the work very visible and enables you to understand what is really happening, whereas before it was simply a black hole that seemed very complex and inaccessible.

It allows you to go beyond your departmental boundaries and understand the total flow. It allows you and your team to take responsibility for the day to day improvements. Small improvements every week add up to a lot at the end of the year. Steady, regular improvement led by the team is how sustainable improvement is achieved.

You understand that your responsibility as their manager is to *see* what's going on and create an environment that places the responsibility of the improvement in the hands of your team, that is doing the actual work and improving flow. To see and understand what's going on requires you as their manager to understand the types of demand that is being received and the variability in processing it. Without this, they are operating wearing a metaphorical blindfold.

CONCLUSION

The reason why method is so important is that it provides a structure that our emotions and behaviours don't possess. For instance, accepting failure doesn't mean ignoring it; it means dealing with it systematically and scientifically.

So, the obvious question is if it is so simple, then why hasn't this way of working become ubiquitous? One reason and I believe the primary one is that we seriously over complicate things with methodologies and tools.

Using a capability chart is simple. However, people feel daunted with messages of statistics and frameworks. In one large manufacturer, I was working with; they had a large internal Lean Sigma team responsible for quality management across manufacturing. I went to see them and proposed an initiative to educate one of the IT departments so that we could introduce some basic principles. They presented me with a three-month training programme, made up of business cases, classrooms and projects. Of course, it never happened. Methodologies frighten people. In the IT world, they are actually debilitating. For example, ask about data management, and you'll find years of education ahead of you. I've worked with two companies that actually banned the term Six Sigma be used with the leadership team because of the perception of complexity. I asked one of the executives why the board had decided this. He told me they felt it was too *"overkill"* for them and they didn't want to frighten people with a large corporate initiative, *"and anyway it would cost too much"*. I also got a condescending quote about the cost-of-quality, to firmly close the subject. So, they did nothing and carried on as they always had.

In addition to this way of working, improving performance is also extremely good for mental health. It's rewarding to feel we're doing something of value. The psychological effects are well studied. People feel more valued and more connected, and our brain gets a shot of feel-good dopamine. The connection is important because positive experiences generate intrinsic motivation. The management at Toyota understood this by not telling people what to do; instead, they set the boundaries and direction, giving their teams the responsibility of what and how to improve. Failure due to trying to do the right thing must never be punished. It must be treated as a learning experience. I hate the expression *"our meetings are talking shops and a waste of time"*. It's not the talking that's the problem; it's what the conversations are focused around and how they are being conducted. Talking is critical.

Organisations are full of contradiction and conflict. We are social beings. It's how we're wired. We need to connect with others, and we always produce better results together than individually. Tribes can be toxic, especially when each has a different agenda. So, it's important to understand any conflicts. In a call centre, I was working with some years ago; there was a complaint from the sales team that they weren't cross and uplift selling enough, which was impacting the top line. There was some animosity between the two departmental managers. When we looked at how the call centre was operating, we quickly realised that the team had a two-minute call duration target, set because there was a view that shorter calls meant more calls would be answered more quickly resulting in more orders being taken. This criticism from the Head of Sales had been present for a few years but had never been addressed. She believed there was a missed opportunity to sell more related products. Her view was that by increasing the call time significantly, sales would increase, and this would more than pay for the additional agents. This argument fell on dry ground because the perspective was on cost, but more specifically, the unit cost of people. Presented with better data and an experimental approach, it was agreed to extend the call time for some of the team. It proved to be a tremendous success, and the Head of Sales was proven to be correct.   Eventually, the call duration limit was removed completely.

It's essential that when we perceive that demand coming from another department is the cause of the disruption in our team, we must approach it empirically to understand what the root cause is, and not emotionally by attributing blame. Nine times out of ten, it will be a policy, a rule or a target or even just plain naivety, that is based on a set of unchallenged assumptions. The principle to remember here is that our thinking is what designs the system in the first place, and it is the way the system is designed that determines its performance. If that thinking was based on a false premise, then taking a helicopter view of this starts to provide a systemic perspective of the situation. However, having said all that, policies, rules and measures usually come top-down, so it's important to gain sponsorship or support from the levels above. If this isn't possible in the first instance, then don't simply present your findings using only data to your seniors. Remember their prefrontal cortex has no emotion. You present a gun, and they see a metal tube and a handle. You have to pull the trigger so they can experience its impact (metaphorically speaking). Remember the housing directors experience and the thought of his mother living in those conditions. In less analogous and anecdotal terms than a presentation, walk them around the team, show them the improvements the team has made, demonstrate the types of demand and show them the impact it has on flow and how the variation impacts performance. Fill the walls with improvement information and use them as a communication tool. Talk to them about stress in the team and that although they care, they feel powerless. Don't hold a formal meeting, walk them to the desk of another impacted department and talk openly about it.   The leadership must really understand and feel the experiences of the team.   Allow the team to talk openly.   Only then will the leadership begin to share any meaningful emotional connection with the problem you are presenting.

This book isn't about telling you how to be a manager or a leader. I wouldn't be so bold. It is simply pointing out that there's a way to see the things that hurt the performance of your team, and there's a more simple way of reducing variation and waste than applying quality methodologies in their full glory. But more importantly, is how people respond, or more accurately, how their brain responds to systems that don't work very well. Deming once said that a bad system will beat the best people every time.

CHAPTER 9

Social Network Analysis

WHY SOCIAL NETWORKS?

In systems theory, there is a central principle that everything is connected and however complicated things may seem there is an underlying order to everything, and however complex, the environment around us seems there are invisible forms and structures that bind everything together into a universal whole.

These connections describe how things work. Stringer's acorn and the British plug are examples of where the environment shapes and determines why things are the way they are. The challenge with a complex system is that it can be difficult to visualise and consequently understand. Our limited ability to see much further than our personal perspective creates grey space in our minds that limits our ability to comprehend the whole. By referring to these connections as a network, we can develop models that start to describe how information is flowing. In particular, we can begin to explain how information diffuses within a social network. However, and more importantly, these models can start to identify why the network exists in the first place and the system conditions that brought about their emergence.

In the 1980's Mark Lombardi, an American artist, mapped out news articles from the newspapers, in a network pattern, to show the connections between political, financial, and corporate entities. His art presented those relationships in such a powerful way that it took the interest of the Department of Homeland Security in the US.

When we consider the organisation as a whole and give it an identity, we typically refer to the company name, its heritage, its brand and its values. Organisational Theory would ask 'but who are we?'

The organisation, as we know it today, is a relatively recent phenomenon. Peter Drucker, credited as being the father of post-war management thinking, developed his theory in the

1940's at General Motors; he prescribed that the organisation is a social system as well as an economic one. He argued the production line created inefficiency because the rate of progress was as fast as the slowest process. A theory Goldratt would pick up on years later. He described how the hierarchical nature of the modern organisation was simply an adoption of the military model, because at the time people didn't know any better, and that layers simply created levels of bureaucracy where rules and policies are divided into ever-increasing levels of invisible controls (systems conditions), that actually generate work, what we'd now call waste.

Before Drucker, the world saw workers as a cost, but he regarded them as a resource. He coined the phrase *knowledge worker* because he saw that how the organisation developed was not due to the few at the top or the advancement in technology but through the creativity and adaptation of the people who actually do the work (remember our two young go-to people). He believed the identity of an organisation is carved from the way people are able to work within an organisation and that social health was the responsibility of the whole, with the leadership taking strategic and directional level decisions. How the individual engages with the whole was not an individual property but a holistic one – and a leadership responsibility.

When we look at many contemporary designed organisation, they seem to either misunderstand or to be ignorant of these golden principles. Over recent years we've seen the rise of the modern organisation with flattened structures and less hierarchy. Apple and Steve Jobs are famous for branding, marketing and products, but he was also revolutionary in his organisational thinking. He wanted harmony in his organisation, not conflict, and so he created what would become the most valuable organisation on the planet with a single profit centre. A concept most management accountants, in companies a fraction of Apple's size would class as impossible. He even designed their headquarters to hold twelve thousand people, in a circular architecture to promote the flow of information and social connections.

People inside organisations are tasked with getting a job done, whether they see the end result or not. They inherently know how to create social relationships; it's how we're built. So, when structures stand in our way, we simply go around them. As James Taylor sang, *"bridges are for burning"*.

The true identity of an organisation is found inside, in how its social systems are arranged, whether this is through design or evolution. The aim then is simply to understand them.

In today's world of social media, social networks have become a very valuable asset, and corporations have realised over recent years that the diffusion of information can describe and even influence behaviours as it spreads. Data, I recently read, especially social data has become the new oil. However, mainstream organisations have been very slow to realise the value of this data, even though most already have it in abundance. The most common types of data are social platform data, emails, telephone logs and even door access logs, anything that connects a person to another person or a location.

When we first look at the data from a social network, it can seem like a knotted ball of complexity. The diagram below represents raw email data:

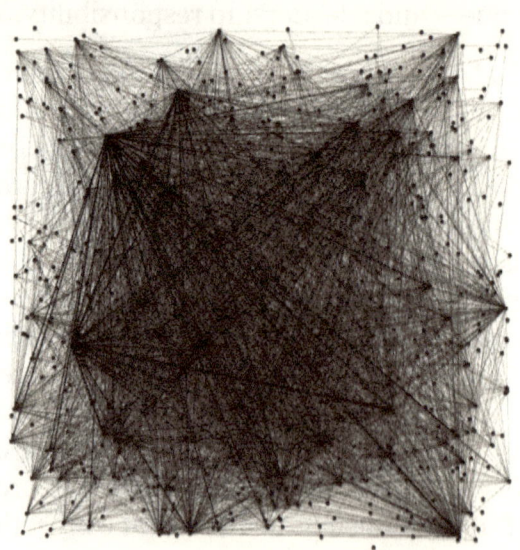

In this format, it is a two-dimensional flat structure, with seemingly no meaning and nothing from which to drive any insight or a deeper sense of understanding. In many ways, this is a nice metaphor for how our minds perceive a complex situation.

Using algorithmic models to determine the intrinsic patterns within these data sets is called Social Network Analysis. There are different models for different types of analysis.

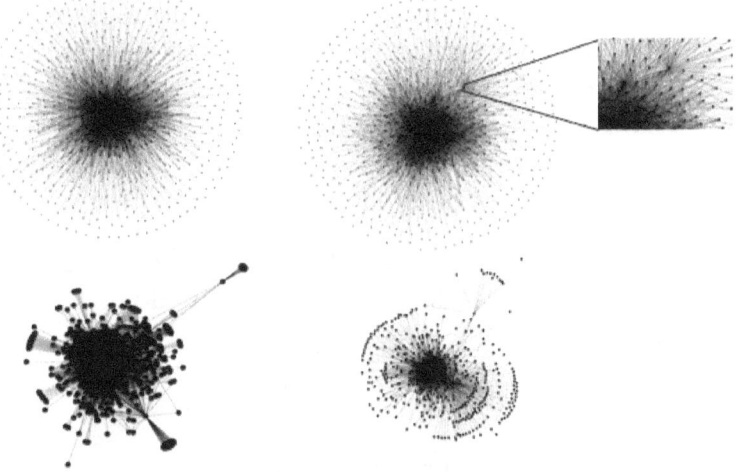

Before studying email to form a social network, it's important to realise that how people use email can tell us a lot about the culture of the organisation. Here are a few clues:

- Large volumes of email are a good signal that there are significant disconnects in the organisation where the formal processes either aren't present or are inefficient.
- Large numbers of emails with certain words can suggest particular patterns, such as the word 'approved'.
- A regular presence of senior managers and executives on copy (cc), can suggest a political or blame culture
- The broad spread of departments can mean a disparate set of responsibilities
- A large amount of attachments, especially spreadsheets suggests off-line information subsystems
- Large amounts of 'fyi' emails can suggest gaps in the formal structures.
- Large numbers of people on emails can suggest a lack of coherence and clarity of responsibilities.
- And so on.

Sentiment analysis can also be a good indication of the mood in the organisation. In one organisation I worked with that I regarded as toxic, where people were extremely dissatisfied, the HR department presented the results of an employee satisfaction survey that provided an overall score of eight out of ten. A big congratulations were sent to the workforce. The reality couldn't have been further from the truth. Analysing, the sentiment of their emails would have painted a very different picture.

If we don't know where we are, how do we know where we're going? And, when we're lost the best thing to do is to stop, look around and assess our surroundings, to try and understand where we are before worrying about where we want to be. In this example, the leadership team were lost, very lost.

However, over and above all these very valuable insights, we're interested in what groups are connected, cliques and communities, and who is at the centre of them.

We have to remember these networks are not often aligned to the formal organisational structures and have not been designed by any conscious choice. They have emerged because of a need in the systemic nature of the organisation. So, the reason we want to understand them is to determine where the systemic failings of the organisation are happening. Understanding emergence is one thing, but it's a snapshot at a particular moment in time.

Now, of course, there are other ways of building a picture of the network, using interview techniques and surveys, for example, and although these can be a useful input into the analysis, they are subjective, whereas email is empirical data, because it is real communication that has taken place. However, if interviews are required, there is a more effective way of running them that can be summed up in seven principles:

1. **Don't prepare questions**. Interviews should be free-flowing and encourage the interviewees to lead the process. However, this approach can cause the conversation to wander too far off track, so it's important to bring it back at times. I remember one humorous situation when I gave this guidance to a young consultant, and he came back with all the person's family background and nothing about the work he did – my failing, not his. Scripting the interview with lists of questions, places boundaries and constraints on the answers even before they've been asked. By letting the interview find its own path we're more likely to come across golden nuggets that surface because of questions like *"please, can you tell me more about that?"*, and, *"why do you send this information to them?"*.

2. **Start with purpose.** Begin the interview with questions that explore what the person thinks about the purpose of their department or function and if they see any alignment with the whole organisation.

3. **Leave the service provider to last.** If the improvement is directly associated with a particular service provider, say IT, then leave that department until the last set of interviews. This allows us to build a picture

of how other departments view them before we speak to them.

4. **Confirm you've understood.** To quote George Bernard Shaw, *"The single biggest problem in communication is the illusion that it has taken place"*. It's critical that we properly understand what we're being told. It's ok to say, *"I don't understand"*, such as asking for clarification on acronyms that might be used. Sometimes drawing pictures can help to get a better understanding, so it's a good idea to ensure there's a whiteboard or flipchart in the room.

5. **Keep it friendly.** The more informal the interview, the better. This is not a job interview; it's a conversation to gain insight and understanding. Humour is not always possible and can even be dangerous, but a little never hurts. It's ok to cover personal subjects like family if it appropriately breaks the ice.

6. **Never Contradict.** The purpose of the interview is to get information from the interviewee, not to validate their understanding. Whether we think their answer is correct or not is irrelevant, it's what they believe that is important.

7. **Two ears and one mouth.** As a minimum, we should do at least twice as much listening as talking. This is an information receiving exercise, not an information broadcasting one. The less talking and the more listening, the better, so a two to one ratio is the minimum we should adopt.

Whatever method we employ, the objectives for understanding the social network are as follows:

- What work are people involved in?
- Who are the central people or most important in the network?
- What departments and external organisations do people belong to?
- How far apart are people in the network, and how many hops does it take to make a connection?
- How prominent are these organisations?
- Does the network contain communities of people from different departments and external companies?
- What is their preferential attachment; in other words, why have certain people become more popular over time?
- What information is flowing and why, and where does it get stuck?

However, ultimately, we want to see how certain dynamics of the network effect how it operates. The social network has become an integral part of the systemic organisational structure, whether the leadership team or management know about it or not.

How well information is flowing across the network and how the network's structure enables it to propagate is an indicator of the effectiveness and efficiency of an organisation. It also provides clues to how potential technology could improve the integration and automation of the work. I say clue because early network analysis is too abstract to determine cause never mind solution, but nevertheless, it is a valuable insight that provides us with much better questions from which to build further enquiry. It also helps describe cultural diffusion, or the spread of ideas that remain intact, especially those that suggest the emergence and expansion of social networks. This may also be useful to understand how views and opinions, based on sentiment analysis, can spread.

Where the rubber hits the road - 11'Cs in actions

Earlier in this book, I presented the 11'Cs model for how cultures are formed. The network can provide real insight into organisational weaknesses caused by certain system conditions and how communities repair these through cooperation and collaboration.

An essential question that must be answered by our analysis is *How resilient is the network?* For example, if one or more very central people were removed, what would happen to the flow of information? Not knowing, could cause severe disruption to an organisation if the organisation is ignorant of the importance of these people in the network. These bridge and go-to people are central to the network. Unlike naturists, they add a tremendous amount of value. Because, paradoxically, they are often the least recognised and are below the management radar in terms of seniority, they are more likely to get affected by a decision the organisation makes to rationalise its workforce. The most valuable asset they take with them, apart from being pivotal in the flow of information, is knowledge of how the organisation really works.

CONCEPTS

To begin with, I'll explain some of the main concepts of social network analysis. *Nodes* are our people, and *edges* are our connections.

So, with a basic model (below), we can see a community where George seems to be one of the more popular people (he is a central node). He is connected to five people (has five edges). One of those is Joe, and we can see Joe is connected to Charlotte and David. Charlotte is one step (hop) away from George. In the famous Kevin Bacon model; most people on earth are only six hops away from him.

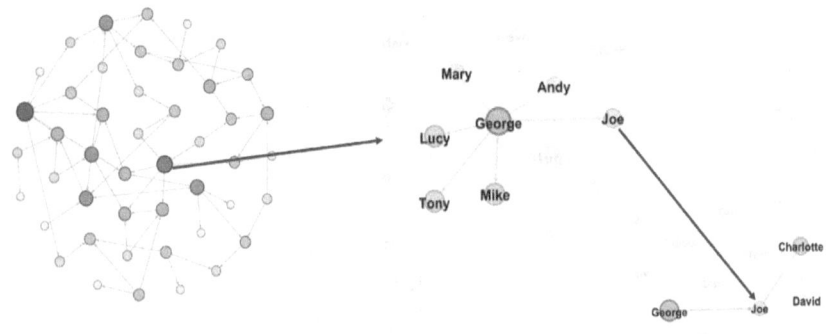

The two metrics introduced here are *degree* plus *degree distribution*.

The *degree* simply states how many edges a node has; for example, Charlotte has some connections coming into her and some going out. This property is called *directionality*. *Directed* means Charlotte sent something to someone else. The term *undirected* would mean two people or nodes, are recipients of Charlotte but not connected directly themselves.

As well as *directionality*, there are other attributes associated with the *edge*, such as *weight, ranking, type* and *betweenness*. *Weight* is the calculated weighting you place on the connection so that it can be the frequency of the communication or the number of emails sent or received. The *ranking* is the importance you put on a particular person. *Type* is how we categorise the people, so it can be by department or internal versus external. *Betweenness* is the role the *node* plays, for example, they can form a bridge between two different communities

We can also provide connections with a positive and negative classification. Meaning we can take a view of the more positive and the more negative relationships in the network, such as using sentiment analysis as a classification mechanism.

However, for our analysis, the size of the *node* will be based on the number of connections in or *weighted in-degree* and *weighted-out degree*. These are very important for identifying the most prominent people in the network, or the go-to people. For this example, in our first pass of the analysis, we'll weight based on the *weighted degree* or the weighting of all the connections in and out. Below we can see Dee is highlighted as being the largest *node* or the person with the most connections; however; she has a zero *weight in-degree* score meaning she's only transmitting information. Now, this may be a very useful analysis for identifying who is authoring the most information or the most information of a particular type, such as email with a subject title, for example, we may want to identify those people that send the most spreadsheets out with the word 'Revenue' in the subject field. In this example, though we're interested in identifying our go-to people, those people that receive the most questions or information, so for this analysis, we're more interested in people with a higher *weight-in* score. Now, when we change the analysis to identify these people in the network, we can see Lucy is by far the most prominent person.

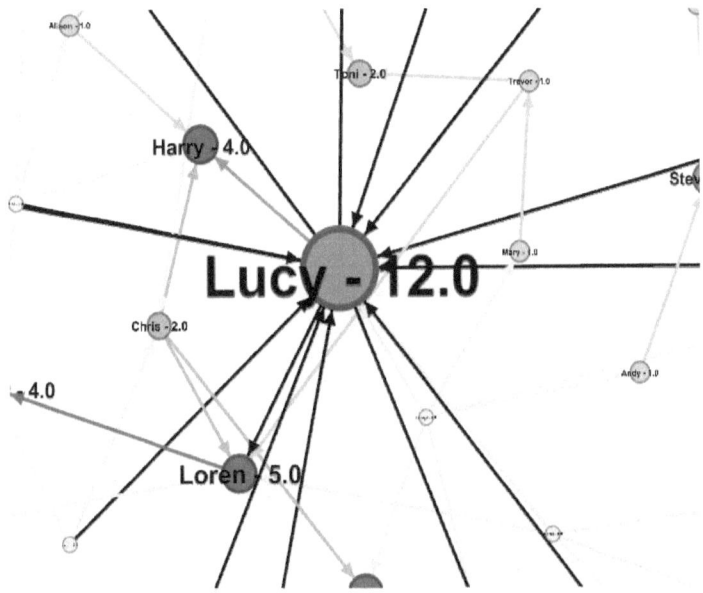

In summary then, when we're analysing connections it's important to think through the scenario we're addressing, to identify whether we're interested in the total number of connections a person has, or whether we're interested in those that have more connections going out or in. A couple of examples; if we are analysing a project community, we may want to identify the more senior people, such as executives with a lot of out-connections. In a normal project, we would expect a smaller number of connections from these people, mainly for the update of communications and direction, but a more significant number of connections may signify the need for their intervention such as approvals to perform specific tasks, suggesting weakness in the process or a lack of formal delegation. Another example could be an increase in the number of out connections from project managers, indicating a need for more updates due to problems on the project. By merely using a timeline effect, we can see a gradual or a sudden prominence of a particular person. Here we can see Lucy has suddenly appeared (below), suggesting she's either new to the role and joining the network for the first time or if she was already present, a change to her role. It could also mean something has changed in the organisation, meaning the information she possesses has become more important.

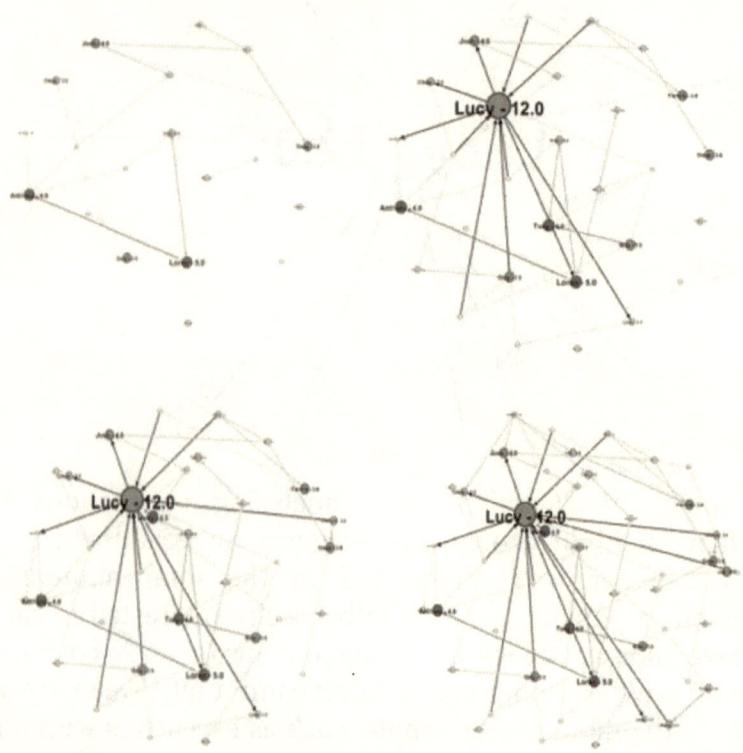

We can also see that other connections are also being formed between people directly and indirectly connected to Lucy, suggesting a small sub-community is emerging.

The other analysis we can perform, especially if we're focusing on a particular subject, is where a document is flowing. Let's say we want to see where a management reporting pack is flowing. What we see is that some of the people we'd expect to be most prominent in the network aren't. We've identified the go-to people, but the more senior people aren't involved at all. This may require more in-depth analysis and even interviews with these people to understand why their actual involvement is limited. The converse is also true. Let's say we have important information in one part of the network that is not propagating. Below Harsha, Tim and Rob could be in the same department as Lucy but are not connected to the same network, prompting a deeper analysis. Are there silos within silos?

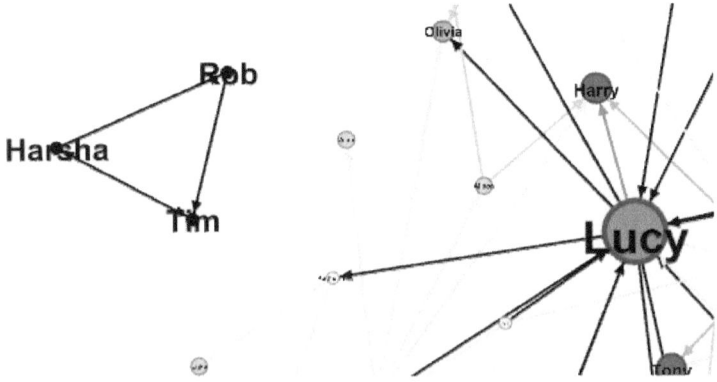

One of the phenomena we'd be very interested to understand is whether there exists, what's called, a *giant component*. The *giant component* in our analysis is a significant number of tightly connected people sat within a broader network that holds the majority share of connections. This suggests a well-established network of knowledgeable people. Their purpose in this network is something we would want to understand, especially if we're tracking information flows.

Identifying the central people in the network is of paramount importance. Lucy is our key person, but merely counting edges is not enough to identify her significance in the network.

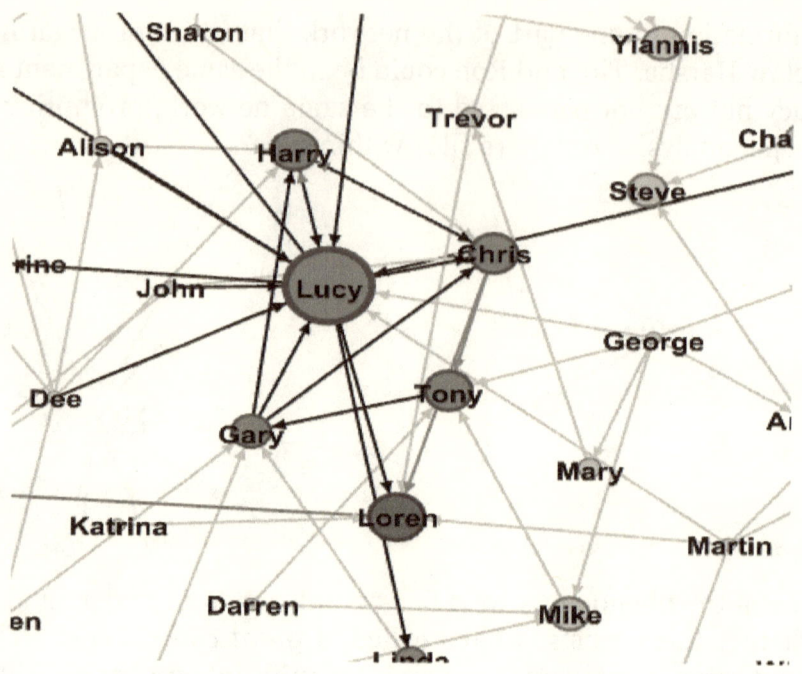

Maybe she just sends many emails? What if there is someone in the network that is important but has a low number of connections?

Below we can see our central node is actually creating a bridge between two networks, so this would be an important insight when thinking about key people making our information flow across the organisation. However, they have a lesser number of actual connections.

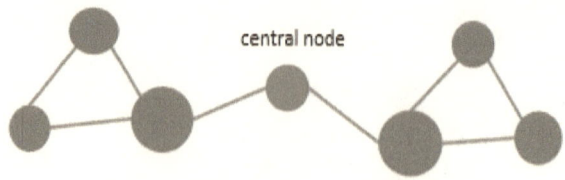

central node

Taking a different perspective. Our central node would only have to take two hops to get to either edge of this network, whereas any of the other nodes would have to take three or four hops.

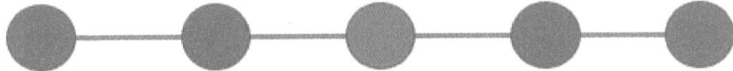

So, in both situations, our central node is looking quite crucial because they are more likely to hold more knowledge of what's happening in the organisation.

This concept is called *betweenness*, meaning how pairs of individuals in the network would be connected to our key person on the shortest path to each other; in this case, our central node. If we now weight the nodes based on the shortest route to each relationship, we get a very different perspective of our central node:

Using this method on our earlier network, we can see that Gary begins to become more prominent, given he's bridging the gap between two groups of people, Harry and Chris, and Roger and Tyler.

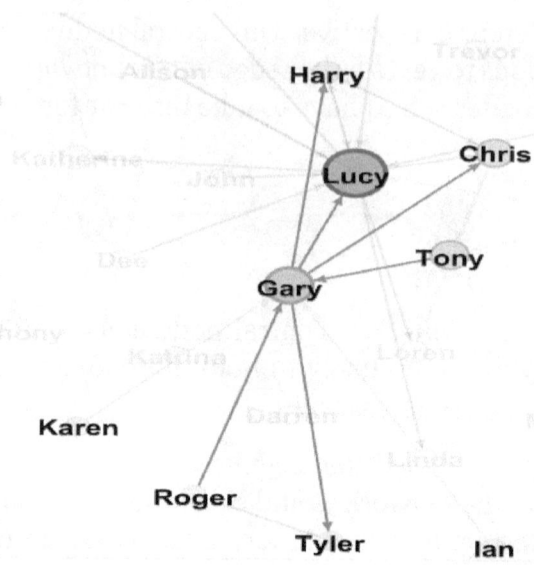

Now if we look at a basic network's resilience, for example, if both Lucy and Gary left the organisation, what would happen to the connections and the flow of information?

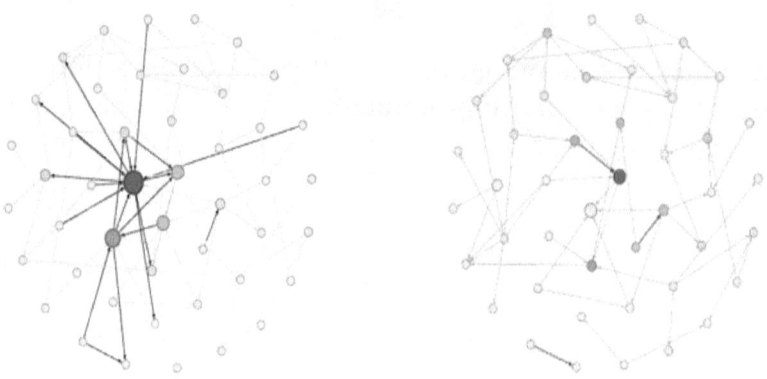

What we've lost is a great deal of connectivity across the network, leaving some people either with a single point of contact or as with Roger and Tyler no connection to the main network at all. It's not uncommon to hear this in many organisations, "*I used to*

*go to [such and so], but now they've left I've no idea whom to go
to".*

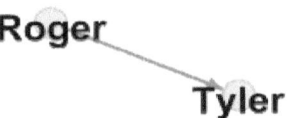

In this case, Roger and Tyler, if they required the information that
was being provided by Gary, would have to find another
connection. Now if Lucy or Gary weren't just passing on
information but authoring it, approving or checking it, then the
network is less easily repaired. When one lady I worked with
only a few years ago went on holiday, none of the IT service
reports could get published. Not only was there no stand-in, no
one even had any access to or knowledge of what she did. For IT
management, she was their go-to person – and a single point of
failure.

COMMUNITIES

The reason why communities within organisations are essential
to our understanding is that although the go-to people provide a
focus, communities provide us with a sense of collective purpose
and if these communities don't align to the formal structures then
we assume there is some hidden or not well-understood
objective. The larger the community, the further away the

leadership's understanding of their organisation. This is why smaller companies go through terrible growing pains, as the founders lose touch with the operation they designed. For some, the pain is too great, and they leave – and start a new small company that brings them closer to the action.

To detect a community, we need to answer a couple of key questions; Can we identify them by merely observing a set of connected nodes? How visible are they based on certain criteria?

In a complex network with hundreds or thousands of nodes and hundreds of thousands of connections, spotting communities with the naked eye isn't practically possible.

The definition of a community is subjective, but we can set some general criteria based on our scenario:

- People that are connected with n levels of separation, for example, we may say each person in the network must be connected to at least four other people in that network.
- People defined by their connections as a percentage of the total population, for example, if a person directly connected to twenty five percent of the network, they would be included.
- People associated with a bipartite group, for example, people that are linked to a specific event, such as a project.

If we take a densely connected network like the one below that I showed earlier; it really isn't clear where the communities are. In fact, it isn't clear where anything is.

Through further analysis though, we begin to see smaller and smaller communities in the network. By zooming in, we start to see patterns that represent departments, teams and people that are most dominant.

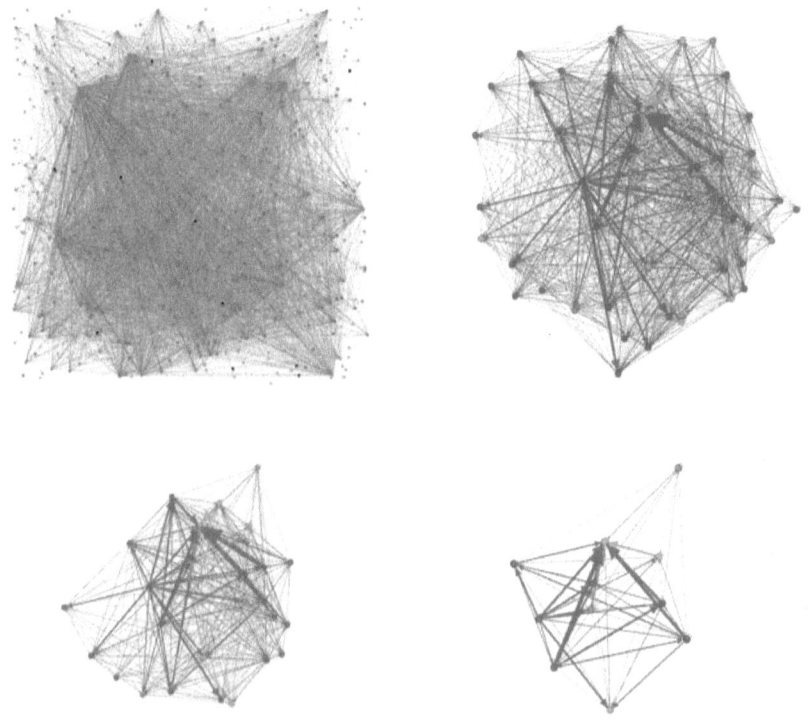

In a larger organisation tracing a specific communication, say a regular monthly report, can be a complicated exercise, especially when much of the information is handled off-line. Once, before I knew anything about social network analysis, it took me weeks in one company to find out where specific files were being sent, and even then, I don't believe I found all the recipients.

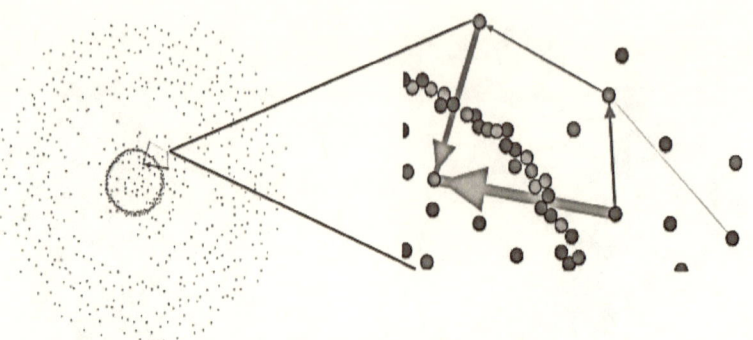

In the example above, we can easily see, buried in a complex organisation that there are five people involved with one person sending the report more often than anyone else. This is represented by the arrow size.

As well as for process performance transformation initiatives, this technique of identifying communities using additional attributes such as departments, internal events (such as projects), sentiment, and the frequency of connections (the number of times two people connect), is extremely useful in other scenarios, for example, tracking illness or absence across the organisation or tracking mood. This can be especially pertinent to organisations that have a significant amount of mental health-related sickness, such as stress. Emotions are contagious – meaning they spread. Taking a regular snapshot is a very powerful way of assessing the social health of the organisation. These patterns in the organisation are not visible elsewhere, including in HR systems. It's easy to imagine how a simple combination of department, projects and sentiment, could identify hidden trends.

HR systems record when someone takes sick leave, but the power of social network analysis is that it can help predict future absence, by surfacing hidden attributes, properties and trends in your organisation that just aren't possible with interviews and surveys.

A note on the legal bit. With the 2017 General Data Protection Regulation (GDPR) it is acceptable to monitor employee communications in the workplace. However, there are clear guidelines for when and how it can be used, and it requires policy, that should already be in place, that complies with expectations of fair use. Even though workplace email is not regarded private, it is recognised that not all communication in the workplace is business-related. An organisation's monitoring policies should be covered by its information security management system (ISMS), best described in ISO 27001.

This documentation should cover why monitoring is required, such as to improve performance and to support occupational health care.   It can also refer to the prevention of theft or improper use of data. It should differentiate between the use of personal and work communications, but organisations have a right if not an obligation to ensure employees aren't emailing confidential work documents using personal email accounts.

The type of analysis I'm talking about in this book is both in the interest of the employer and the employee as long as the legal bit is covered, which it should already be through your GDPR policies, so there should be no reason at all why email can't be used.   If you are denied, remember our thoughts on system conditions. We must pursue them, however difficult, until we get to the root. And, then and only then should we make a decision of whether a policy is legitimate or not.

CASE STUDY

Background

Several years ago, I was involved in a high-profile project to establish an executive management information system for a very large organisation. One of the first objectives was to install virtual servers in their data centres and install the software on them. Because it was all virtualised, we didn't need to buy any new hardware so the task should have been straight forward. We needed twelve servers, and the software was estimated to have taken no more than half a day per server with two or three installations running in parallel. Taking into account all the necessary admin, the total estimate was around twenty days or four weeks. The project had Board level visibility, so everyone reporting to the Steering Committee played the positive party line, and to prevent any difficult situations, we added fifty percent and presented six weeks.

There were several suppliers involved, each with their project manager. Each was responsible for taking their project demands and then coordinating that demand back into their respective back-office functions. To ensure alignment, I set up a daily 9am call where I would run through the plan. I also decided to invite the CIO to attend a few of these because I knew if push came to shove his say so would get the job done. Everything was lined up. I had my plan, and all the other necessary mandated project documentation. I'd spoken to all the partner project managers, and everyone was very confident. The CIO was onboard – this should have been a walk in the park.

The first few days seems to go reasonably well. Everyone was positive and committed to getting the job done. However, towards the end of the second week, a couple of tasks had slipped. My CIO stepped in, but the cause was an unaccounted-for holiday with one crucial resource. We eventually found a replacement person, but by that time we'd lost a day – we had two weeks of buffer, so no harm was done. Then came more trouble. We discovered a software platform that was required to comply with a specific firewall policy, for which I had not accounted, and each of the new firewall rules had to be individually impact assessed. Also, an incorrect naming convention had been applied to one of the databases that were installed, and consequently had to be recreated. The security seemed to take forever, and the architecture design review was reviewed again because of all the firewall questions.

All in all, it turned into a firestorm very quickly. Towards the middle of the project, every 9am call was intense and aggressive.

To make matters worse after five weeks, we were less than halfway through, and the CIO stopped attending the 9-am calls. My friend had a term for what some call *firefighting*; he called it *street fighting* and my goodness did it feel like that. None of the project managers had personal disagreements, but some had personnel issues, in the form of blame and suppliers trying to defend reputations. You see, their back-office functions managed work using queues on a last-in last-out basis. When my project came along, it immediately jumped to the top of every queue, and the suppliers didn't like that, mainly because they'd already made promises they now couldn't keep.

After ten weeks, people were burnt out. It had been a hard slog, and a few people decided to take some leave. Throughout the project, we had been giving regular updates to the Steering Committee that contained all the reasons for why the project was running late. However, towards the end, the pressure was so great that even the CIO openly blamed the CFO for budget cuts. It wasn't a pleasant time for anyone involved.

The total duration of the project to install all twelve servers was twelve weeks, one-week per server, more than double the original estimate and three times what we'd originally calculated.

The CFO wanted answers, so a *root cause* was commissioned, responded to initially by a *lessons learnt* exercise from all the suppliers. It was proposed to the board by the CIO, and that seemed to satisfy everyone temporarily. However, after four weeks, nothing had come back, and the expression I heard used was "lessons learnt? This is more garbage observed". Recognising we needed something better I proposed we look at the communication that took place between the three central project managers. I gained permission to take their email folder containing those messages related to the project and started a social network analysis.

Analysis

The question I started with was *"given the high degree of input from all the parties involved, why was the delivery one hundred percent later than planned?"*. The question was based on people working long hours and weekends. It also considered the high degree of executive sponsorship, and that our project was prioritised over all other projects.

I'd been in the trenches on this project since the beginning, but what I saw in the analysis even surprised me.

It became immediately apparent that there were far more issues here than simply a bunch of inefficient processes and a few people off sick. A *lessons learnt* exercise was clearly totally inadequate because the issues were systemic and much more intrinsic than could be determined by extracting fragile and unreliable memories.

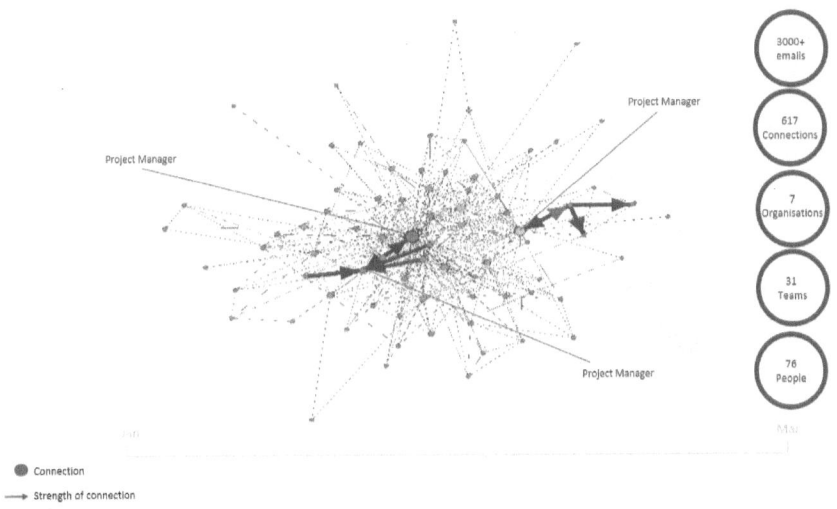

Project Manager

Project Manager

Project Manager

3000+
emails

617
Connections

7
Organisations

31
Teams

76
People

● Connection
⟶ Strength of connection

Over three thousand emails from three project managers paled into insignificance when the analysis identified seventy-six people were actually involved, from an original of around twenty on the plan.

There were seven organisations and thirty-one individual teams involved, with over six hundred connections between them.

An analysis of these connections across the organisational groups showed the extent of back-office functions. It read like the titles of a blockbuster film. So many people and so many connections.

Breaking it down further by function showed that the firewall issues were only a tiny part of the problem. This troubled me because the perception I had after the event was that this was a majority contributor to the delay. When I went back over the project plan, there it was, the firewall issues had only resulted in four days delay, five if the weekend was included. I attributed my warped memory to be down to the stress at that time – the firewall issue caused a storm. The CIO involved the head of security, and all manner of resentful favours were being pulled.

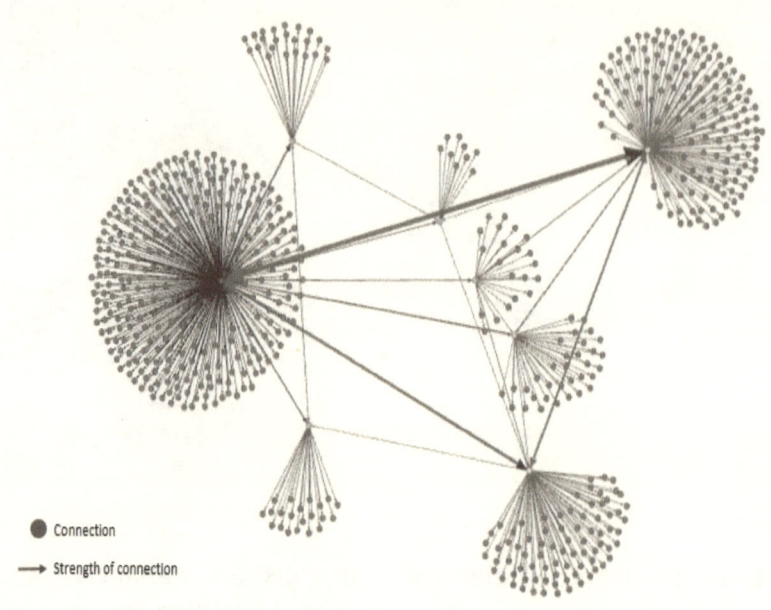

Connection

Strength of connection

People outside of the firewall team thought they were overly difficult and even unhelpful. People inside the firewall team thought the project was being ignorant and reckless.

The other finding the functional perspective identified was the amount of time spent by the executives on this small project. During the email analysis, I was careful to pull out only communications for work instructions, so I knew that these communications were instructional and not simply questions or updates. When I took a closer look, they were mainly approvals.

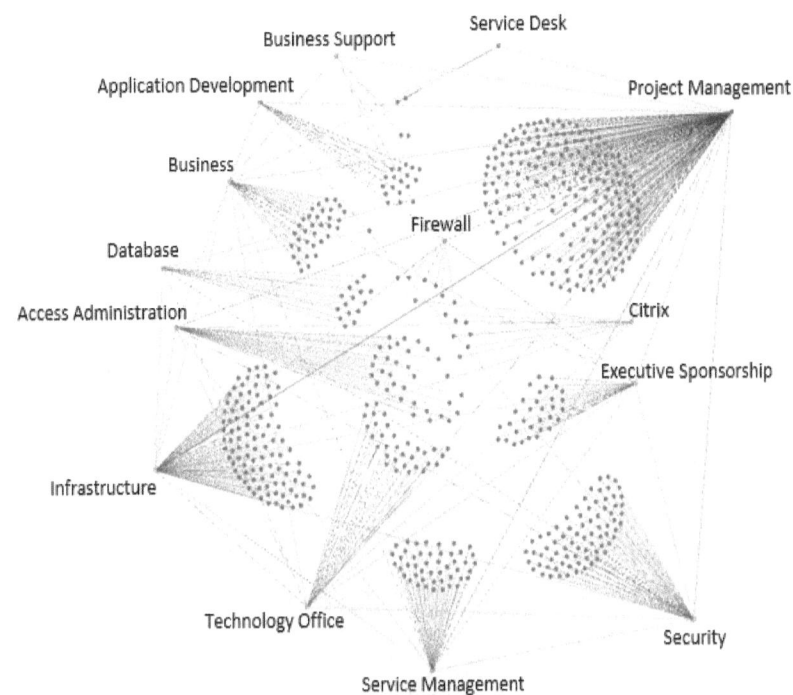

The project plan also suggested that security was an area that caused some significant delay. A deeper look started to explain why. It showed four teams involved with low levels of connection between them, and that some of the tasks, such as approvals, were duplicated.

In one case one security team was approving another security team's request; all behind the scenes, that could only be pieced together by combining all three projects managers email data – in other words, grey space that was invisible to everyone.

When I eventually presented my findings back to the CIO, his reaction was *"I don't know if to laugh or cry"*.

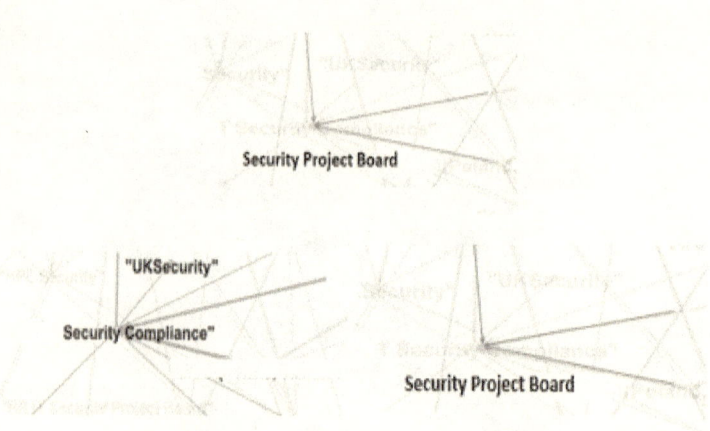

CONCLUSION

My assessment back to the CIO described a complex arrangement of people, teams and organisations, with duplicate and overlapping responsibilities. I demonstrated that most of the large number of connections between people did not align to any of the formal processes, nor did they respect the organisational structures.

This non-linear view of the world was completely contrary to the linear perception that was held in the mental models of the managers in those organisations, which was based on process workflow, approvals and service level agreements (SLA). The queues in each department meant that every day was a surprise and that no department had any idea what was coming down the pipeline until it hit them. This gave them no ability to capacity plan. Consequently, because this project was of the highest priority, all the other projects were deprioritised without prior warning, creating a ripple effect across the whole organisation that went systemically unseen but felt by each individual project, creating a win-lose situation.

The large number of handoffs between people was causing conflict across the whole network through misunderstanding and miscommunication. Interpretation of instructional emails was regularly incorrect, even in the simplest of examples; for instance, one form that had to be completed stated a database port defaulted to x number. If no number was presented, then, x would be used. The port was missed by mistake, and so the whole database had to be scrapped and recreated. The two people involved, the person that created the specification and the person creating the database were three hops from each other on the network, so no communication between them was possible, and the people forming the bridge were not skilled enough to identify the mistake.

So, you can see that from the starting position, a *lessons-learnt* exercise might have seemed plausible, but in reality, proved to be totally inadequate. The systemic problems were caused because of the very construct of the system itself. After further conversations with the IT leadership team, the root cause of these systemic issues was attributed to the organisation structure, supplier contracts and service levels agreements. All of which were established before any understanding of the different types of demand that would be passing through it, was understood. It is an extremely common mistake to define the organisation structure (*who*), before understanding the demand and designing the processes (*what*). Systemically it meant that the entire IT function was incapable of managing the flow of demand and unable to flex capacity to absorb fluctuations in this demand proactively. It also meant the whole system was full of non-value failure demand. It was impossible to estimate the percentage of failure demand across the whole system, but in my small project, I can safely estimate this to have been fifty percent, at the very least.

For the CIO, it meant bigger problems. At the same time, like our project, he had around a hundred other projects all running through the same system.

CHAPTER 10

How to Study Your Organisation as a System

GO SEE

Study

The principle Cho laid out at Toyota was *"Go See"*, and it is at the heart of systemic improvement. Regular observation must be practised, so it becomes habitual. To make it effective, however, we must observe the work where it's being done. Not in a meeting room, over the phone or on a report. We must observe the actual work, the people doing the work and the way the work is done. Only then is it possible to see the reality of the situation. Identifying where waste is being created and why it exists in the first place.

It's important to start by understanding what our customer wants and the purpose of our organisation. Keep it simple. For one utility company I worked with, we simply defined it as *"Providing an uninterrupted supply to all our customers, with the least amount of leakage as possible"*.

Use the VoC method to help you if you need to.

To see, we must capture data. As Deming said, *"without data, you're just another person with an opinion"*.

Our goal is to understand the flow of demand for two reasons. Firstly, to provide a better service for the customer and secondly to make the work more effective (right first time) and increase efficiency (speed).

A quick point to note here is that efficiency is always a by-product of effectiveness.

This is only achieved by first taking a helicopter view of the situation. Therefore, the data we collect will not be very detailed but holistic across the process.

To begin collecting data, we start by defining the start and end of the entire process for the task we're trying to carry out. It's important to understand the true start and true end of the process. To make sure we've done this, we can simply ask conditional questions, such as *"before this step can start, condition X must be met"*. Here we'll use a Human Resources example for the Hire & Induction process. So, our starting condition would be something simple like *"before the hiring process can start the recruitment process must have been completed."*.

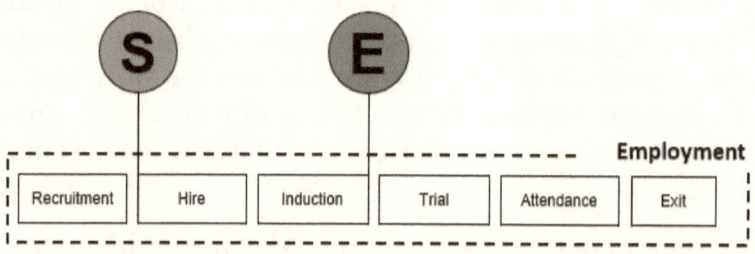

I just want to pause here and highlight a very critical point. When we map the processes, we're not mapping formal structures or functions. We're describing how the work really happens. At this stage, we'll take an aggregated view to see what the current performance looks like. So, when we look at the six sequential process boxes above, it may seem here like we've simply plotted the sequence of functions, but we haven't. We've created these boxes based on real observation of the stages the demand for new temporary staff goes through. It may differ from how the formal organisational structures are set up. This knowledge was available because the work done prior to this included the teams that run these processes. The role of the central team is to purely guide them through the method, up to the point where they become knowledgeable enough not to require any further assistance. This approach, of teaching people to fish so they can feed themselves, is known as experiential normative learning.

Now, you may be thinking that we haven't set the start and the end, at the first and last step. This is ok because we will perform a systemic check during our improvement phase, when we will test our proposed changes against those processes before and after our focused or in-scope processes, to confirm that nothing we are proposing will compromise them. We will also check the areas of the business that may be above or below our scope, for example, I mentioned earlier about management measurements set above our changes that created a conflict between the two levels, that compromised the lower managers ability to operate. This is a critical point that both Lean and Six Sigma ignore.

Once we've understood the start and end positions, we then map the high-level set of steps for each end to end process. To do this, we can simply follow the thing we're trying to measure and record its journey; in our example, a new employee.

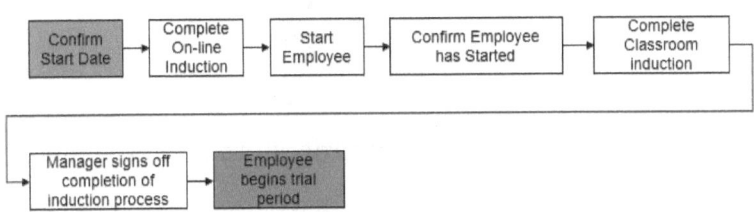

Ok, so now we have our process mapped. Again, this process was mapped, not by looking at a document or holding meetings and workshops to ask people what they do. This knowledge was gained by observing the process first-hand, by the teams that do the work supported by the central team – this is so critical. In the previous chapter, we talked about Social Network Analysis (SNA). In my project case study, neither the process documentation nor people's perceptions of it bared any resemblance of what was really happening. The SNA was purely an insight into where to "Go See". The central team's role is to facilitate the mapping of the whole system by working across many smaller teams each working on improvement in their own respective areas.

Now we have our process we want to establish how it's performing and to do this; we want to measure the variation from start to end. To know what to measure, we need to define our Critical To Flow (CTF) metrics. A CTF metric is one related to a process step that directly contributes to the flow, so by nature they are throughput metrics and non-conformance metrics. To define them for our Hire & Induction process, we'd follow the guideline of Voice of The Customer (VoC). To do this, you will have to speak to them. In this case, it is our Hiring Managers.

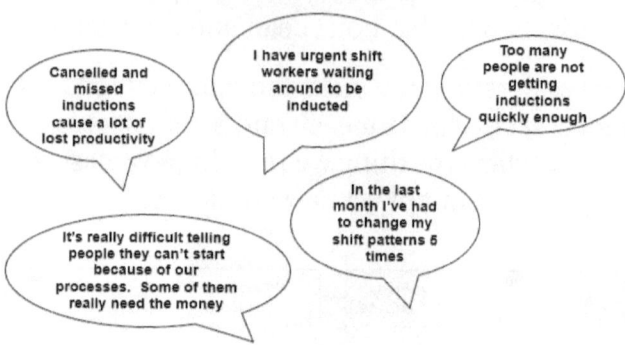

We then simply map these onto our process and plot the metrics.

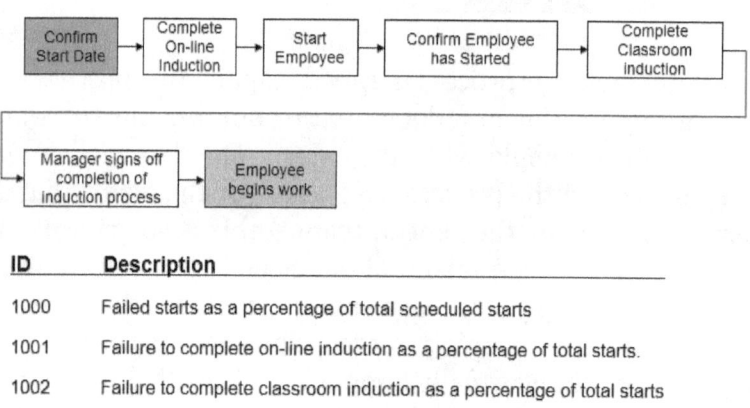

ID	Description
1000	Failed starts as a percentage of total scheduled starts
1001	Failure to complete on-line induction as a percentage of total starts.
1002	Failure to complete classroom induction as a percentage of total starts

At this point, some may question whether we require the VoC; after all, we seem to have all we need, namely the process and the demand. The reason why the VoC is also required is that we don't want to do the wrong-thing-right. We want to be certain what it is the customer really wants. It isn't enough to assume the demand they present us with is want they really want, and that everything we're doing is required.

Before going any deeper, we need to go back up and connect or map back to the high-level end to end process and define the end to end metric.

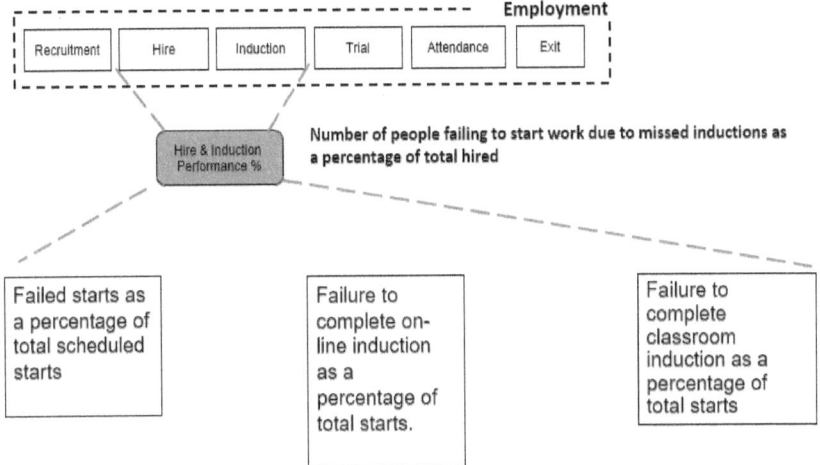

This gives us a first view of the system and how we want to measure it.

Now we will measure the variation of our high-level end to end, or critical to flow or CTF, metric. To do this, we'll create a capability chart. After this, we'll repeat the same process for each of the sub-metrics.

To do this, we need to capture some data. If we can't get the data we need from a database or a spreadsheet, then we'll need to capture it manually.

In our example, we have collected ten weeks of data. It's possible to buy expensive software such as Minitab and SPSS to produce a capability chart, but for this example, we'll create one using Microsoft Excel. It's simple, and it's cheap!

	A	B	C	D	E	F
	Data	abs	Mean	Mean MR	UCL	LCL
5	58%		0.7	0	1.2	0.1
6	84%	0.26	0.7	0	1.2	0.1
7	78%	0.26	0.7	0	1.2	0.1
8	62%	0.06	0.7	0	1.2	0.1
9	38%	0.16	0.7	0	1.2	0.1
10	50%	0.24	0.7	0	1.2	0.1
11	81%	0.12	0.7	0	1.2	0.1
12	90%	0.31	0.7	0	1.2	0.1
13	58%	0.09	0.7	0	1.2	0.1
14	56%	0.32	0.7	0	1.2	0.1

The MS Excel formulas to calculate the columns are:

	formula
abs	ABS(A6-A5) : (Leave first row blank - B5)
Mean	SUM($A$5:$A$14)/COUNT(A$5:A$14)
Mean MR	SUM(B$6:B$14)/(COUNT(A$5:A$14)-1)
UCL	C5+(2.66*D5)
LCL	IF(C5-(2.66*D5)>0,C5-(2.66*D5),0)

And that's it! We have our calculated data. Now, all there is to do is to create a simple chart.

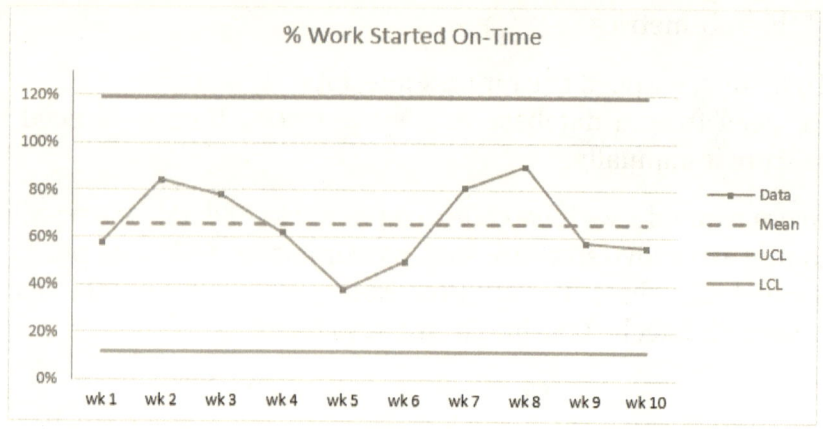

We can see that we have a significant variation, ranging from 40% to 90%. From here, we need to look at the sub-metrics to determine where the variation is the highest; this is what Goldratt meant when he talked about seeking out the most significant bottleneck.

So, we repeat the same process and produce capability charts for each of the sub-CTF-metrics.

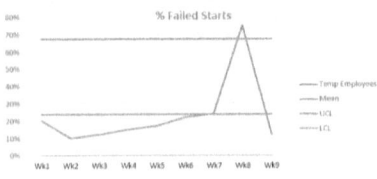

And then map these to the overall process

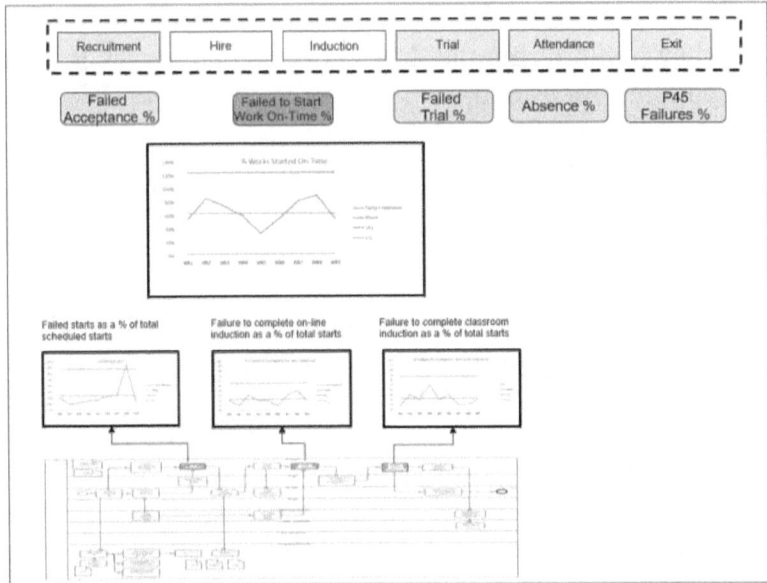

So now we can see the performance of the Hire and Induction processes. From a first look at the data, it's clear to see that most of the variation is coming from the Failed Starts CTF.

Adopting the Goldratt method, this is our biggest constraint, so it's vital to examine that area to see what's going on. At this stage, we need to take a more in-depth look at those process steps we plotted on our process map when we observed the actual work being carried out.

When we get into the next level, we are interested in one principle and three key points:

Principle: It's all about the customer's demand.

Key Points:

1. How demand is handled. We know already that the flow gets slowed or even interrupted because of handoffs between groups, so we want to understand where, when and why this happens.

2. We want to understand what system conditions are embedded into the design of the existing process and if they're hindering the flow of demand. These will come in the form of assumptions, rules and policies. We need to ask why and for what purpose? Is this policy valid? We can't take the experts word for it either. We want to see the evidence in writing, for example, a statement from a regulator.

3. The definition of value, when assessing it for a particular process step, can be very subjective, so to make it simple, our definition is: "*does it support the flow of demand*". If it hinders it in any way, it is non-value. Now all non-value processes are wasteful, but some are necessary, so we want to put them into one of two categories, Necessary and Non-Necessary. For example, a manager's approval may be necessary or non-necessary. Identifying invalid or

erroneous system conditions can turn steps from necessary to non-necessary.

When we analyse the process steps, we want to know the Inputs (what comes in), Process (what happens to the demand once it has been received), Output (where it goes next). Plus, any equipment, such as IT applications that are used.

Over the years, I have used several process mapping methods, but a good one is IDEF0. IDEF0 was developed as far back as the 1980s by the US government. It is hierarchical in nature and makes for a very intuitive diagram.

In a typical structure, we start with the main function that then cascades down into more detail propagating the inputs, outputs, controls and resources.

The controls are those things such as policy. The resources are those things that do the work such as a person or a computer.

System conditions may be part of a defined control, so need to be understood to check they are not impacting throughput.

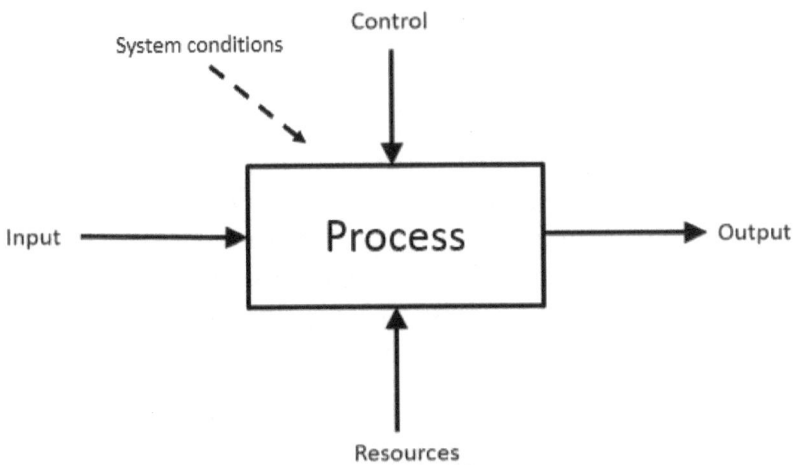

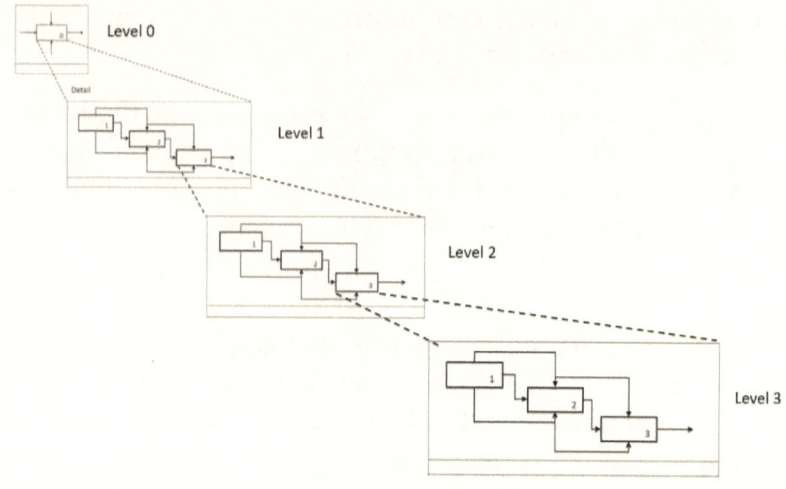

The thing to remember about process mapping of this kind is that it records the steps taking place, and IDEF0 identifies what resources and controls are in place, but they lack some additional information that is useful to help describe what is really happening, such as time and whether the step adds value or not.

As an improvement to this, the Lean movement created, what they called Value Stream Mapping or VSM. It was a reinvention of what Toyota called material and information flow mapping. The purpose is to simply identify those steps in the process that contain or create waste and to reduce or remove it.

When we write down the steps, I find it extremely useful to use a method called swim-lanes. This simply places horizontal lines on the process map to show who is owning a particular process step. We then connect the process steps to show the flow and the hand-offs. As part of the flow VSM classifies waste into three categories, Non-Value-Adding (NVA), Necessary but Not-Value-Adding (NNVA) and Value-Adding (VA).

NNVA's are the most significant cause of grey space in a process, so we need to zoom in and check whether they are truly necessary, especially policies and regulatory controls. These are the system conditions that can often go unchallenged in a Lean improvement but can often be the most damaging to performance, so it is vital they are explicitly identified during the mapping exercise. Usually, if some internal authority stipulates its necessity, then the improvement team backs away, and it goes unchallenged. However, we don't back away, we want proof, and until we do, we keep on challenging unless someone much more senior tells us to stop.

To categorise waste, we will use the DATACHEAT model described in the Methodology Dogma chapter, but just to recap here is the definition.

D	Documentation	Missing, incorrect or unnecessary i.e. must be purposeful
A	Approvals	Duplicate or unnecessary approval
T	Testing	Duplicate or overlay burdensome testing or checks
A	Autonomy	No authority to complete a task
C	Capacity	Bottlenecks or queues holding up the work
H	Hold	External constraint holding up the work - e.g. supplier lead-time.
E	Error	Fault needing a specialised team involvement - i.e. IT system
A	Ability	Lack of knoweldge and skills to complete task
T	Time	Time involved in completing a task or process step

A critical point; We don't want dogma. If you feel that there are better definitions of waste for your situation, go ahead and change them. I came up with these because they seem to fit my situations in IT much better than the seven or eight wastes that Lean provides.

Lost time can be a result of all the wastes above so as part of the modelling exercise it is a good idea to track time across the process, a common practise in VSM.

While producing the map, it is also a good idea to colour code the steps (boxes) and the waste categorised flows (inputs and output arrows). It just makes things a little more visible.

Red = The step is a definite waste (NVA)

Amber = The step is non-value but necessary (NNVA)

Green = A step that directly promotes the flow (VA)

The following picture allows us to see that there is a problem in the centre of the end to end process that is impacting hundreds of appointments.

This bottleneck is where we would begin our improvement initiative (next chapter). And once that is completed, we would simply move on to the next most significant bottleneck.

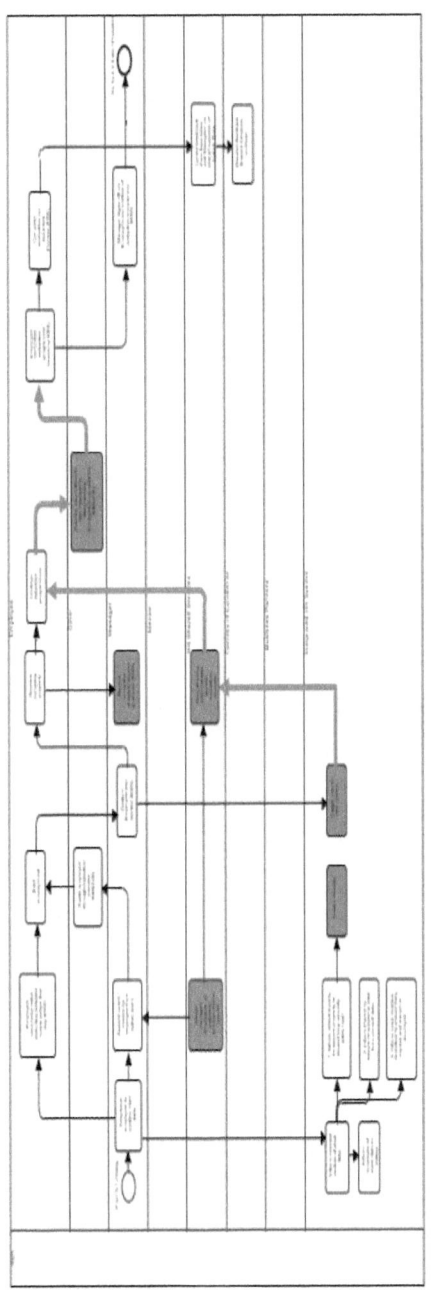

Process ID	Waste	Type	Description
2.6	Approval	Input	Approval has already been provided in 2.2. 125 delayed starts impacted
2.12	Hold	Throughput	103 appointments held waiting for security to be completed.
2.14	Test	Throughput	No need for further checks. All appointments experienced 1 or 2 days delay due to second approval
2.15	Capacity	Output	Incomplete employee details sent. Had to re-work for 56 employees
Etc….			

SECTION 4

IMPROVING

CHAPTER 11

Design

"Design is not just what it looks like and how it feels. Design is how it works."

Steve Jobs

THE CRISIS

The term *problem-solving* is thrown around in most organisations so much these days that it can lose any specific meaning, so it's essential to define it more succinctly.

Organisations approach problems in typically four ways:

- **Ignore:** In many organisations' problems, even those that occur regularly are simply ignored, and their causes remain in grey space.

- **Resolve:** Problems are resolved using the existing know-how and skills. If this lacks method, it can be only temporarily effective, because it isn't systemic and often doesn't get to the root cause, so inevitably the problems return and drift back into grey space.

- **Solve:** Problems are addressed using methods and tools to eradicate the root cause, but don't fundamentally change the nature of the whole solution.

- **Dissolve:** Problems are resolved through the design of new solutions that radically change the way the work is carried out.

These can be categorised into five flavours of approach in the broad spectrum of organisational capabilities:

- **Reactive:** Organisations with no particular method or process for solving problems. In this situation the term *reactive* can often be substituted for *firefighting*, meaning that people are just responding to issues as they arise, where every day is a surprise, and there's no real way of planning for future errors. We see this most commonly in organisations that have siloed structures, and batch and queue mechanisms.

- **Responsive:** Organisations where some processes are present to deal with specific errors in a more controlled manner by defining mechanical triggers for actioning a particular resolution. These practices tend not to be systemic across the organisation and are usually present only in critical business areas such as manufacturing processes and warehouse management.

- **Proactive:** Organisations with method in place, especially those using techniques such as statistical process control, are more often proactive in their approach by implementing early warning alerts and preventative measures. In these situations, there is typically a presence of process quality found in only certain parts of the organisation. The areas of the organisation least likely to have these measures are the supporting functions, such as HR, customer services, sales, marketing and finance.

- **Interactive:** Organisations with a process of ongoing improvement, as Goldratt called it (POOGI), will have a continuous flow of improvement initiatives running across the organisation. Some call this Continuous Improvement (CI). There will most certainly be a methodology based culture that is present in most if not all the areas of the organisation.

- **Creative:** Organisations that have moved beyond CI can design solutions that don't merely correct problems by improving the way work is being done, but they implement solutions that remove the potential errors altogether by changing the entire situation. Russell Ackoff called this dissolving problems. This requires a more inclusive, multidisciplinary and creative approach than mere process improvement techniques.

Ironically, organisations typically in the reactive category rarely acknowledge they're in a crisis. Their way of working becomes so normalised to them that a better way of working is dismissed as unnecessary and a waste of time and effort. In an earlier example I cited, this was the prevailing attitude until we presented the crisis, that was their management current reporting and planning capability:

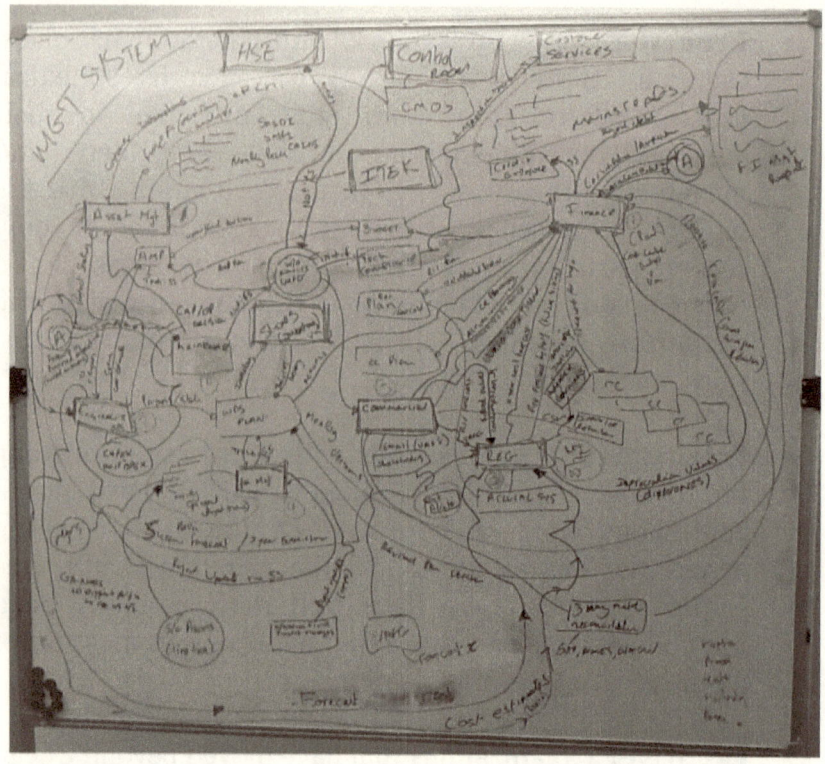

The offline and informal nature of the information flows meant that no-one person in the organisation had any idea what each department was reporting, the source of the data and how this was impacting their ability to make informed decisions. By performing this analysis on the current state meant that people could see the crisis for the first time, giving them choices. Before this, no choice was possible. The first step in our improvement initiative must always be to understand the current situation to provide us with choices.

In the methodology Design Thinking, *Ideation* is a central concept where a group with the responsibility for implementing a specific improvement use Socratic techniques to iterate ideas and concepts to formulate potential options. In this approach, it is standard practice to experiment with prototypes in real environments to test out ideas and assumptions. The reason why this approach is particularly powerful is that it places *practice solutions* in real-world environments much more quickly than traditional methods that typically build solutions in laboratory conditions, such as a waterfall style project before exposing it to the environmental conditions in which it must operate. The problem with artificial environments is that they ignore the properties of a system that exist purely because of the environment in which it exists. An aeroplane in a vacuum won't get very far and neither will a new software solution developed and tested outside of its natural habitat, the organisational social system. (Notice I didn't say organisational structure).

The other important aspect of the ideation concept is that it follows the golden rule of improvement *'never define the who, before the what'*. The number of times I've experienced organisations struggling with the systems they have implemented because they designed their organisational structure before their ways-of-working; resulting in erroneous structures and commercial contracts that actually hinder their ability to operate. Additionally, when organisations guess about the levels of demand before implementing an outsourced service, they always end up with much higher costs than they estimated.

Ideation consists of three main phases:

- **Idealisation:** Design without constraints; with the exceptions of (a) technological viability – there's no point designing something that requires technology that doesn't exist in the real world (b) It must be legally or regulatorily compliant – we don't want to break the law.

- **Experimentation:** The implementation of prototypes and pilots to prove the solution is practically viable. This may bring an understanding of other constraints and environmental conditions that the new design must be able to handle.

- **Realisation:** The implementation of the final solution bringing together all the learnings from the iterations of idealisation and experimentation.

Following this approach not only brings together the environment and the solution, it includes the customers and consumers into the early design phases of the improvement.

Customers are those that purchase, and consumers are those that use. I've had enough confused stares from my children at Christmas and birthdays, to know the difference.

Although this can be a powerful and even inspiring process for those that are involved, it can often be difficult for them to let go of their current views and beliefs, especially in the early stages. It can be difficult to imagine a world where their current ways of working that they have practised over many years, no longer exist. The assumptions that hold these beliefs in place must be surfaced and challenged. It's advisable, however, to treat such situations with care so as not to offend anyone and that may cause them to disengage. The best way to do this is to ensure they're involved in the examination of the current situation, as described in the previous chapter. And, it's particularly important not be judgemental. People can often feel quite protective over their existing practices, especially if they were personally involved with the implementation of them.

To test the systemic nature of the solution, it must satisfy the steps before and after it, and the levels above it and below it, in the organisation. A departmental solution, for instance, must work for teams within that department and the division of which it is a part. An example of a change that didn't consider its environment at all was commissioned by Gordon Brown in 1999, the then UK Prime Minister. He implemented a new tax credit system that severely damaged the ability for the Inland Revenue Department to process claims correctly. To prevent a political disaster by causing harm to vulnerable families, many of the internal controls were abandoned, resulting in wrong assessments and payments. At the time the Government was reported to have been in melt-down with blame being banded around everywhere. It was reported a few years later that the catalogue of errors and lack of controls led to an overpayment of £1.8 billion in tax credit claims.

There can often be a temptation to look for quick-wins or low-hanging-fruit as it can be referred to, to add some early value. Although in principle it sounds plausible, even sensible, in practice it can often lead to problems later down the line, like the child that ties knot after knot in their shoelaces to the point that there is no more lace to knot and it all needs painfully unpicking. It's ok to implement quick wins if they have been systemically tested against the containing environment, and they don't implement degrees of complexity that hinder the longer-term ambitions. The Greek's have a nice saying *"temporary has a habit of becoming permanent"*.

The more quick wins that are implemented, the more complexity is added to the system as a whole. In fact, most quick wins aren't worth the effort or the distraction when considered against the context of the larger scheme of change, because the threshold at which the cost outweighs the benefit or *diminishing return*, is usually quite soon after implementation. The quick wins are typically done to add value to a politically motivated situation, to a detached leadership, rather than being implemented to add value to the work being done and the broader environment.

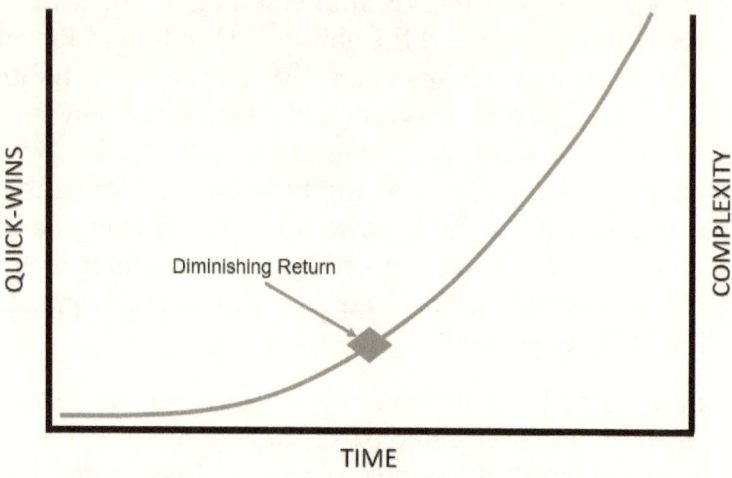

ROOT CAUSE ANALYSIS

Root Cause Analysis (RCA) is the process of identifying the basis (the root) of a problem that is occurring; predicated on the assertion that every effect has a cause. Over the years as quality management techniques have developed, there have been a number of methods and tools spring up, some more sophisticated than others. The simplest of these is the original; The 5 Whys.

The 5 Whys, is the process of asking *why* five times, and in doing so, we assume we'll find the true cause (it can often take a few more whys than five, but I don't want to ruin a good story).

Unsurprisingly, the inventor of this method was the founder of Toyota, Sakichi Toyoda (1867 - 1930). It became the early defacto method in Toyota, and every employee had to adopt it in their day to day working practices. After some time though they realised that the simplicity of it was prone to error. Nevertheless, it is still very popular today, and in my view, because of its simplicity, is a very powerful method.   Let's take an example.

Q1. Why was the customer's order delivered late?
A1. Because the goods were not despatched as promised.

Q2. Why did we fail to despatch on time?
A2. Because the stock was not available?

Q3. Why was the stock not available?
A3.   Because the stock safety level (SSL) was set too low?

Q4. Why was the SSL set too low?
A4.   Because the master data in the IT system had not been updated?

Q5. Why was the SLL master data not updated?
A5.   Because we need better master data processes.

From this straightforward example, it shows that that the root cause is poor master data processes that are failing to update the safety levels adequately, causing the stock to run out, and preventing customer orders to be satisfied on time.   Or does it?

Well, actually, it doesn't.   This is a real example from a situation I was involved with many years ago.   There had been a series of customer orders that were failing the *next day* premium delivery promise.   So, an RCA was commissioned to determine a solution.

Soon after the improvement of the master data processes started, it became clear that this wasn't the real cause.   What we found when we did a systemic check and brought all the parties involved into the RCA was that the answers to questions four and five were different from the original pair.   The real answers where:

Q4. Why was the SSL set too low?
A4.   Because there was a marketing promotion running on those products and we quickly ran out of stock.

Q5. Why didn't we order more stock to cover the campaign forecast?
A5. Because the marketing team didn't tell product management about the campaign.

This example was one of the reasons why Toyota developed more sophisticated methods, such as the Ishikawa (fishbone) diagram, that took a more standard approach by including default dimensions (equipment, process, people, materials, environment, management).

The 5 Why's is effective because it is simple, but it is extremely prone to misapplication through assumption. When coupled with a systemic mindset, it can be an extremely effective technique. Outside of manufacturing and engineering, I have experienced very few examples of thoroughly applied RCA. In one embarrassing situation, myself and the organisations Master Black Belt met with the Service Manager from the main IT service supplier. He opened the meeting by stating that they (the supplier) were taking the recent service failings seriously and had commissioned an RCA. When asked about their approach, he replied, *"erm...not sure...a fishy diagram of some sort"*.

I went on to find out that the supplier a month back had deployed a *Lean* approach using a mandated e-learning course. Waste is not just costly; it can also be extremely dangerous.

When RCA is coupled with a systemic approach, were cause and effect is regarded as non-linear, and relationships are identified through the creation of causal diagrams described earlier in this book, it can become a potent approach. Doing it every day makes it habitual and a way of thinking. Another very effective method from Goldratt is The Current Reality Tree (CRT).

The reason why I believe most shy away from RCA is that the organisations they work in are too siloed, and as my earlier example demonstrated, root causes are not aligned to departmental structures. A customer's demand flows across and through an organisation, not down it.

Deploying multidisciplinary teams that represent each area or department, to carry out RCA is essential for getting to the root of problems. Managing failure in this way, by deploying community founded RCA to find systemic solutions to causes, can never be subjected to politically motivated blame, and the reporting mechanism to the leadership team must be a supportive one. When organisations introduce contractually based service level agreements (SLA's), where there is a financial penalty for failure, it is impossible to achieve systemic solutions in this manner. Rather than resolving problems, politics kick in.

DESIGNING

In situations that require more than a process improvement, it is necessary to design with a systemic mindset.

The Teams

The design process has two fundamental objectives. Firstly, the solution must meet the customer's demand. Secondly, the solution must make a systemic change to the organisation.

To ensure both objectives are met, the project will need to consist of two teams; a core or primary team, and a supporting or secondary team. Both teams need to have a multidisciplinary makeup to cover all areas of the organisation that will be directly or indirectly impacted by the change.

The core team will be made up of customers, consumers and people with direct involvement in the design and build of the solution. If there is no direct involvement, then these people will fall into the supporting team. These people could be from HR, Legal, Architecture, to name a few. Within the second team, the leadership that is sponsoring the change will also need to be present.

In terms of involvement, the core team will be full time for an intensive period. Depending on the size or complexity of the problem this can range from a week to a month, although it is better to make the design phases around two to three weeks, to ensure that the change is not too big.

To ensure the supporting team are involved and kept up to date with the progress, it's generally a good idea to do regular feedback sessions; at least once a week at a minimum, but more frequently is better if it's possible to get their commitment.

It's essential that for the duration of the design work to have a dedicated room with plenty of wall space to hang paper and sticky notes.

Step 1: 'Go See' - Experience the problem

Before coming up with solutions, it's important that a thorough study of the existing situation has been carried out. As we've discussed in earlier chapters, this could involve social network analysis, process mapping and measurement, waste identification, classification of demand value and demand failure and even a range of interviews. However, most importantly, for design work to be effective, the team must experience the work, that would be subject to the improvement, first-hand, and this may even involve doing the job itself for a while. I worked a shift in one plant to get a better understanding of how the work was done and how it was managed. The understanding I gained through the interaction with the environment and the guys running the line would have never been possible in a meeting. The value of this in a broader team is to be able to bring all the experiences and observations together, enabling different perspectives and viewpoints to be surfaced.

Step 2: Share the observations

To do this, each person simply takes their observations and writes them on a sticky note. Once all the sticky notes are presented, they are then grouped into categories associated with the route the demand takes, also known as the journey map or the experience map.

Once everything has been categorised lay them out across the process.

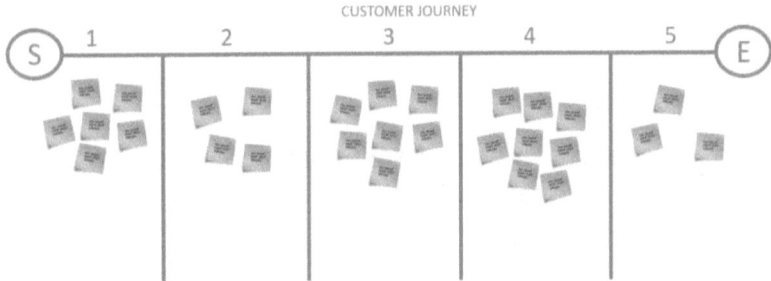

The graphic above shows a very simple example, but in practice, it's typical to fill a full wall.

The next step is to identify the pain points in the end to end process. This can be done in a variety of ways. As we've discussed earlier, if the data produced in the process measurement identified a critical bottleneck, then this can become a focal point. If the pain point was identified through experiential observation, as this can become a little subjective, it's important to get a weight of feeling about it from the team and check it against the data. The recording of these can be done by simply applying sticky to the sticky notes causing the largest pain points.

Once all the observations have been recorded, simply tally them to identify the most troublesome areas, and this will give the improvement initiative a focus and an early scope for change.

Step 3: Identify the goals

In a similar approach to a method called the Goal-Tree developed by Eli Goldratt (the subsequent step after the Current Reality Tree), we will create our goals by simply inverting the negatively worded pain points the team have voted on.

The team spend most of their day firefighting known issues

Demand failure needs to be identified and reduced to decrease the amount of failure demand that is being received.

Very often, this approach will present goals that would not have been thought of before the exercise.

Step 4: Create Personas

By taking the time to observe the work first hand, discuss, categorise and identify the main problem areas, as well as defining the goals, the team should now have a good understanding of the situation that needs improving and the people that it will impact. It is at this stage we can create the personas.

A persona provides a more specific profile to customers and consumers of the system. Personas are like character definitions in a play, for example, the personas for an HR solution may include the HR manager, the line manager and the employee. Each persona describes the role of each specific person; their purpose and objectives, how they're measured or what they measure their area against and a few meaningful quotes from the real people.

The reason why we describe the measures against each persona, whether these be measurements used on them, by them or both, is because once we look at all the personas, collectively we want to spot any measures that we would need to be considered by the solution. We also want to identify any conflicts between them that would cause our new solution problems.

As the project continues the personas will be referred to regularly to check if the needs of the customer are being met, and this may mean that the personas will change at times as we understand more through testing our ideas.

Step 4: Ideation

Now we have all our background information it's time to get creative. The best way to do this is to follow this simple three-step process:

1. **Individual:** Each person comes up with some ideas. This can be in the form of words and pictures. No ideas are crazy at this stage. The purpose here is creativity, not practicality. The two viability constraints will be tested later.

2. **Team:** Individuals are then placed in teams of no more than six people. We should ensure that there is a mix of disciplines in each team. Everyone then presents their ideas to the rest of the team. The team then formulate a

single idea that can simply be one of the presented ideas, a further developed idea or a brand-new idea that came out of discussions after every idea was presented.

3. Group: The same process is followed at the group level as it was in the teams. Just a point of caution here; even in a well bonded and collaborating group, early tribalism can set in during the team phase when people begin to become precious about their team's ideas – humans tend to believe they're correct. During the group session, it's common to observe a psychological effect called loss aversion. Loss aversion is a theory developed by Daniel Kahneman and Amos Tversky. Their work focusses on the psychology of decision-making that won Kahneman a Nobel Memorial Prize in Economic Sciences in 2002. The theory implies that a person who loses something loses a greater level of satisfaction than the person who gains it. In our example, the person that loses their idea to that of another team's idea will lose more satisfaction in that process than the satisfaction gained by the team whose idea was selected. This can create an imbalance in the group with some people feeling less satisfied with the process than others. The way to mitigate this is to address it directly. It may sound a little out there, but it's incredibly worthwhile talking about this before and after the exercise. Ignoring feelings can cause those feelings to develop. The team is still in the early stages, so we don't want any negativity from creeping in. Ask them how they're feeling. Ask them if they feel a sense of loss and ask them to focus on those feelings and to think them through. This mindful approach of focusing on emotions, especially those you can feel in your stomach (our second brain), tends to dissipate them.

The benefit of this approach ensures that everyone gets a chance to participate and input their ideas. Jumping straight into groups and not allowing individuals to contribute means that the most dominant, the person that shouts the loudest, will get their way. We want to avoid this at all costs because the dominant person is seldom correct no matter how senior they are, and it can even be the more senior the person, the more wrong they are. At this stage we're not trying to remove wrongness we're trying to promote the best ideas, so everyone must have the opportunity to participate.

The final step of ideation is to make it real by firstly applying our two viability constraints; is it technologically possible? And is it regulatorily and legally compliant?

Once this is done, we can now get down to more practical limitations the solution may come across. A good technique for doing this most effectively is *Break-It*. This involves throwing all kinds of negative scenarios and situations at your new idea to see if it holds up. This is run by a facilitator using a brainstorming approach but in the negative form. If under this bombardment, the idea breaks, record the reason why it broke and continue. At the end of this process, we'll have a list of reasons why our idea doesn't work. People tend to be far more effective at breaking things than creating them.

Before jumping into the solution, we first create a storyboard. To create the storyboard, we will use everything we've learnt so far. We will start will the process and the main observations, the personas, our selected ideas and our thoughts on what would break it. The storyboard then tells the story of the customers' experiences with the new solution.

Once the storyboard is created, we then need to look at solutions to our *break-it* scenarios. A brainstorming session is a good idea for this. It may be necessary to go back up the process, step by step to see if a possible solution or change of idea can be found, however, typically solutions or mitigations are found quite quickly because during the ideation sessions many things will have been thought through already, so at this stage we should be dealing with the exceptional situations.

Step 5: Playback

At this stage, it's time to test our ideas on our customers and consumers. Of course, we still haven't built anything here but remember we're not testing a solution we're testing an idea. The way to do this is to mock-up our ideas using the least amount of technology as possible.

Some teams I've seen have used Microsoft PowerPoint to simulate software screens and wireframes (wireframes are simply the relationships between screens), but the most compelling demonstrations I've seen have simply used paper and sticky notes. In one playback we built both the paper and the electronic versions. The customer's feedback was that the paper version was far more powerful.

During the playback sessions, customers have a real talent for throwing a spanner into the works, and undoubtedly, they will in ours. It's important not to get defensive. Remember, they haven't given us a requirement, nor have we built anything; we're simply testing an idea. If we lack some vital data, then our idea will have to be adjusted. However, also remember your customer has not been through the process we have, so it is important that they feel at this stage that they too can contribute. You want, in fact, it's critical, that the customer normalises their thinking into your idea by having the opportunity to shape it.

It may be necessary to take a little more time to explain why your idea looks the way it does and explain the thought processes that went into formulating it.

Let's get what neither of us wants and compromise

We're at a delicate part of the design process, and it can be at this stage that compromises can creep in because people don't want to lose their ideas. So, whilst putting self-interest aside and outweighing the needs of another over our own might be an act of kindness, it isn't the form of compromise we want. Neither do we want a compromise that exposes our new solution to a danger of failing.

The problem with this kind of close collaborative working is that we can compromise by creating a settlement of some kind between two opposing views.

When we're considering the purpose of a whole system, there must be clarity on how the parts of that system can be designed, in such a way as to ensure that they work together to achieve a shared goal.

The word compromise originates from two Latin words, com, meaning together and promittre, meaning to promise. When we bring a decision down to a social level, we can fall into the trap of agreeing on a course of action to avoid conflict.

We're trying at this stage to come up with the optimal solution that directly contributes to the purpose of the whole. Therefore, in this context, compromise, should always be treated as a dirty word. We must try at all costs not to agree on compromises as they always  result in something being lost. If compromises present themselves, go back through the process and examine what you've missed or discussed them openly with the team to determine why they're being proposed. Playback sessions are not a one-off event; they are an ongoing process until both the team and the customer are satisfied with the idea.

Step 6: Simulate

The next step is to find the remaining actors that match our other personas and have them run through our paper-based solution. This will mean we will have to fill in the gaps and act as the missing parts, such as a computer or a delivery service. Although this exercise can be a lot of fun, it's also extremely powerful because, for all our wonderful and intellectually brilliant work, it can be fundamentally flawed due to the blindness to our biases. Confirmation Bias is a psychological condition that leads us to believe something is true because of past experience and a desire for something to be true. It is quite common in IT for a developer that has a great solution in mind to be convinced that the problem they're solving is the correct one. This condition causes us to stop gathering further information in the belief that we have enough understanding. Furthermore, it causes us to reject new information that contradicts our beliefs. By having real people naïve to our ideas run through simulation, with a fresh pair of eyes, it can bring a very valuable dose of reality to the situation. To this end we mustn't be upset if several issues arise with our design, this is the point of the exercise, to test its feasibility while we're still very early in the process; the phrase fail fast is commonly used to describe this.

Even if the amount of issues means the design phase must be extended, it will still be much more cost-effective and efficient than building a wrong design into the real solution and then having the change it later. If this happens using *red, amber, green* statuses to communicate progress can create emotive responses, especially if they're *red,* and therefore can be damaging to momentum, so I would advise against using such methods.

Step 7: Build It

The premise of this step is that the solution builders have been part of the design process. It is a fundamental error to consider steps 1 to 6 as a requirement definition phase to be passed on to an external agency, that hasn't had any involvement thus far, in other words in this kind of intimate process, outsourcing the build doesn't work.

Before building, we have to decide what to build and in what sequence. It may be that in our solution we have many features that would take a long time to develop and deliver, so here we should prioritise those features in terms of difficulty and the amount of value they will add. (The word feature is often used to describe IT functionality, but it can be used to mean anything from a process to a report; anything that stands alone as a solution in its own right). A simple four-box diagram allows us to perform this prioritisation:

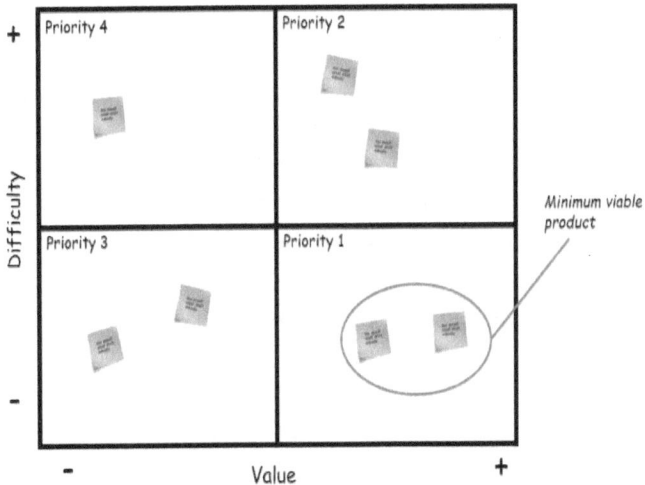

The term Minimum-Viable-Product or MVP means – the features that can be delivered at the fastest possible pace while adding the most value. The word viable can often be misrepresented as simply being technically functional, but viable also means addressing a customer's need, and therefore, if the new product or service does not meet this condition, then the solution is not viable. Ideally, these will sit in the Priority 1 quadrant but sometimes to make a product viable features from other quadrants also must be chosen. With this picture, it is possible to create a high-level release plan.

Now we have identified the scope of our MVP we need to map out all the capabilities that make up these features. It's important here to only include the capabilities that were part of our simulation. It's a very bad idea to cheat and bring in new capabilities that did not form part of the simulated design.

To map out the capabilities list them in the sequence of use underneath the features we've selected. Because we've only selected a sub-section of features and capabilities used in our simulation, it would be wrong to assume the solution remains viable, so it's time to take a step back and look at our solution holistically, as a whole, using the storyboard. Take time to walk through the storyboard and identify any areas that are still uncertain or cause for concern. We can use red labels or red sticky notes to highlight these areas that require further examination. Running through this process may again lead to going back up the process, changing the design and running new simulations. But, it's all worth it in the end, because you'll not only have a solution the customer wants, but you'll also know what features in your release plan will create even more value, which is in itself is a good story to tell. I've noticed over the years that customer's like a succinct release plan so they can see what's coming. We'll also know that the change is systemic in nature because we have tested its compatibility against the environment in which it has been implemented.

CONCLUSION

Design Thinking is a method just like any other that came about because people needed a more effective way of working. The problem it is trying to solve is creating solutions to systemic problems, by bringing people, ideas and skills into a safe environment where creativity can flow out of the collective experience.

It is not a magic wand. Not all Design Thinking exercises produce ground-breaking solutions; in fact, few will. James Dyson is famously reported to have created over five thousand failed prototypes before eventually patenting his Dual Cyclone vacuum cleaner.

And as with all ways of working, Design Thinking requires practice. It is an extremely iterative process. This approach does not fit into the traditional corporate way of working, with business cases, sequentially based plans and set objectives. Because learnings at any step can mean going back to an earlier step or even back to the drawing board, space must be created for the team to operate within, without the pressures of hierarchy and deadlines imposing constraints that result in suboptimal solutions. Now having said that, even Design Thinking is not a free for all, with no obligation to time and cost. Within an organisational context, there is a threshold between creative iteration and the dogmatic pursuit for innovation. This is why time boundaries should be set. However, adding a few extra weeks to get to the right answer is always worth it in the end.

CHAPTER 12

The Fourth Generation

SOCIAL POWER

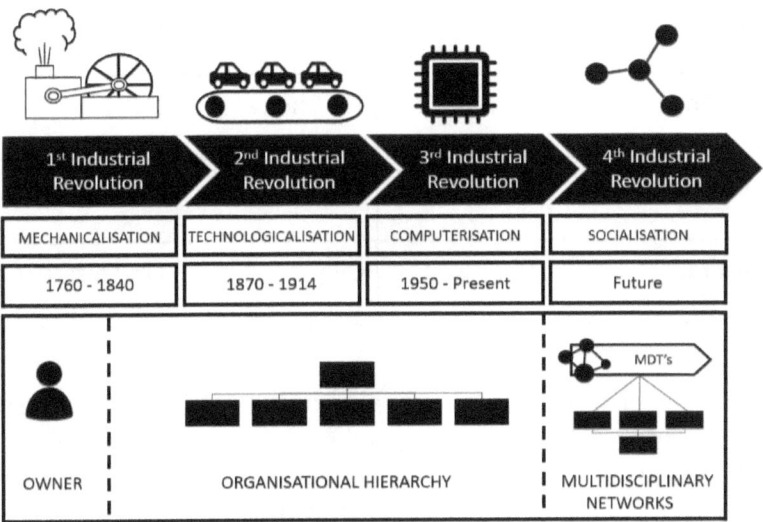

1st Industrial Revolution	2nd Industrial Revolution	3rd Industrial Revolution	4th Industrial Revolution
MECHANICALISATION	TECHNOLOGICALISATION	COMPUTERISATION	SOCIALISATION
1760 - 1840	1870 - 1914	1950 - Present	Future
OWNER	ORGANISATIONAL HIERARCHY		MULTIDISCIPLINARY NETWORKS

There is much talk about the 4th Generation of industry being driven out of the move towards digital technologies, such as internet of thing (IoT), artificial intelligence and quantum computing. However, if the challenges to organisational transformation, since Peter Drucker coined the phrase *knowledge worker* in the post-war corporate world, have been socially and culturally centred, how does more mechanical invention help? To try and understand this, we can refer back to Russell Ackoff's definition of system types we discussed in chapter 1.

	Parts	Whole	Example
Deterministic	No Choice	No Choice	Car
Ecological	Choice	No Choice	Nature
Animate	No Choice	Choice	Person
Social	Choice	Choice	Organisation

As we've discussed throughout this book, organisations are social systems, and social systems are tricky because not only does the whole system exhibit choice, so do the individual parts. Imagine if your right leg decided one day that it doesn't want to go for a walk while the rest of your body does. Moving very far, fast, is going to be tricky. When individual parts of an organisation don't agree and make different choices to the rest, the chance for systemic change is lost.

Some may respond to this and say that is what the leadership's authority is about, but again, this is like grabbing your leg and making it walk. You may well make some progress but not for long, and you won't get as far as you would like.

This view that people don't really have a choice, that work is carried out purely under instruction led authority, has caused organisations to regard people as deterministic systems falsely, and that process is what determines their productivity, the ultimate source of cost. In today's organisations, the influence of leadership can be seriously exaggerated, causing change agents to focus more on top-down change strategies than bottom-up. The reality is that workforces do have a choice and they can and do block change in its tracks if they regard it as a threat or disruptive. In one very large corporate a manufacturing unit openly referred to themselves as the mafia, *"don't tell the ********

mafia how things are going to be done" they told a programme board meeting I attended. A union representative told another programme board that any slight risk to the payroll and they'd have everyone out picketing. People do have a choice, and they do exercise it.

The more disconnected the leadership is from the work, the more choice these functions typically have. Leadership in many organisations struggle with the concept of control versus controlling. It is quite common to see that organisations can go through phases of centralising and decentralising. They try and decentralised to provide more flexibility to its individual business units and respond to markets more effectively, and then centralise again because they lose control. This oscillation is because of misunderstanding a systems principle that improving the performance of an important part often reduces the performance of the whole.

When we reflect on the view that the fourth industrial revolution is about *digital*, that is concerned with deterministic systems; it's clear that this does not respond to the social problems being experienced inside organisations. It is also clear that in themselves, deterministic systems don't solve the problems inside social systems. Furthermore, deterministic systems, like A.I. that can make probabilistic based decisions, can be intellectually damaging to the workforce. A few years ago, I toured a plant that had deployed an A.I. system for running the entire line. The operators simply had to keep the needle on the electronic dashboard dials in the green segment to ensure the plant was running optimally. Whilst this was impressive, it did leave me with the foreboding feeling that over a period, the workforce would lose their intellectual curiosity that had introduced A.I. in the first place. There were already signs that their earlier passion for quality management and problem-solving was being degraded, as the machine seemed to be making their efforts redundant. My concern at the time was that although A.I. was running the production line better than ever before, much better, it was by its nature deterministic, and in so being, could only respond to the task in which it had been developed. Any changes to the environment or the conditions of the plant would mean that it could quickly become obsolete, as the problem it was initially designed to solve no longer exists. In many ways, the A.I. system seemed to be biting the hand that feeds it, and in so doing was sealing its fate, and theirs.

The question concerning what impact these new technological capabilities is driving, especially those concerned with advancements in A.I. is causing a kind of cognitive dissonance in many organisations today. On the one hand, it is the ultimate worker – with all the intellectual capability of a demigod and the ability to operate machinery at high levels of efficiency, and on the other, it causes job losses. The easiest way to consider the future is to reflect on the past. The first three industrial revolutions have always followed the same pattern of introducing technologies that either complimented or replaced the workforce. The same principle can be applied this time around.

ARTIFICIAL INTELLIGENCE

I'm sorry Dave, I'm afraid I can't do that

Teaching A.I. to perform specific tasks is like training a puppy. In the beginning, we do more fetching that he does, but after a while and a kilo of doggy treats, he joins the dots between doing the right thing and getting a reward. The reason why A.I. is so powerful is that, unlike humans and puppies, it can look at the whole system in its entirety and run simulations to trial different scenarios before concluding. This ability to perform highly complex computations in very short periods of time, to draw probabilistic conclusions is why everyone needs to sit up and start to pay attention. It will, without doubt, change the industrial landscape. The ultimate question is, *how?* And will it replace the need for social systems inside organisations? The answer is not yet, and not for some considerable time.

The most sensible response is to understand where A.I. can have the most impact. Machines have already been introduced only when they could perform some repetitive task better than a person could, and where it was cost-effective. This is largely where the fear of A.I. is being driven out of. New technology has always led to job losses because it has always been based on increasing labour efficiency, and whilst this is also true for A.I. is not the only implication. The computational capabilities of A.I. not just improve labour it also improves knowledge through data insights. In the very near future, many of the repetitive, data-centric tasks undertaken by clerical staff will be done by A.I. Just as the computer removed the need for an army of account clerks down to a few, so will A.I. remove the need for them altogether.

But, as we saw with the introduction of the computer into business, as certain human tasks were made redundant, new tasks and skills emerged to work with the computer. And so, this is what is likely to happen with A.I. New tasks required by a very differently minded and skilled workforce.

Hold your horses!

I'm told early prospectors would have scouts ride ahead, and if they saw anything dangerous or suspicious they would shout out "*hold your horses*" to the main train. Well, I think organisations should think seriously about moving into the A.I. space without first understanding how it will impact them. A.I. is not yet an off-the-shelf product; however, there will be companies out there that tell you that it is and that it's easy to implement. The challenge with A.I. is that it doesn't solve the cause of the weakened performance that organisations currently experience, because, at its core, it is just another deterministic system.

A common view is that organisations need to digitise their processes to start the A.I. journey, and although this is true to some extent, they must first understand what and how to digitise. Simply slapping in new software does nothing to improve performance systemically. The fact that many will ignore this warning means that the digital and A.I. hype cycle will continue for many years, at great cost to the bottom-line, with many causalities. It also means that A.I. will not become a ubiquitous ingredient to transformational improvement for many years to come. Those that do tread cautiously and take-on a systemic way of working will lead the way, but like the quality movement over the last fifty years, those that benefit the most from A.I. will be the selective few.

The myth that A.I. is some kind of crystal ball that can predict the future is one of the reasons many will rush in, and the reason why many will fail. A.I. isn't a god, and it is not omniscience. A.I. does nothing to predict the uncertainty of the external world. A.I. has a computational brain that requires inputs and points of reference, and the ability to correlate, to enable it to form conclusions. Nassim Taleb famously coined the phrase "*Black Swans*" to mean those events that are impossible to predict, such as the rise of the internet and the tragedy of 911. For some, these black swans have given them an advantage; for others, they have been the cause of their demise. He refers to this phenomenon as the turkey being invited to the Thanksgiving dinner. Given these events aren't possible to predict (the turkey has no idea what Thanksgiving entails), Taleb suggests that organisations are better off ensuring they are more robust or Antifragile, as the title of his book puts it, to deal with them should they occur.

Let's take a simple example; what if we owned a property business and calculated the value of properties in a particular area, to better predict future prices and to forecast our future revenues. We enter all our drivers and throw in some additional attributes, such as the number of rooms, plot size, parking etcetera, and we base our assumptions on all things being equal to past events. However, what we don't know is that in a boardroom on the other side of the planet, a conversation is being had about the future of the plant that underpins the socioeconomic conditions in that area. This conversation is taking place because the product they make there is quickly becoming obsolete, and upgrading the plant's machinery and upskilling its workforce doesn't seem to make economic sense.

Of course, we cannot know about what the owners of the plant are discussing, so we must acknowledge that even the most advanced A.I. in the world won't save our business if we don't ensure we can protect it from adverse situations like this. We also must acknowledge that future revenue and growth predictions are predicated on unknown circumstances. Given the plant's economic condition drives social wealth in the area, the conclusion we must arrive at is that we must answer the question, how would we survive should the plant close? The generic answer to this is a change of perspective – one that places a lens on the fragility of our business model, and the interventions necessary to make it more robust.

Two ways to think about A.I. is *task-driven* or *narrow* (artificial narrow intelligence – ANI), and adaptable or *general* (artificial general intelligence – AGI).

The later, AGI is, well, somewhat in the future – a *one-day* dream. This is the kind of machine, like HAL 9000 from Stanley

Kubrick's film *A Space Odyssey 2001* and Holly from the British science-fiction comedy *Red Dwarf,* that can exhibit adaptable human behaviour. For all the recent advancement in A.I., it doesn't yet have the adaptability of a rat's brain.

ANI is a computational model that has been trained with large amounts of data, to perform a specific task without the need to be specifically programmed to do so. These models are becoming ever more common and are quickly finding their way across many industries in all manner of applications. In only a few years they will be ubiquitous in virtually everything we do. However, these models are built using algorithms and statistics to calculate probabilities. The fact that they can make decisions does not mean they are intelligent, in a self-aware perspective – in other words, A.I. can make decisions against a set of calculated scenarios, but it doesn't possess the ability to choose. It doesn't have any intrinsic motivation, causing it to suddenly try something new for the sake of it, to see what happens. From this perspective, A.I. is very much concerned with automation rather than true intelligence. It is trained on a specific task, and that is what it will focus on until the end of its days. The human job, therefore, is to define what these tasks that we give to A.I. should be. The implication will be some tasks will disappear altogether, and some will be greatly enhanced, and some will be entirely new.

Machine Learning

In 1959, the same year Taiichi Ohno introduced the Kanban system into his Toyota factory, Arthur Samuel defined machine learning (ML) as *"field of study that gives computers the ability to learn without being explicitly programmed"*. ML, a subset of A.I., has become the prominent application of A.I. In general terms it an algorithm that through repetition and adjustment can increase the accuracy of probability of a certain phenomenon, based on historical data. There are three main categories of ML; 1. Supervised, where we feed a model with a specific outcome in mind, like the probability a machine will breakdown.

2. Unsupervised – when we're looking for insightful patterns without any specifics in mind. 3. Reinforcement learning - where we're trying to achieve an optimum, such as winning a computer game or finding the most efficient way through a maze.

The latest capabilities on ML are based on a neural network design. It is essentially a computational model inspired by the structure of the human brain, consisting of interconnected layers of algorithmic nodes or neurons, where each neuron in one layer feeds into every neuron in the next layer.

In more recent years a subset of ML called *Deep Learning (DL)* has been developed. It simply refers to more layers in the neural network, enabling a much more granular breakdown and distribution across ML algorithms. Essentially, the more complex the problem being assessed, the more layers we'd expect to see in the network. These models are particularly effective in complicated scenarios, such as image and facial recognition.

If you fancy a play with a neural network, a great choice is Google's open-source Tensorflow Playground. It is packed with useful information, and you can play with the simulator, adjusting values to see the results.

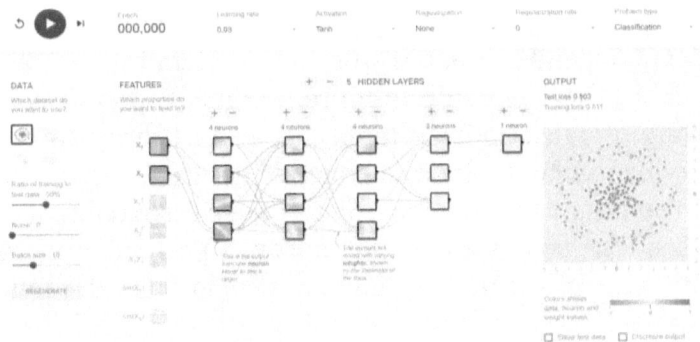

https://playground.tensorflow.org

Before moving off the subject, a quick note on variation, to avoid any confusion. The process of systemically reducing variation is necessary to improve effectiveness; in other words, doing repetitive things right the first time. When we're dealing with problem solving or creative design, we want as much data as possible, to look at a situation from many different angles, providing us with alternative perspectives from which to base our conclusions. Over time we hone the data down to something that precisely aligns to our given situation. So, in the beginning, an ML exercise will require lots of data or Big Data, but in the end, the model may only require narrow and specific data.

MULTIDISCIPLINARY TEAMS

We've discussed throughout this book that perceptions are determined based on vantage points. Vantage points can be considered as skills and experiences, or disciplines. How one person with a particular background approaches a problem can be very different from a person with different experiences. From this, it's tempting to conclude that the greater the diversity within the team, the more effective that team should be, due to an increased array of perspectives from which to consider solving the problem. However, we don't want too many cooks in our kitchen, so it is important to get the balance right. The balance of an MDT depends essentially on the problem that we're trying to solve, but there is a minimum requirement when it comes to improving organisations systemically. As I discussed earlier, when trying to understand the systemic nature for any particular point in an organisational environment, it's essential to look at it from all sides. So, if we want to improve a particular process, as a minimum, we will need to include people from the following perspectives:

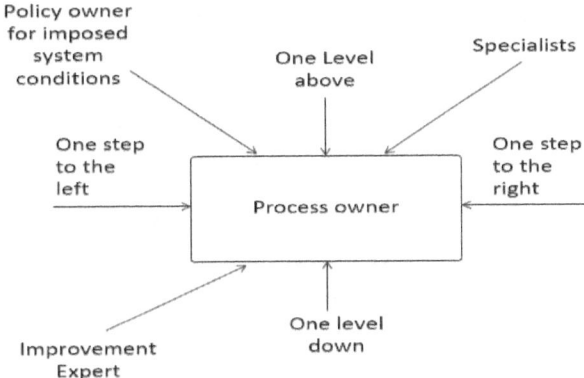

Success is a team effort, so it's important that all the participants know why they've been selected and how they can contribute.

Improvement Expert: A central expert needed to facilitate the improvement initiative and ensure the correct approach is taken.

Policy Owners: It is highly unlikely we will be successful if we try and approach a change in policy without this person's involvement. All that will result is conflict, escalation and stress. Most functions that impose policy, such as security, internal controls, legal, HR, external regulation etcetera, will probably assume their role on the team is to ensure compliance to their respective policy or policies. But it is critical that the expectation is set that the scope of their role also includes the need to provide empirical evidence to the legitimacy of the relevant policy or policies, and to help remove or adjust it if deemed acceptable and necessary.

Left, Right: These people effectively represent the supplier or the customer of the part of the business you're focusing on, so having their involvement ensures that they are consistency involved throughout the change.

Top: These people are usually imposing something. Such as a way of measuring or reporting. Having these people on board will drive out any inconsistency in the hierarchy.

Bottom: These people are usually an operation process. It can be quite common that people above them assume they know what they do, but in reality, this is seldom the case, so as with customers (right), ensuring they are involved is essential because they will directly be impacted by the change

Specialists: It is important to understand what specialist skills we're likely to need on the team, especially for I.T. and data analysts. The work can often involve handling and analysing large amounts of data, so having these people involved can be very helpful if the activity is data-intensive and analytical models need to be built.

General guidelines for creating an MDT

- **Check disciplinary boundaries.** We need to be careful to determine the correct disciplinary boundaries. If the level of input needed is simply reference information or expertise that requires active involvement, then it is better not to include them in the core team.

- **Set the right team size.** Team sizes will vary, but too small, and it's likely there won't be enough coverage to create a systemic change. Too large and the team becomes more difficult to manage. Somewhere between five and ten is usually fine.

- **Get commitment.** This may sound a little draconian and a little arbitrary, but have each person write down how their discipline can contribute. Include that in a contractual document that they sign. This provides an anchor of commitment if issues arise. It also provides clarity of their role. Without this, resentment in the team can set in because of ambiguous responsibilities.

- **Set values.** Have the team agree on a set of values that should be kept throughout their time together. I'd suggest a few light-hearted ones, so as not to make it too serious.

- **Agree on methods and tools.** Discuss and agree on the use of methods and tools upfront. Create a scope map, an approach and a schedule. Pull this together to form an overall plan. But remember, less is more and only use the ones you really need.

- **Promote inclusion.** We're looking for ideas that form as a property of the whole group rather than from one discipline or one person, so it's important to promote inclusion and ensure each person in the team has the ability to share their views. A good idea is to have each person introduce themselves, their role and their responsibilities.

- **Create visibility.** Visibility is of primary importance to ensure clarity and cohesiveness. Having members of the team running in different directions behind the scenes will result in a sub-optimal outcome, so making sure everyone is aware of what is being worked on and by whom is vital.

- **Practice sharing ideas.** The team should practice sharing ideas. This may sound a little lame, but it is quite common for some people to be defensive and passive-aggressive in the beginning as they try to establish themselves. This must never be met with open criticism or retaliatory aggression. These situations usually resolve themselves as people become more familiar with each other.

- **Encourage dialogue**. Do not always follow a prescribed agenda or a desired outcome. Run dialogue sessions, as

David Bohm described. Simply position the subject and let the conversation flow, as dialogue is a process that allows ideas to flow and develop across the team. They sound simple, but in practice, they are quite a skill. The team must learn how to talk less and listen more, suspend their views and be more reflective on what others are saying. Receiving candid feedback can be very challenging for some, especially when it's not delivered well. It's also important to recognise that the emergence of shared understanding and new ideas is not guaranteed, so it's important to keep trying. Some people may get frustrated and think it is a waste of time, but gently remind them that this is not a talking shop as some critics may suggest, but a process of discovery and that it takes time and effort to find those golden nuggets.

- **Practice challenging assumption.** From the early stages have the team practice surfacing and challenging assumptions and beliefs. Most people not only don't know how to do this effectively; they don't even think to do it in the first place. It is essential the team get used to doing this.

- **Learn each other's language.** The team will be made up of people from different areas of the organisation and from different disciplines. It is a good idea for each person to prepare a list of common words and acronyms unique to their area and present this back to the team.

- **Discuss ways of working.** How some people report upwards, run meetings, escalate problems, perform analysis and document findings and can be very different, so it's important to find some common ground. This generation is obsessed with uniformity, because of the many reasons discussed earlier in this book, but resist the temptation to impose standards. Let the team define the way they want to work.

- **Use the 11 C's model.** Let the group adjust it if they feel a better model reflects their environment, but ensure you build a reference to which to refer to if issues arise and relationships in the group are threatened. Moving the subject of personal conflict away from the individuals involved, towards something extraneous, such as a reference model can be very effective for diffusing and resolving a disagreement. This works because both parties share a common focus on the model rather than focusing on each other's differences. Moderate conflict is a good thing when it is focused on the idea, but if it becomes personal, then I have found that it usually happens in some idiosyncratic manner, where it is more about language and semantics than any material difference. In these moments it's important to take a step back and calmly facilitate an explanation from each party and then draw parallels between them. In this situation we're trying to find a shared agreement, a win-win if you like, and definitely not a compromise.

- **Agree on how to meet.** Get a routine going and agree on how and where to meet regularly, whether this is online or face-to-face. Split the meetings into two categories. The weekly general update, where people can provide a longer narrative on what they're working on. And, the more frequent, daily if possible, quick ten to twenty minutes, and only have the team present issues and blockages that they need help with and take any problems that need longer conversation out into a separate meeting.

- **Share success**. Ensure everyone in the team is explicitly recognised.

- **Have fun.** It is fundamentally essential this is a fun experience for the team. Some helpful hints are; keep it positive, promote inclusion, keep it relaxed. Resist the pressure of deadlines; with this statement, I am not saying ignore the plan; I am saying the plan can be a barrier to success because the outcome is the objective, not a date. However, it is important to ensure communications are clear and regular, so everyone is aware of the current status. To inject some fun, it can also help to arrange a few social events in the beginning.

- **Observe.** Finally, we must constantly observe the team. Keep a close eye out for conflict, anxiety and language. If you start to hear the word *them* instead of *us* when referring to members in the team address that quickly because it's a sign the team have lost cohesion, and inter-team alliances and coalitions threaten the robustness and unity of the team

The concept of the MDT approach is well established within health care and the sciences. However, across business, it has been slow to catch on. This seems to be because businesses have concentrated more on performing specific tasks than solving problems, and as a result, they have not developed the skills or the practices for doing so. As the founders of industry have proven throughout the decades, specialising repetitive tasks increases productivity; however, creating segregating specialisations into silos inhibits creativity and does not enable systemic thinking.

MDT's are not mini-project teams; they are a continuous process of introducing improvement into an organisation. They are much less temporal than projects and are in place to reduce waste over the long term. To clarify this point further, we can think about interventions purely as solutions, a one-time effort – like a project. But they are also an ongoing process.

The MDT approach is a completely different way of thinking and designing organisational structure.

THE FUTURE ORGANISATION

It takes two to tango

Until Peter Drucker defined people as Knowledge Workers, organisations thought of employees as deterministic in nature; that all they required was instruction, and they would respond. Since Drucker, knowledge has been attributed to the furtherment of information, and that more of it would result in greater productivity, and if greater productivity was not achieved, then it must be down to poor communication and not enough information – and the cycle continues producing more and more information. This drove initiatives like management information and Business Intelligence to the top of the CIO's priority list for over twenty years, as business leaders were shouting for more data and better insights into performance and growth opportunities. However, on the whole, these mechanistic approaches failed to deliver on their promises. People simply choose not to use their new software, or if they did, they didn't know how to use it effectively, to drive better insightful decisions. The more the problem persisted, the more information was produced until managers had more information than was possible to consume. But the information systems kept on being developed with ever-increasing levels of sophistication. The more reporting and analytics software was delivered, the more redundancy was produced. Over the years, all the data management and information systems that I have audited, have never had less than fifty percent of redundant data in them; that is data that has not been accessed in more than a year. This creates what is known as the Meier Condition (1963) or *information overload;* people become so saturated with information that they don't know what is useful and what is not. To compound the issue, searching or drilling into down has been shown to create a small dopamine response, making us feel good. This is why people that perform internet searches often continue to search even after they've found the answer to their question. People literally have become addicted to data. In contrast to having a positive effect, more information can be extremely negative. In a highly politicised organisation with power-silos, increasing information has the opposite effect. Rather than improving the situation, it exacerbates the conflict between them because now each is armed with harmful data about the other, where the insight is not used for improving performance but for blaming each other and putting each other's dirty laundry out for all to see. As a response security teams have had to design systems that segregate data between user groups. One generalised observation I've made over the years, is that the larger, more sophisticated the internal role-based security model is, generally the more politically motivated the organisation.

Russell Ackoff referred to a supportive leadership style as more akin to a democratic organisation, where its members have more considerable freedom to make the right choices. In cultures like Toyota, freedom manifests itself as an inclusive workforce, that includes cleaners, having the ability to stop the production line if they see a problem.

In the organisation of the future, it will mean the creation of multidisciplinary teams to solve problems systemically. GE had a term for this, although it wasn't exercised in the right way, *boundarylessness*. Meaning people could get involved for the greater good wherever that took them. But as one leadership trainer told me in one class "*be careful Mark, boundarylessness is like being on the roof of a tall building with the lights out, there is an edge, and it's a long way down*".

What is required is not a word but an organisational construct that enables people to mobilise across networks without any cliff edges or the need to go between the formal structures where their efforts and achievements aren't visible.

The socio-systemic model

In 1972 Stafford Beer presented his, now famous, Viable System Model (VSM). He described it as a system that is an organisational structure capable of meeting and adapting to the demands in a changing environment, or in other words capable of autonomy.

We see large organisations come and go because they become out of sync with the environment in which they operate, (I won't mention Kodak, damn it, I just did!). The world we live in today is becoming more socially connected than ever before. The current population in 2019 is seven point seven billion. Four point two billion of those people use the internet with three point three billion people using social media platforms. More than ninety percent of large retailers are online, and more than eighty percent of small to medium-sized businesses offer some online presence. Facebook alone gets sixty billion messages a day. Youtuber's upload three hundred hours of video every minute. Twitter has one point three billion registered users. I could continue with the mind-blowing numbers, but it's easy to see how our world has changed in such a very short period. To give you some idea of how short, Google launched on the 15th of September 1997. That's just over twenty years ago. In that time, the number of searches on their platform has risen from ten thousand a day, to five point five billion. To suggest that organisations will remain in the same and in a similar construct as they did at the turn of the twentieth century is simply not realistic; in fact, it's delusional.

Within the next ten years, social media is predicted to continue to grow exponentially with more organisations using it for customer engagement. Employees will become increasing normalised to a socially accessible and connected world. The generations to come will simply take it for granted. The CEO then is your social-media shaped teenage gamer of today. The dynamics of society are changing; not because humans have changed, but because modern digital technologies enable us to be more socially connected. Organisations that have divided people into silos have created conflict that results in waste and lost productivity, to the point of almost being dysfunctional, won't survive the next ten years, never mind the next twenty. People adapt and respond to create connections regardless of the hierarchy and despite the difficulties. These networks form out of necessity to keep the organisation moving – but it's a struggle and very inefficient. The leadership of the future will not only understand this, but they will also work with this knowledge to observe and design better organisations. It is absolutely possible with simple statistics to distinguish between a trend and an out of control situation. Leaders looking at the data of an improving trend, may miss the data that provides the perspective showing the distress and lowering morale of the team. Leaders of the future will learn to have both sets of data.

Organisations that are multidisciplinary focused will bring people together with a broad range of disciplines to focus on the start and end of the customer journey and everything in between.

Quality management has focused heavily on manufacturing. However, most of the lost productivity and waste these days is lost in service and support processes. Thousands upon thousands of emails, documents and handoffs, all generated because of unnecessary silos and methods of measurement that divide and create a politicised agenda within tribalistic cultures. Interestingly, when I've observed self-forming social networks, I've found no politics, just people wanting to get the job done but as soon as management get involved the politics appear.

A socio-systemic model brings together the concept of new technologies, such as A.I. and the social model of MDT's. It redefines the way organisations need to structure themselves and directly addresses the failings of traditional functional and matrix models. It does this by creating a systemic concept into the social fabric and enables cohesive networks to be built. Consequently, the use of data and information inside an organisation is driven towards purposeful outcomes.

Because the nature of a socio-systemic model is heuristic and provides a holistic approach that includes the ability to determine a systemic course of action, the informal social networks are no longer required, as the gaps between the formal structures have been bridged.

The organisational leadership of the future will have four primary shifts in their focus.

1. **Systemic Throughput.** Understanding how customer demand is flowing through the organisation and why it is getting stuck and taking time to observe the work first-hand, to understand bottlenecks and inefficiencies, and considering the whole organisation from an end to end perspective to determine where conflict exists, resulting in productivity constraints.

2. **Everyday analytics.** Implementing A.I. technologies to predict and automate – all available in a digitally enabled boardroom, without the need for spreadsheets and performance reports full of retrospective, rearview metrics where this month versus this time last year is the only level of visibility. They will make it a mission to understand variation and will drive the systematic eradication of it, by understanding where and why most of it exists — connecting the organisation from the boardroom to the shop floor and from left to right by tracking customer demand. The leader of the future will do as Cho did in the 1950s. They will stand in their organisation and observe, but now they will also *see* by using the digitised and calculated data being presented to them in real-time as they watch the work. They will be able to see that the seemingly normal process in front of them is actually statistically out of control and that the impacts further downstream, are yet to come. The boardroom will be a living breathing performance knowledge centre with a finger on the pulse of the organisation. This won't, paradoxically as some see it,

create a more detached leadership, but will invite them into the working areas of their organisation, prepared with better questions and insights.

3. **Multidisciplinary Networks.** Leaders will be systematically eradicating the reasons why people find it hard to do their job and understand why social networks have emerged inside their organisation and be able to respond with a dynamic MDT capability. This makes multidisciplinary teams the default response to problem-solving and for long term intervention. The socio-systemic model will become the organisational model of the future. The failed silo and matrix structures will be a thing of the past. Multidisciplinary teams will have two primary objectives; (1) to process the throughput of demand as quickly as possible without undermining quality. (2) To increase creativity for growth. Costs will fall like a stone.

4. **Supportive Leadership.** The organisational hierarchy will be metaphorically inverted so that their role will be to support the dynamic nature of the MDT's processing customer demand. The age-old problem with autocratic leadership that has been hugely ineffective will be replaced with empowered groups, all focused on systemic change, and the Human Resources manifesto will be centred around a collective agenda, where personal performance will be for the betterment of the whole.

Regular not continuous improvement

Cardiovascular exercise is more than walking, or a gentle jog, it requires some exertion to get the heart pumping. Many make the mistake that a healthy lifestyle, involving taking a brisk walk, keeps you fit, it does not. The adage 'No Pain, No Gain' is very true. But who wants pain, right?

Well, for many that partake in strenuous exercise the feeling of discomfort caused by DOMS (delay onset muscular soreness) can feel strangely satisfying and rewarding, while much lesser pain, say that of a mild headache can feel so much more unpleasant. A little self-induced pain is weirdly pleasurable. Moderate exertion, both physically and mentally, is very good for us, but not all the time.

Here lies a problem with the Continuous Improvement messages. They sound like a constant burden, immediately turning many people off. It's like knowing you must do strenuous exercise every day; it would be horrible. This may sound like I've contradicted the whole concept of quality management, but not at all. All improvements should start with the condition that is causing a degradation in performance, increasing cost or causing the customer pain or both. It is vital that the question "*what problem are we trying to solve?*" is asked first. I hear some so-called Design Thinkers say that the problem may shift, and the design work defines something not previously known about, and what results is an entirely different solution (innovation they often call it). However, it's a mistake to go looking for problems. Design work that sets out to solve a clearly defined problem but discovers an alternative, more valuable way of resolving the situation is fine, very good in fact, but it's not fine to do *improvement* for its own sake.

The human condition does not like monotony. Regular strenuous exercise in moderation is much better than both constant low-level exercise or one-off extreme exercise, like training for a marathon every day and then after the race never running again. Continuous improvement baulks against our nature. I don't want DOMS every day, but occasionally it feels good. Some say we must normalise improvement so that it becomes part of the work itself, and while I agree with the sentiment, I disagree with the interpretation many apply to it. Constant improvement is tiring and even stressful.

Improvement should be regular, not continuous. Regular small improvements that build over time make a very fit organisation. I used to be a regular long-distance runner (long but not extreme). One morning I was running down the banks of the River Thames near London. I was running at a decent pace (7-minutes per mile or 13.8 kilometres per hour). I'd been out for around thirty minutes when a group of guys all geared out in black shorts and black vests overtook me. These guys looked fit. As they went past, I kept up with the last guy and said good morning. We were now running at a fast pace (fast for me), so talking was difficult. The last guy smiled and said hello back like he was sat in a chair; he looked about 50, wow! I asked him "*h...h... hey, you guys are pretty good, any tips?*", he answered, "*rest more than you run...but run...a lot*". After a few minutes, they were gone.

The answer to large improvement is to build from small and do it regularly. Without an understanding of the whole, improving parts in isolation can be seriously damaging, and consequently brings no benefit. I've heard organisations regularly talk about launching a continuous improvement program that has no method of measurement in place from which to baseline the nature of their organisation, and how it would improve the satisfaction of their customers demand. It's also common to hear departments or functions state that CI is high on their agenda. Continuous improvement isn't an agenda; it's a lifestyle. So, what to do? On the one hand, we shouldn't change a department in isolation, and on the other, the organisation is too large to be taken on in one go. And, surely the 'start small and build' approach is paradoxically anti-systemic? The answer is small is best. Less is definitely more when it comes to improvement. Large changes can hurt organisations, but small ones, not so much - usually. For example, take a twenty-kilogram weight and drop it from your waist height on to your foot and experience how it feels. Then take a thousand twenty-gram weights (total weight of twenty KG's) and drop those on the other foot one at a time and compare the difference. (actually, don't do this, I'm just trying to make a point). The small changes can be made in a systemic fashion if they are deployed using MDT's and approached in the correct manner.

A final remark, CI can often be confused with optimisation. The two couldn't be more different. Optimisation causes weakness, single points of failure. Redundancy creates strength and resilience. Most people, when they say, "*we need to optimise*", have no idea what they're saying. Building resilience into the system adds value in times of stress. CI is also about this.

When people blindly use the economy of scale argument not to take action, saying the initiative can't scale against the current backdrop of large scale failure, they fundamentally miss this point, the point Goldratt shouted from the rooftops, that focused intervention on areas of constraint removes waste and removes failure demand, *increasing* capacity. It is counterintuitive to those that are stuck in traditional thinking that redundancy increases cost.

MDT's are by their very nature, demand failure and failure demand killers. They eradicate waste like nothing else does.

MDT's practising small and regular improvements will shape the next generation of organisation.

CONCLUSION

Above all, organisations must **Study** their working practices and understand it's social dynamics and how demand is being treated; to **Find** where the main constraints are and then systematically **Break** them, either through continuous or discontinuous improvement methods. Or as my mentor, Russell Ackoff put it, *"continuously dissolving conflict while increasing choice."*

The fourth industrial revolution will require the need for more advanced technology, but this alone will be insufficient to solve the systemically damaging social problems, experienced in the third industrial revolution.

The socio-systemic model of the future, coupling multi-disciplinary teams with new technological capabilities such as artificial intelligence, will transform the way we approach organisational transformation.

Epilogue

Before we end, I'd like to thank you for reading this book.

I hope I didn't overly offend anyone along the way; my only intention was to highlight our current mode of working, that is based on our pattern of thought and our assumptions and beliefs, that is a result of the way we've been educated, either through the education system or in the workplace.

We have a powerful capability that often goes underutilised, that of self-reflection. We always have a choice, even in the most difficult and toxic environments. If your gut is saying something that doesn't feel right, it most likely isn't; our intuition is a powerful thing.

Become uncommodified. Do what you feel is right not what people tell you is right. You'll be astonished what you can get done. Remember, small improvements create large gains over a period. I encourage you to read. I find those that get stuck in the mental mud are those that don't.

There is a joy in joining the dots between the thoughts of a great thinker and the problems we experience every day, and this, in turn, generates our mental energy and slowly things begin to make more sense. It's a shock to the system when you first read something written decades ago, or even further back, that describes our current situation. The understanding of different subjects that somehow join up can bring a new perspective to the work. The number of people I've met over the years that have said they hate their job is truly sad. It's all so unnecessary.

Go slow to go fast. Take your time and reflect on your past and your present and be hard on yourself. Ask questions such as, "*am I really successful?*" "*do I deliver valuable work, really?*" "*does what I do ever make any meaningful difference?*".

Turn the situation of fear on its head and stop worrying about the small day to day failures and think about the bigger picture, but don't try to solve everything all at once. Remember, ongoing improvement is about direction, not perfection.

Make things practical. Go see. Walk and talk with your team and managers from other departments to share thoughts, build knowledge. Work with them to try small things out and build on those. Make problem solving, analysis and measurement a passion.

Baseline your team's performance. Understand where you really are, not where you think you are. Reflect over the years and ask yourself *"have we really improved over that time?"*. And, don't kid yourself by making up narratives about how bad it used to be. Fight the cognitive dissonance with all your might. Test your improvements empirically not anecdotally. Reassure your team and colleagues, talk them through a few basic principles of systems, flow and measurement. Get their ideas and thoughts.

Put things you're told into two buckets (1) assumption, or (2) fact. Drive hard on system conditions to prove, without question, whether they sit in category (1) or (2), and only accept those that are in category (2).

Before jumping in ask, yourself the most important question *"what problem are we trying to solve"*.

Don't solve processes top-down. Instead, get underneath the work and really study it, to flush out those grey spaces.

Observe your surroundings and decide whether the work is being done by an informal social network or by the formal structure and processes – you'll be surprised what you find.

Above all, ABOVE ALL, lose the ego. I hear terrible advice from people that say apologising is bad. Be meek and be kind. Meek is not weak. Encourage people, be sympathetic to those that are still stuck in the mental mud. Recognise you won't change the world until you change yourself.

Think systems!

Goodluck.

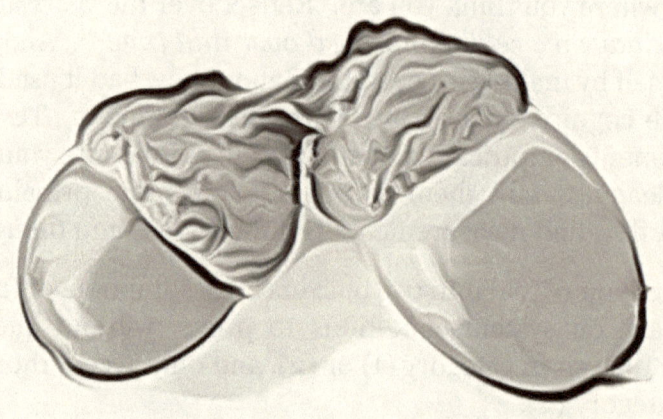

necessary but not sufficient

References

Anthony J. Bradley and Mark P. McDonald - (2011) - The
Social Organisation - (1, 4, 17, 42, 167-178) :
Gartner Inc : Harvard Business School

Chris Argyris - (1992-1996) - On Organizational Learning -
(7-36) : Blackwell Publishers Inc.

Daniel Kahneman - (2011) - Thinking Fast And Slow - (80-81,
156-165,203-204,382-384, 236-240, 311-312,
352,) : Allen Lane - an imprint of Penguin
Books

Domenico Lepore and Oded Cohen - (2010) - Deming and
Goldratt - The Theory Of Constraints And The
System Of Profound Knowledge - (58-88) : The
North River Press

Donald J.Wheeler - (1993,2000) - Understanding Variation -
Second Edition - (23-42) : SPC Press

Donella H. Meadows - (2009) - Thinking In Systems - (4-6,
14, 25-72,111-114) : Earthscan

Eliyahu M. Goldratt - (1990) - What is this thing called
Theory of Constraints and how should it be
implemented - (9,26,28-33,90-95) : North
River Press

Eliyahu M. Goldratt - (1990) - The Haystack Syndrome -
North River Press

Eliyahu M. Goldratt - (2008) - The Choice - The North River
Press

Eliyahu M. Goldratt with Eli Schragenheim and Carol A. Ptak
- (2000) - Necessary But Not Sufficient - The
North River Press

https://www.psychologytoday.com/gb/blog/beyond-the-
doubt/200910/the-uncertainty-paradox

https://www.psychologytoday.com/us/collections/201010/th
e-power-perception

https://www.sciencedirect.com/science/article/pii/01918869
94900485

https://www.sciencedirect.com/science/article/pii/S0272735
811001334

https://www.theatlantic.com/health/archive/2015/03/how-uncertainty-fuels-anxiety/388066/

James P. Womack and Daniel T. Jones - (1996) - Lean Thinking - (15-89, 189-218) : Touchstone Books

John Gøtze, Anders Jensen-Waud - (2013) - Beyond Alignment - Applying Systems Thinking in Architecting Enterprises - (12-13,17-19,21-2330-31,33-34, 45, 52-54, 57-65, 97-98, 101, 121-125, 128-146, 189-197, 320) : College Publications

Journal List Social Cognitive and Affective Neuroscience - *Feeling emotional: the amygdala links emotional perception and experience - PMC2555454 - Adam K. Anderson*

Mal Owen and John Morgan - (2000) - SPC In The Office - (75-103) : Greenfield Publishing

Malcolm Gladwell - (2008) - Outliers - Penguin Group

Matthew Syed - (2015) - Black Box Thinking - John Murray

Max H. Bazerman - (2006) - Judgement in Managerial Decision Making - (13-39, 62,68,131,171) : John Wiley & Sons

Nassim Nicholas Taleb - (2007) - Skin In The Game - (13, 24-25, 55-56,128-129, 161, 230-232) : Random House

Nassim Nicholas Taleb - (2011) - The Bed of Procrustes - Penguin Group

Nassim Nicholas Taleb - (2014) - The Black Swan - (41-56,62-83, 312-313, 363-365) : Random House

Nassim Nicholas Taleb - (2018) - Antifragile - (72,76,111-119, 267-273,311-315,) : Random House

Peter F. Drucker - (1990) - The Essential Drucker - (8-10,14-20,52-57,61,69,71-73,84-90, 180,183-191,198-202,203-205,218-224,225-243,244-255,256-262) : Elsevier Ltd

Peter M. Senge - (1990,2006) - The Fifth Discipline - (x-xi,17-26, 27,93-99, 163-171, 210-211,280-281, 325) : Random House

Robert B. Cialdini - (2007) - Influence - (114-166) :
    HarperCollins
Russell L. Ackoff - - Re-Creating the Corporation - (3-6,9,11-
    15,21-25,36-39,52-53,82-84,93,102-
    103,105,116-123,150-154,157-158,159-163,164-
    167,172-174,226,251-255,260-261,264,266-
    271,273,286,288-291) : Oxford University Press
    Inc
Russell L. Ackoff - (1999) - Ackoff's Best - (3-6, 27-33, 37-42,
    44-45, 46-53,99-103,128-135,168-170,268-289)
    : John Wiley & Sons Inc
Russell L. Ackoff - (2008) - Difference That Make A
    Difference - (7-10, 19-21,30-31,54-55,56-57,94-
    95,119-120,124-126) : Triarchy Press
Russell L. Ackoff & Herbert J. Addison - (2007) -
    Management f-Laws - Triarchy Press
Russell L. Ackoff & Sheldon Rovin - (2005) - Beating The
    System - (15-17, 45, 115-116, 139-141) : Berret-
    Koehler
Russell L. Ackoff with Herbert J. Addison and Andrew Carey -
    (2010) - Systems Thinking for Curious
    Managers - () :
Russell L. Ackoff, Jason Magison, Herbert J. Addison -
    (2006) - Idealized Design - creating an
    organisations future - (3-33, 61-80, 103-116,
    117-118, 197-201, 202, 210-211,246-249, 252-
    253,258-259) : Prentice Hall

Viktor Mayer-Schöberger and Kenneth Cukier - (2013) - Big
    Data - (146, 158-163,196) : John Murray
W. Edwards Deming - (1982,2000) - Out Of The Crisis - (4,
    18-23, 47, 90-92,156-166, 167-169, 180-181,
    183-247, 297-308,309-370) : The MIT Press

Index

www.ingramcontent.com/pod-product-compliance
Lightning Source LLC
Chambersburg PA
CBHW020730180526
45163CB00001B/179